SIZING UP U.S. EXPORT DISINCENTIVES

J. DAVID RICHARDSON

SIZING UP U.S. EXPORT DISINCENTIVES

Institute for International Economics
Washington, DC
September 1993

J. David Richardson, Visiting Fellow at the Institute for International Economics, is Professor of Economics in the Maxwell School of Citizenship and Public Affairs at Syracuse University. He is also coeditor of *International Economic Transactions: Issues in Measurement and Empirical Research* (1991) and *Issues in the Uruguay Round* (1988).

INSTITUTE FOR INTERNATIONAL ECONOMICS
11 Dupont Circle, NW
Washington, DC 20036-1207
(202) 328-9000 FAX: (202) 328-5432

C. Fred Bergsten, *Director*
Christine F. Lowry, *Director of Publications*

Cover design by Supon Design Group

Printed in the United States of America
96 95 94 93 4 3 2 1

Library of Congress Cataloging-in-Publication Data

Sizing up U.S. export disincentives /
J. David Richardson.
p. cm.
Includes bibliographical references and index.
1. United States—Commercial policy. 2. Export controls—United States. 3. Foreign trade regulation—United States. 4. Competition, International. I. Title.
HF1455.R48 1993
382'.64—dc20 92-37854
CIP

ISBN 0-88132-107-9 (paper)

Marketed and Distributed outside the USA and Canada by Longman Group UK Limited, London

The views expressed in this publication are those of the author. This publication is part of the overall program of the Institute, as endorsed by its Board of Directors, but does not necessarily reflect the views of individual members of the Board or the Advisory Committee.

Contents

Preface

The Institute has conducted extensive research on the impact of trade barriers throughout the life of its research program. The analysis by Gary C. Hufbauer, Diane T. Berliner, and Kimberly Ann Elliott in *Trade Protection in the United States: 31 Case Studies* (1986) has been widely used to generate estimates of the total costs of American restrictions. Elliott, Jeffrey J. Schott, Wendy E. Takacs, and I quantified the effects of the most important "voluntary" export restraint agreements in *Auction Quotas and United States Trade Policy* (1987). William Cline derived the definitive estimates for the most heavily protected manufacturing sector in the United States in *The Future of World Trade in Textiles and Apparel* (2nd ed., 1990). Cline and I estimated the impact of American and Japanese protection in each other's trade in *The United States–Japan Economic Problem* (2nd ed., 1987). Marcus Noland and I recently produced a contemporary estimate for Japan's barriers to US exports in *Reconcilable Differences? United States–Japan Economic Conflict* (1993).

Import barriers, including their implementation via "voluntary" export restraints, are the traditional focus of trade analysis and were the subject of all these studies. It has become increasingly apparent, however, that American trade flows—and perhaps those of a number of other countries—are also significantly affected by export barriers. Pathbreaking estimates of one dimension of this issue were developed by Hufbauer, Schott, and Elliott in *Economic Sanctions Reconsidered* (rev., 1990).

But the present study by J. David Richardson is, to our knowledge, the first comprehensive effort to catalog and "size up" the entire range of such barriers in a single country. It therefore employs a series of new and creative methodologies and uses several data sets in innovative ways. We hope that his study—in addition to whatever contributions it may make to current understanding and policy—will presage a series of further and more refined analyses of a very important issue, as did some of the initial studies of nontariff barriers to trade (NTBs) in the early 1970s.

The Institute for International Economics is a private nonprofit institution for the study and discussion of international economic policy. Its purpose is to analyze important issues in that area, and to develop and communicate practical new approaches for dealing with them. The Institute is completely nonpartisan.

The Institute is funded largely by philanthropic foundations. Major institutional grants are now being received from the German Marshall Fund of the United States, which created the Institute with a generous commitment of funds in 1981, and from the Ford Foundation, the William and Flora Hewlett Foundation, the William M. Keck, Jr. Foundation, the C. V. Starr Foundation, and the United States–Japan Foundation. A number of other foundations and private corporations also contribute to the highly diversified financial resources of the Institute. About 16 percent of the Institute's resources in our latest fiscal year were provided by contributors outside the United States, including about 7 percent from Japan. The Alfred P. Sloan Foundation provided partial support for this study.

The Board of Directors bears overall responsibility for the Institute and gives general guidance and approval to its research program—including identification of topics that are likely to become important to international economic policymakers over the medium run (generally, one to three years), and which thus should be addressed by the Institute. The Director, working closely with the staff and outside Advisory Committee, is responsible for the development of particular projects and makes the final decision to publish an individual study.

The Institute hopes that its studies and other activities will contribute to building a stronger foundation for international economic policy around the world. We invite readers of these publications to let us know how they think we can best accomplish this objective.

C. FRED BERGSTEN
Director
August 1993

INSTITUTE FOR INTERNATIONAL ECONOMICS
11 Dupont Circle, NW, Washington, DC 20036
(202) 328-9000 Fax: (202) 328-5432

Acknowledgments

This project, more than most, has had a long gestation. C. Fred Bergsten has had it in his mind for more than 20 years, and Thomas O. Bayard contributed to much of the earliest work along these lines. I have benefited greatly at all stages from their studious patience and their thorough critique. Two sturdy commentators who likewise followed this project carefully from its earliest to its final stages are Howard Lewis, III and Judith A. Youngman. They and the four faithful research assistants who succeeded each other (Philip J. Ruder, Pamela J. Smith, Daniel M. Bernhofen, and Mursaleena Islam) deserve Distinguished Service Medals. So do Anthony ("Corporal XD") Stancil of the Institute staff, as well as Christine Lowry and Valerie Norville, whose editorial input was superb. Brigitte Coulton and Michael Treadway are also appreciated for their assistance during production and indexing.

In addition to those above, several other people read final drafts of the manuscript in its entirety. They deserve special thanks for their extensive recommendations: Richard N. Cooper, Edward E. Leamer, Theodore H. Moran, Peter Morici, and Christopher A. Padilla.

Earlier drafts of this study benefited substantially from critical commentary by Donald L. Alexander, Steve Charnovitz, William R. Cline, James C. Cruse, I. M. Destler, Robert S. Dohner, Thomas A. Dorsey, Geza Feketekuty, William F. Finan, Isaiah Frank, Ellen Frost, Gary C. Hufbauer, Anne O. Krueger, Mordechai E. Kreinin, Allen J. Lenz, Jane-yu Li, Boyd McKelvain, Allan I. Mendelowitz, Marcus Noland, Ernest H. Preeg, John H. Qualls, Howard Rosen, Philip K. Verleger, and by colleagues and participants in seminars and study groups at the Institute for International Economics, Michigan State University, Purdue University, and Syracuse University.

Finally, although they may never choose to read the book very carefully, Karen, Kris, and Laura have played vital roles in the pleasure with which I have written it.

SIZING UP U.S. EXPORT DISINCENTIVES

Overview and Summary

Overview

Recent debate over American competitiveness has focused largely on US macroeconomic policies (the budget, monetary and exchange rate policy), on US structural impediments (managerial myopia, labor relations), and on foreign macroeconomic policies and trade barriers. Largely ignored have been our own domestic microeconomic policy impediments to US exports. These may deter many billions of dollars in sales annually, and thus rival some of the other elements in importance. They may specially afflict our most competitive sectors, "shooting ourselves in our best foot forward," as one wag put it.

This study aims to provide a detailed quantitative assessment of the export deterrence of a number of US policies. The assessments may then be compared with estimates of the effects of budgetary imbalance, exchange rate misalignment, and foreign tariff and nontariff barriers on US competitiveness.

The study also aims to assess "passive" export restraints, such as inadequate export promotion and finance, and compare US practices with those of its chief competitors. All such restraints may inadvertently impair US export competitiveness. But no one knows how much, nor which are most important.

Of course, many of these export-deterring policies serve important objectives. They seek to limit US sales abroad for security or foreign policy reasons (e.g., export controls and sanctions against Cuba and Iraq). Others serve important objectives such as health, safety, and protection of the environment.

But export success is an important objective, too, for many reasons. Exports are important because they employ workers in jobs with higher real incomes than could be earned otherwise. Exports are important when they allow fixed resource costs (e.g., R&D or marketing) to be spread across a larger customer base. Exports are important when they increase the density, and hence the intensity, of competition. Exports are an important form of diversification and self-insurance for a firm and its workers. Exports are important as a barometer of a firm's competitive success, and also as a catalyst. Successful exporting is winning one's share of the "away games." Actively seeking to achieve export success can sharpen incentives to innovate and tighten up a firm's organization, enhancing its internal efficiency.

Production abroad through overseas affiliates has many of these same benefits from a firm's point of view. And US export disincentives sometimes encourage such production. But the benefits are not the same for US workers, communities, and any other immobile resources. Therefore, they are not the same from a national point of view. One cost of export disincentives is "export diversion." The more severe cost, however, is export extinction.

This project aims to size up the cost of US export disincentives. The project does not assess the benefits of these XDs for national security or welfare. That is an important and challenging project of its own. Some of the benefits could be shown almost certainly to be worth the export costs; other benefits might be questionable. That project is the natural and needed counterpart to this one.

The term "sizing up" is used deliberately, in preference to terms such as "measure" or "estimate." The distinction is the degree of empirical accuracy or precision one can reasonably expect. This study is the first comprehensive effort to size up US XDs. All the techniques employed in this project—surveys, simulations, statistics—produce order-of-magnitude estimates of the size of individual disincentives and describe a range of their potential effects on aggregate US exports. Narrowing the various ranges requires considerable judgment and more research. Given the newness of empirical research in this area, sizing up is thus the intellectually honest description. The techniques are analogous to those used in early research on sizing up nontariff barriers and to those used by businesses trying to establish "benchmarks" against which to size up their own competitiveness.

Important conclusions include the following:

- This study estimates that US exports forgone due to US export disincentives (XDs) range as high as $40 billion annually in the mid-1990s, depending on how one adds up the calculations (there are important methodological issues in the adding). The estimates center on a range from $21 to $27 billion in the mid-1990s,[1] in which a range of from $4 billion to $14 billion could be ascribed to multilaterally agreed export restraint rather than to US unilateral initiative. Though many of these XDs are necessary costs of maintaining national and global security, at least some seem questionable. The overall estimated impact is notable when compared with estimates of trade barriers in other areas, such as the $9 billion to $18 billion estimate by Bergsten and Noland (1993) of US exports deterred by Japanese trade barriers.

- Export controls for national security or antiproliferation purposes seem to be especially strong XDs, accounting for two-thirds to three-quarters of our estimates. Controls for foreign policy reasons, inadequate official support for export finance, and sector-specific regulatory burdens seem to discourage US exports moderately strongly. Fixed costs of meeting export control or regulatory requirements also discourage US exports moderately strongly. But it is hard to detect any significant export deterrence from environmental controls or other across-the-board regulatory burdens on US industry. Nor does inadequate export promotion or reliance on direct taxes that are ineligible for border adjustment seem to have any significant export deterrence.

- Though the surveys, simulations, and statistics generated quantitative estimates of lost US exports that varied for the most part between $10 billion and $40 billion, the qualitative ranking of XDs by relative severity was remarkably consistent. The statistical and simulation experiments found export controls to be considerably more severe XDs than believed by the experts surveyed, but found broad tax and regulatory burdens to be considerably less severe XDs.

- Those XDs that are quantitatively significant seem to have especially strong effects on exports of chemicals, machinery, equipment, and instruments, often believed to be some of the most dynamic sectors in the US economy and important sources of technological impetus and favorable spillovers. Those that raise fixed costs tend to force newer and smaller firms out of exporting entirely, blunting still further the capacity for these sectors to lead growth dynamically.

- Not reflected in the $21-27 billion central estimate are barriers to US export competitiveness that are the indirect, "once-removed" cousins

---

1. The very bottom of the range is $7.3 billion. But several features could lift the entire range of estimates. One important example is that exports of weapons themselves raise special problems of measurement and security and are not treated explicitly in this study. However, exports of products with "dual use,"—that is, both military and civilian—are affected significantly by many XDs and are an important focus of the project. Second, no attempt is made to quantify a "perverse multiplier" effect of certain XDs that is described in Chapters 2, 3, and 4; in industries with dynamic and other economies of scale, foreclosure in some export markets hurts competitiveness in all by raising costs worldwide.

of direct XDs: inadequate education, skills, productive capital formation, and technological impetus. Statistical sizing-up results suggest the export efficacy of several important old and familiar friends—policies to boost capital, education and labor skills, and appropriable technology.

Policy implications are detailed in chapter 6 but can be summarized here. Since US export controls seem so strong an XD, this project underscores two conclusions from a succession of National Academy of Sciences studies and workshops (1987a, 1991, 1992). US export controls, whether for national security, antiproliferation, or foreign policy should be implemented with:

- maximal multilateralism, to meet the clear objectives of export controls more effectively without symbolic display, and with an explicit goal of smaller sacrifice of US and multilateral exports;
- a commitment ultimately to abstain from unilateral export controls, with immediately increased sensitivity to "economic security and to foreign availability," especially in light of the heavy incidence of such controls on leading sectors of the US economy.

To help attain these objectives, I also recommend the following:

- auxiliary mechanisms to enhance the target efficiency of export controls: specifically, annual, timely "sizing-up" reports using the methods of this study or better ones; accessible and automatic foreign-availability investigations[2] that cover export controls for any purpose, including foreign policy sanctions and antiproliferation; official support for and supplementation of end-use and end-user monitoring and intelligence.

Since officially supported export finance also seems to have moderately strong effects on US exports in leading sectors, this project supports recommendations that:

- official US export finance programs be supplemented to make US capital goods competitive in financial terms with those of overseas rivals, especially in projects and procurements where private financial markets are inadequate—for instance, many public infrastructure proj-

2. Foreign availability investigations are aimed at establishing whether items subject to US export control could be obtained in adequate quality, quantity, and timeliness from countries that are not maintaining such controls.

ects in developing and transition economies are often financed by mixed credits. Recent agreements on official finance should, of course, be respected and strengthened further.

Since this project finds indicators of indirect XDs manifested through inadequate public policy toward education, capital formation, and technology, it supports a "back-to-basics" recommendation that:

- growth-enhancing policies toward human, physical, and technological capital be endorsed not only in their own right, but also for their favorable US export spillovers.

Background

New strands are emerging in the ongoing US debate over America's growth and competitiveness in the world economy. Policymakers and business leaders have become increasingly concerned that policies undertaken for security, environment, foreign policy or other good reasons discourage US exports. They are also concerned that policies undertaken abroad to support competitiveness, such as export promotion and finance, are not pursued vigorously by the United States. Discussion of these export disincentives (XDs for short) is still quite muddled. There is little consensus on what constitutes an export disincentive and still less on how quantitatively important they may be, individually and in the aggregate.

Nor is there a clear answer to why exports are important relative, say, to any other productive activity. The United States has historically been able to afford a certain nonchalance about its export competitiveness. It was never the most important thing. But today the cost of such nonchalance regarding exports is rising.

This project helps clarify the policy discussion of self-inflicted export disincentives. It first catalogs alleged XDs and then goes on to "size up" scattered quantitative estimates of these disincentives. The cataloging task is similar to that undertaken recently by Bergsten (1988, chapter 6) or by Frank (1990) for the Committee for Economic Development, but this study seeks to provide a more detailed inventory. The task of sizing up is similar to that undertaken by Morici and Megna (1983) for certain US XDs or by the National Academy of Sciences (1987a) for national-security export controls, but this book aims to be more comprehensive and cover all alleged XDs.

This assessment of the nature and size of alleged disincentives is an essential precondition for informed discussion of whether policies should be changed to ameliorate their disincentive effects on US exports. The other important part of informed discussion is how well policies succeed in achieving their objectives for security or environment and how those objectives should be traded off against the export goal. This study does not address that issue.

For some, the study may seem a return to broad themes treated in the reports of the US President's Export Council under President Jimmy Carter (1980) and President Ronald Reagan (1984, 1988). But the stakes today are higher, the issues have changed, and those reports supplied little quantitative guidance. Exports have become much greater engines of macroeconomic growth and microeconomic discipline, and hence liberalizing forces, in the United States and elsewhere. US policies toward former enemies, corporate and personal taxation, antitrust, regulation, and foreign corrupt practices have all been modified substantially. Policies toward the environment, product liability, export subsidies, tied foreign aid, education, and infrastructure have become more prominent in discussions of US competitiveness. Proliferation of arms supply capability is a growing concern, as is the way that apparently innocent exports and other commercial ties may help unreliable countries to become suppliers of nuclear, chemical, and biological weaponry. Fear of uncontrolled proliferation is replacing the Cold War as a motive for US and multilateral export controls.

It therefore seems timely to reconsider the cost of XDs, and to do so quantitatively this time. Chapters 1 and 2 introduce the sizing-up exercise with data, conceptual distinctions, extensive illustrations, and a discussion of why exports are increasingly important to US prosperity.

Chapters 3, 4, and 5 are the heart of the attempt to size up the cost of US XDs. They are a sequence of survey, simulation, and statistics. Chapter 3 records the results of formal and informal discussions with exporters and export experts. Chapter 4 summarizes recent numerical approaches to sizing up the cost of US XDs and adds some new ones. Chapter 5 develops two new econometric approaches to the same enterprise.

Chapter 6 summarizes the results and discusses policy implications.

Contents

Chapter 1 is an overview of the importance of exports to the American economy. It begins with a review of the recent data on US export performance and that which can be gleaned from surveys and profiles of typical firms exporting from the United States. US exports have risen dramatically as a share of GDP, not only since the trough of 1985 but also since the previous peak in 1980. But they have not recovered their historical share of world export markets. Surveys suggest, however, growing export consciousness among small and medium-size US firms, which might translate, on one calculation, into as much as $13 billion of additional US exports in the long run. Certain XDs are shown later in the study to place such new exporters at risk.

The focus then turns to the reasons policymakers should care about US export performance and why they might be concerned about policies that, while undertaken for legitimate economic, social, or security reasons, may nevertheless impede US exports. Economic reasons for caring about US export performance include innovation, scale economies of many types, and competitive discipline associated with producing for a global market, as well as more traditional gains from international trade. They also include important reasons the United States might care about the structure of its exports and not merely the aggregate level and whether its firms do business from US locations or from affiliates abroad.

Chapter 2 addresses definitional and conceptual issues, using extensive real examples. How should export disincentives be defined? For example, should they be net or gross of positive policies that serve to promote exports? The most important distinctions drawn are between "demand-constricting" and "cost-inflicting" XDs, and in the latter case, between those that inflict extra fixed costs and those that inflict extra variable costs. Demand-constricting XDs such as embargoes are more potent than cost-inflicting XDs such as tax disadvantages. And fixed-cost-inflicting XDs are more potent than variable-cost-inflicting XDs, in part because XDs that affect fixed costs lead to a shakeout in which new or small exporters die and an industry is left less dynamic and less competitive.

Chapter 2 also introduces the important issues of "additionality" and "avoidability"—how XDs confronting only some product lines, firms, or industries, and those affecting only some sources or destinations, often get offset by compensatory exports of other products, firms, or industries from other sources or to other destinations. The US export ban on logs from federal lands is a classic example of a (merely) apparent XD because offsetting exports from unregulated lands "undo" it. With such offsets, apparent XDs are almost never as severe as they seem to overall export competitiveness, nor should their estimated effects be blithely added together.

But the one case in which such "redemptive" offsets fail is export controls that constrict demand in high-technology and other scale-intensive sectors. Then zero offsets are to be expected, and perverse offsets are possible. XDs in constricted markets can make exporters less competitive in unconstricted markets, not more, and hence less competitive globally across the board. As a rule XDs in constricted markets yield no incentive to catch up in unconstricted markets. This is an important conclusion of the sizing-up exercise. It is the principal reason export controls have especially large quantitative impacts that leading sectors of the US economy bear heavily.

Chapter 3 provides an ordered catalog of alleged XDs, based on formal and informal surveys. The ranking, by degree of consensus over apparent quantitative importance, is noncontroversial. But by comparison with calculations in later chapters, the rank-order judgments of informed commentators[3] varied in an interesting way. They understated the severity of the most severe XDs and overstated the severity of the least severe, according to the simulation and statistical calculations in later chapters. Chapter 3 summarizes these findings, using real cases to illustrate.

Chapter 4 begins by assembling existing estimates and guesstimates of the quantitative significance of several important export disincentives, done with varying degrees of empirical rigor. This chapter also takes a first stab at distinctive sizing-up methods, using the fairly simple technique of numerical simulation. Such simulation models have been widely applied to size up the effects of nontariff import barriers and to "benchmark" a firm against its rivals, and are generally thought to be instructive, if not definitive. The simulation models in this chapter are distinctive in their explicit treatment of imperfections in competition and market structure. Because of these, it turns out (somewhat surprisingly) to be possible to draw conclusions about the relative potency of various export disincentives. Embargoes and export controls are particularly potent XDs, and fixed-cost XDs are more potent than variable-cost XDs. Among other things, variable-cost-inflicting XDs can be more readily shifted to and shared among workers, shareholders, customers, and suppliers than demand-constricting XDs or fixed-cost XDs. This makes them less problematic as XDs but sometimes more problematic as distributional shocks.

Chapter 4 also employs the simulation methodology to provide a range for US export deterrence due to inadequate export finance, running from $0.5 billion to $3.1 billion of forgone exports, and concentrated on heavy machinery and equipment.

Chapter 5 applies somewhat more sophisticated econometric techniques to selected export disincentives. The econometric results ratify the conclusions from chapters 2 through 4. Demand-constricting XDs have large effects. Cost-inflicting XDs have small, if any, effect. Two different approaches are pursued. The first is particularly well-suited to demand-constricting XDs, and the second, to cost-inflicting XDs. Each seeks to answer the key counterfactual question: what would exports be with less or none of a specific XD?

---

3. The Institute for International Economics hosted study groups in November 1990, January and July 1991, and July 1992 at which industry representatives and policy officials helped identify what they view as the most important disincentives in various industries. We have followed up contacts made in these study groups over the telephone and in interviews and meetings.

The first approach examines 1989 and 1991 data on cross-importer variation in US exports for both aggregate and industry categories. It tries to explain the variation using aggregate indicators: real income, population, and distance. Residuals from econometric regressions are examined for countries whose trade makes them outliers. The former communist bloc and countries that are targets of US sanctions and antiproliferation controls turn out to be suspiciously large negative outliers, especially in high-technology sectors and especially relative to other countries with radically different culture or politics from the United States. The figures are open to a variety of alternative interpretations, most of which suggest sizable US exports forgone. The largest of these reach almost $20 billion of forgone exports for 1989 and above $25 billion of forgone exports for 1991. Two-thirds to three-quarters of these forgone exports are from chemical, machinery, equipment, and instruments sectors that are the most technologically intensive by the usual measures. Compared with results from the same econometric approaches to British, French, German, and Japanese exports in 1989 and 1991, the United States is still an outlier in exports from these key sectors. As much as $11 billion in 1989 and $14 billion in 1991, however, could be ascribed to multilateral agreement among these trading partners, though ambiguity exists in distinguishing voluntary multilateralism from US-coerced multilateralism.

The current relevance of these calculations is then discussed. Liberalization of national security controls since 1991 has almost certainly increased US export potential to former Cold War rivals. But tightening of US antiproliferation controls since 1991 may merely have changed the justification and added extra names of trading partners that are targets of US and global concerns about war and terrorism. Some are small, but others, such as China, India, and Iran, are quite significant. High-technology sectors still appear to bear the principal burden of anti–nuclear proliferation controls.

The second approach in chapter 5 examines US state-by-state data on cross-regional variation in 1987–89 exports for both aggregate and industry categories. It tries to explain the variation using indicators of state comparative advantage such as endowments of labor, capital, land, and resources, as well as technological indicators such as patents. It then adds in various alleged XDs that vary across US states, to see if they help to explain the cross-state export variation. One XD in question is "environmental regulation," sometimes alleged to reduce the international competitiveness of certain high-profile US tradeables. A second is direct income taxes, alleged to put all US exports at a competitive disadvantage because of the inability to rebate them on exports or charge them to imports (as our trading partners can do for their predominant indirect taxes). A third is inadequate government export promotion, and a fourth is inadequate public infrastructure.

The cross-regional econometric perspective presumes that such cost-inflicting policies also may *increase* the international competitiveness of at least some sectors—for example, pollution control equipment or exports that do not depend much on public promotion or infrastructure, such as many services. Resources will move from more burdened sectors to less burdened sectors over the years prior to the three on which the cross-section "snapshot" is based. Regulation, taxes, and export promotion might thus change the structure of trade, but not necessarily or predictably its overall volume.

That, in fact, is often the pattern of the results. Neither taxes, environmental regulation, nor export promotion have any discernible negative or positive effect on overall US exports of manufactures. States with higher direct taxes do seem to have lower exports of electrical and other equipment, but this seems to be offset by higher exports in other manufacturing sectors. The results for environmental regulation and inadequate export promotion give almost no support to the belief that they are important export disincentives, even at the sectoral level, though the empirical measures are suspect in both cases.

Finally, states with more public capital do tend to have higher exports of manufactures, especially transport equipment. But a dollar of private capital is estimated to generate more than two and one half times the exports that a dollar of public capital does. In fact, one of the most arresting conclusions from chapter 5 is the significantly greater exports enjoyed by US states with comparatively large professional work forces and patent and capital stocks. A hidden US XD of great quantitative importance, though indirect, may be inadequate government support for private acquisition of technology, education, skills, and productive capital.

Chapter 6 sizes up the sizing-up exercise and adds detail to the policy conclusions summarized above.

1

Exports and American Competitiveness

Until recently, US exports have had a low profile. The largest firms, of course, have always exported.[1] For many others, exports just "weren't their thing." At least two generations of American students have learned about exports almost as an afterthought, as the quid pro quo for high-quality, price-competitive imports, or as the *X* before *M*, long after *C*, *I*, and *G*,[2] and important only in its ability to top *M* or its failure to do so. US government policies toward exports in their own right have been scarce,[3] although policies toward national security, foreign aid, and industrial regulation had important spillovers to US exports.

Until recently, exports were an eddy in the mainstream of US economic activity, and both government and the public could afford to treat them with some nonchalance.

No more.

Exports have begun to grow strongly as a share of US economic activity, as have concerns over the competitiveness of US goods and services

1. 64.3 percent of 1987 exports of US manufacturers came from establishments employing 500 or more workers. Such large establishments represented only 6.4 percent of the number of manufacturing establishments exporting. However, exports of wholesalers and retailers (43.8 percent of total US exports, including their exports of some manufactured merchandise) were somewhat less concentrated on large firms (*US Department of Commerce News*, ITA 92-40, p. 3).

2. *X*, *M*, *C*, *I*, and *G* are standard shorthand in most economics textbooks for, respectively, exports, imports, consumption, investment, and government spending.

3. The US Export-Import Bank dates from 1933 and Webb-Pomerene Associations from 1918. Both are described below.

in world markets. More and more US firms see inviting opportunities for export growth and diversification into new markets. And influential voices have urged the US government to abandon export nonchalance and embrace active export promotion.[4]

This chapter documents the growing importance of exports for the US economy, first numerically and then conceptually. The conceptual treatment assesses old and new reasoning about why exports are beneficial. The assessment aims for balance: exports may be too important to neglect, but they should hardly be treated as a mercantilistic holy grail. The conceptual treatment also raises an important question: how many of the national benefits from exports can be attained alternatively by selling goods from US-owned facilities abroad? The basic answer is some, but not all.

Data Profile

Over the past 14 years US exports have been subject to strong crosscurrents: rapid appreciation of the dollar, then depreciation; internationalization of important markets; revolutionary technological change in transportation, telecommunications, and other sectors; and surging foreign direct investment from Europe, Japan, and elsewhere.

Internationalization alone has created a striking increase in US export dependence. Exports have risen as a share of US GDP from 8.5 to 11.7 percent between 1980 and 1992 (see table 1.1a and b). The dollar-driven slump in export dependence from 8.5 to 7.2 percent between 1980 and 1985 was reclaimed three times over between 1985 and 1992 (11.7 percent). In fact, table 1.1a shows that export growth created more than 40 percent of overall US output growth during this period, though exports were on average less than 10 percent of output. Though the role of exports as an engine of growth has been widely reported, neither the size nor duration of that role is well-known.

At a more disaggregated level, sectors as diverse as the following all had export dependence that exceeded 25 percent of total sales in 1990: oil field machinery (77 percent), aircraft (48 percent), semiconductors (42 percent), mining machinery (36 percent), computers and peripherals (36 percent), construction machinery (29 percent), industrial/analytical instruments (29 percent), and machine tools (28 percent) (Competitiveness Policy Council 1992, figure 3). Even traditionally import-sensitive

4. For example, Cooney (1991) for the National Association of Manufacturers, or Competitiveness Policy Council (1992, 1993a, b). The Clinton administration appointed an interagency Trade Promotion Coordinating Committee in 1993 to streamline US official export promotion programs and to make them more effective.

Table 1.1a Contribution of US exports to recent US growth, 1986–92 (in billions of 1987 dollars, except where noted)

Year	Growth of US exports[a] over previous period	Growth of US GDP over previous period	Export growth[a] as a share of growth in GDP (percentages)
1986	20.4	124.7	16.4
1987	34.4	135.5	25.4
1988	57.6	178.6	32.3
1989	50.2	119.4	42.0
1990	38.2	39.5	97.0
1991	29.4	−56.5	n.a.
1992[b]	32.0	107.6	29.7
1991 over 1985	230.2	541.2	42.5
1992[c] over 1985	262.2	648.8	40.4

Table 1.1b Base-period totals for US exports and GDP (in billions of 1987 dollars, except where noted)

Year	US exports	US GDP	Share of exports in GDP
1980	320.5	3,776	8.5
1985	309.2	4,280	7.2
1991	539.4	4,821	11.2
1992[c]	576.2	4,939	11.7

n.a. = not applicable

a. Exports of goods and services from the national income and product accounts.
b. Third quarter of 1992 over third quarter of 1991 at annual rates.
c. Third quarter of 1992 at annual rates.

Sources: Economic Report of the President 1992, table B.2, pp. 300–301; US Department of Commerce, Bureau of Economic Analysis Press Release 92-49.

sectors such as autos and steel increased exports, albeit from very low levels.[5]

Though exports have been strong in the internal competition for US resources, they have been weak in the external competition for world customers. Contemporaneous with growing US export dependence has

5. US-resident auto plants exported 318,000 passenger cars in 1991 to countries other than Canada, roughly 5 percent of their 1991 production, and plan to double or triple their exports during the 1990s (*Wall Street Journal*, 8 November 1992, B1, B6). The 1992 value of US auto exports (Canada excluded) was $22 billion (*Wall Street Journal*, 18 January 1993, A1, A6). Steel firms such as Allegheny Ludlum and USX are modest exporters of stainless and electrical steel and seamless pipe used in oil and gas drilling (*Wall Street Journal*, 17 January 1991), A6).

been shrinking US shares of global export markets—one of the classic measures of a nation's competitiveness. Table 1.2 shows trends for a number of manufacturing categories and for manufactures as a whole. The losses in global export shares were especially dramatic during the early 1980s as the dollar appreciated and have not been fully reclaimed during the dollar reversal of the late 1980s.[6] The rate of trend loss in competitiveness was, however, least pronounced in the most competitive US sectors, especially high-technology equipment and instruments (tables 1.2 and 1.4; Cooney 1991, 14). US trends in global export competitiveness differ from those of Germany and Japan, its chief rivals. Table 1.2 shows that Germany has maintained roughly stable shares across most sectors, while Japan has gained somewhat in higher-technology sectors and surrendered export shares in sectors such as steel and textiles, in which its productivity edge was low or negative.

Declining US export competitiveness is more closely linked to geography than to nationality. Table 1.3 shows that US multinational firms and their majority-owned overseas affiliates have maintained a very stable 17 to 18 percent of world export markets over more than two decades. Although US-domiciled parents have lost shares, their foreign affiliates have gained back virtually all that was lost. Competitiveness "originating" in US management decisions has been in essence transferred abroad—perhaps, as we will see, because of export disincentives.[7]

Table 1.3 also reveals that US-domiciled multinational parent firms have lost export shares more slowly than the nonmultinationals that are included in the export trends of the United States as a whole. Table 1.4 sheds further light on these trends. Losses are minuscule between 1982 and 1988 for the highest-technology exports, and US export shares of global high-technology trade actually increase between 1977 and 1988. Declining US export competitiveness is instead concentrated in medium- and low-technology manufactures. And in all but low-technology categories, US multinationals and affiliates consistently "outperform" the geographical aggregates that include nonmultinationals. It is also significant that the disparity between US corporate and geographical performance is most pronounced in the higher-technology categories. There is reason to think, as we will see in chapters 3, 4 and 5, that export disincentives have had an especially large effect in high-technology sectors.

Yet hopeful indicators of resurgent US export performance can be detected in a number of recent surveys. Lenz (1992, chapter 6) is one

6. US exporters have recovered most of their 1980 share of exports by rivals within the Organization for Economic Cooperation and Development but have lost shares to non-OECD rivals.

7. The same pattern shows up in scattered data on global production. Berry, Grilli, and López-de-Silanes (1992), for example, estimate that US auto firms accounted for 34 percent of world production while the geographic United States accounted for only 28 percent.

Table 1.2 US, Germany, Japan: shares of world exports, selected categories, 1980–90 (percentages)

SITC group	1980	1986	1989	1990
Iron and steel[a]				
US	4	2.5	3.5	3
Germany	15	14.5	13.5	14
Japan	20	17.5	13.5	11
Chemicals (SITC 5)				
US	15	12.5	14	13
Germany	17	17	16.5	17
Japan	4.5	6	5.5	5.5
Machinery and transport equipment (SITC 7)				
US	17	n.a.	15	15
Germany	16.5	n.a.	15	16
Japan	14.5	n.a.	18	16.5
Office machines and telecom equipment (SITC 75, 76, 776)[b]				
US	20	n.a.	18.5	17
Germany	10	n.a.	7	7
Japan	21	n.a.	25.5	22
Automotive products (SITC 781–784, 7132, 7783)[b]				
US	12.5	10	11	10
Germany	21	20.5	21.5	21.5
Japan	20	25.5	22	20.5
Textiles (SITC 65)				
US	6.5	4	4.5	4.5
Germany	11.5	12	11.5	12
Japan	9	8	5.5	5.5
Clothing (SITC 84)				
US	3	negl.	2.5	2.5
Germany	7	7	5.5	6
Japan	negl.	negl.	negl.	negl.
Total manufactures (SITC 5–8, less 68)				
US	13	11.5	12.5	12
Germany	15	15	14	14
Japan	11	14	12.5	11

SITC = Standard International Trade Classification
negl. = negligible

a. SITC revision 3, division 67.
b. All included in SITC 7.
c. Less than 2.5 percent.

Source: General Agreement on Tariffs and Trade (1992), *International Trade 90–91*, tables IV.23, 29, 34, 39, 43, 47, 54 and comparable tables from earlier editions of the same GATT annual publication.

Table 1.3 US, US multinational parent, and overseas affiliate[a] shares of world exports of manufactures, 1966–88 (percentages)

	1966	1977	1982	1985	1988
US	17.1	13.2	14.6	13.4	12.4
US MNC parents	10.7	9.2	9.4	9.4	8.1
US MNC affiliates[a]	6.6	8.3	8.2	8.9	8.9
US MNC Total	17.3	17.5	17.6	18.3	17.0

MNC = multinational corporation
a. Majority-owned overseas affiliates of US multinational parent firms.

Source: Lipsey (1991a), tables on pp. 12 and 13 and related text, and Lipsey and Kravis (1991), table 1.

Table 1.4 US and US multinational firm[a] shares of world exports, selected categories, 1977–88 (percentages)

	1977	1982	1985	1988
"High technology" manufactures[b]				
US	18.8	22.0	20.7	21.5
US MNCs	28.8	33.3	32.6[c]	31.1[c]
"Medium technology" manufactures[b]				
US	15.6	15.9	14.3	12.8
US MNCs	26.5	24.1	24.7[c]	23.7[c]
"Low technology" manufactures[b]				
US	8.3	9.1	7.5	6.8
US MNCs	8.3	8.1	8.3[c]	7.5[c]

MNC = multinational corporation
a. US multinational firms encompass US parent firms and their majority-owned overseas affiliates.
b. Technology level is defined by the research and development intensities of the industries from which the exports originate; classification carried out by the National Bureau of Economic Research from United Nations trade data.
c. Figures were extrapolated from 1982 on the basis of the industry of the affiliate.

Source: Lipsey (1991a), table on p. 19 and related text, and Lipsey and Kravis (1991), table 5.

of the most extensive; tables 1.5 and 1.6 summarize two others. The unanimous message is that US firms may be beginning to cultivate a true "export culture." Small US firms are turning increasingly toward export markets, and small, localized exporters are marketing to a wider array of destinations.[8] Lenz (1992) assesses these trends as "too little,

8. See also "Little Companies, Big Exports," *Business Week*, 13 April 1992; "Small US Companies Take the Plunge into Japan's Market," *Wall Street Journal*, 7 July 1992, B1; and "America's Little Fellows Surge Ahead," *The Economist*, 3 July 1993, 59–60.

Table 1.5 Export performance of 160 manufacturing firms from a typical Midwestern state by type of exporter, 1990[a]

	Passive small[b] (n=51)	Active small[b] (n=59)	Active proximate[c] (n=25)	Active global[c] (n=25)
Exports as a share of sales (averages)				
1989	1.2	1.9	11.1	23.5
1992[d]	1.1	8.8	15.4	28.2
Ratio of periods	0.9	4.6	1.4	1.2
Density (average number of customer countries)				
1989	0.8	2.0	6.0	19.4
1992[d]	0.7	5.1	9.3	25.2
Experience (average years exported)	5.2	4.3	7.5	10.3
Employment (average total)	18.8	82.2[e]	154.7	696.8
Average percentage loss in employment without exports	0.0	0.6	4.0	21.4

a. Random sample of 500 out of 8,761 firms from industries in SIC groups 20–39 from Harris Publishing Company data base; 160 usable returns from 176 responses to a survey instrument. Unrevealed state is fairly typical of the United States as a whole, according to data supplied by Kotabe and Czinkota (1991, 2). Categories correspond respectively to Stage 1, Stage 2, Stages 3+4, and Stage 5 exporters in Kotabe and Czinkota (1991, table 1). Passive exporters fill only unsolicited export orders; active exporters solicit orders. Proximate exporters ship only to countries that are geographically close or that have a similar culture; global exporters ship indiscriminately.

b. Exports equal less than 5 percent of sales.

c. Exports equal more than 5 percent of sales.

d. Expected value.

e. Two firms were omitted by Kotabe and Czinkota from active, small exporters because of their unusually large absolute size. Neither, they report, was an outlier in terms of ratios, but one had 3,000 employees and the other 7,600. Including them in the average employment figure would raise it from 82.2 to 253.3.

Source: Kotabe and Czinkota (1991).

too lean" to make a quantitatively significant difference in near-term US export competitiveness. Yet his data show more than 250 firms with less than $500 million of sales per firm expecting to increase export dependence from 21 to 27 percent of sales between 1989 and 1993, and 30 firms with sales between $500 million and $1 billion increasing export dependence from 12 to 15 percent of sales. If these numbers are scaled up using US Department of Commerce data that suggest there are more than 100,000 US exporters in this size range (*US Department of Commerce News*, CB 89-92 and accompanying table "Business Profile of 100,118

Table 1.6 "Small" members of the National Association of Manufacturers by share of exports in total sales, 1988–92 (n = 2,105)[a]

Year	Zero	<5%	Total 0–5%	5–10%	11–25%	>25%	Total 5–25%
1988	44	30	74	10	7	7	24
1989	48	30	78	12	4	4	20
1990	37	35	72	18	4	4	26
1991	35	36	71	15	5	9	29
1992	34	39	73	14	8	5	27

a. Sample of 8,200 small NAM members surveyed for 1992. 2,105 usable surveys were returned through 28 February 1992. Percentages of respondents not responding with data for 1988, 1989, 1990, and 1991 are, respectively, 3,2,2,0.

Source: "NAM Small Manufacturers Operating Survey," Question 10, provided courtesy of Christian N. Braunlich, executive director, Small Manufacturers Forum, National Association of Manufacturers.

Exporters"), the result could be an increase in US exports of as much as $13 billion between 1989 and 1993—no small potatoes from admittedly small exporters.[9]

Table 1.5 suggests similar encouragement. Active small exporters, serving only two countries for less than 2 percent of their sales in 1989, project that their customers will rise to five countries by 1992 and their export dependence to 9 percent. Somewhat larger exporters ("active proximate"), making up half of the small firms surveyed, see customer countries rising from six to nine and export dependence rising from 11 percent to more than 15 percent.[10] Finally, the survey summarized in table 1.6 suggests steady attrition in the number of small US firms that never export.[11]

Whether this growing export consciousness will be choked off by cyclical strengthening in the United States and weakening in Europe and Japan is a worrisome question. US export growth to the rest of East

9. Lenz (1992, 504–05) also shows that these smaller firms are much less likely than larger, established firms to rely on overseas affiliates for foreign sales. Of course, as they become more significant exporters, they, too, might gradually move production locations in the same direction as their larger rivals.

10. An internal Department of Commerce document (RVargo/TD/TIA/OIT/9-11-89) that works from the same 1987 reconciliation of exporter and establishment data documented in footnote 1 finds that half of all US exporters of manufactured products export to only one country, fewer than one in five export to more than five countries, and the most popular customers are Canada and the United Kingdom, respectively.

11. Other data in table 1.6, though somewhat erratic, also support the notion of growing export culture among small US firms.

Asia and Latin America is still very strong. Some recent surveys see US exports flattening in 1993, others see continued export deepening.[12]

But why does all this attention to exports and competitiveness really matter?

Why Are Exports Important?

Some answers are obvious, familiar, and can be treated briefly. Others are more subtle and spring from changes in both the global trading environment and the means for analyzing it. The first two benefits from exports are familiar from discussions of macroeconomics. Two others are familiar from microeconomics. Five others from microeconomics are less familiar but perhaps increasingly relevant to the modern economy.

The microeconomic benefits in essence explain why, apart from considerations of employment and trade balance, a nation might benefit from more exports. That is, they explain why having larger export shares[13] in overall economic activity might be beneficial to a country. They also explain why some sectors' exports may be "better" than others, or why export-related jobs may be better than others. Most of this study reasons from a similar perspective.

Some Familiar Macroeconomic Answers

Jobs. Exports are important when they provide jobs for otherwise unemployed workers and resources. It is likely that US unemployment rates would have been considerably higher if exports had not grown so robustly in the late 1980s (see table 1.1a and the discussion above). However, this benefit is not unique to exports. Any extra spending—say, consumption or investment—could have reemployed the unemployed.

Exports are also important if the jobs they provide have special attractiveness compared with other jobs. This in fact tends to be true and is discussed as a microeconomic gain from trade below.

The Trade Balance. Apart from employment, exports may be important when the trade balance is important. For example, if the United

12. The *Wall Street Journal* (17 December 1992, B2) summarizes a bleak forecast from the National Association of Manufacturers, but more recent surveys are more reassuring (*Wall Street Journal*, 18 January 1993, A1, A6; 30 March 1993, 36; 21 April 1993, A1; 4 August 1993, A2). In August 1992 a Dun & Bradstreet survey of 5,000 US companies found 62 percent expecting increased exports, 33 percent flat exports, and only 5 percent declining exports (*Wall Street Journal*, 27 August 1992, A2).

13. Having larger export shares with constant levels of employment and trade balances implies having larger import shares, too. Microeconomic evaluations often assume this and leave employment and trade-balance effects to be analyzed by macroeconomics. But see box 1.1.

Box 1.1 The ambiguous effect of export promotion on the trade balance

Few of the benefits of exports described in this chapter depend on the trade balance—even though exports are, of course, by definition its "positive" component. That is just as well, because the impact of export promotion (and trade policy in general) on the trade balance is ambiguous. A case could be made for the effect being positive, negative, or zero.

Positive. Simple intuition seems clear. The trade balance is $X-M$, so it must be more positive with more exports; promoting exports would improve the trade balance.

Zero. A floating exchange rate system undermines simple intuition. Policies that promote demand for our exports cause increased demand for dollars, hence a stronger dollar in the foreign exchange markets, and hence compensating, dollar-induced declines in exports and rising imports. Export promotion would have little if any effect on the trade balance. The same would be true, for that matter, for almost any border policy.[1]

Negative. Just as floating rates undermined the simple intuition with which we began, so does mobile international capital undermine the case for no effect. US export promotion increases the returns on export-oriented investments in the United States and discourages similar investments abroad, especially by any multinational firm that has a choice between sourcing from the United States or sourcing from an affiliate abroad. Most of this effect of export promotion would represent a one-time cross-border reallocation of corporate assets, discussed in greater detail in table 1.7. But there is also a recurring effect whenever economies are growing (McCulloch and Richardson 1987, 54–56): proexport policies will cause yearly increments to a firm's investable funds to be also reallocated toward the United States. Strong US export prospects will encourage yearly replacement investment, plant expan-

States is concerned about reducing or financing trade deficits, then "more exports" has considerable appeal over other broad alternatives: import compression, sales of US-owned foreign or domestic assets, increased US indebtedness to foreigners.

But would promoting exports really influence the trade balance? The question is more subtle than it appears and has no unambiguous answer, as box 1.1 shows.

Some Familiar Microeconomic Answers

Gains from Trade. Exports are important when they are the means to obtain unique or uniquely desirable imports. Exports are the quid pro quo for imports in the classic account of gains from international trade. They are the cream of the nation's competitiveness exchanged for the cream of overseas competitiveness, what our workers and resources produce best traded for what theirs produce best. Without exports and imports, each nation is left producing more milk and less cream. How-

sion, and facilities upgrading in the United States and discourage it abroad. Larger US and smaller foreign investments annually for these purposes will imply a larger steady-state US capital-account surplus and a correspondingly larger steady-state current-account deficit.[2] So export promotion may actually increase the current-account deficit because of its ongoing impact on investment incentives.

The ambiguity is clear. No one knows whether boosting exports may improve the trade balance, leave it unaltered, or worsen it. Fortunately, resolution of the ambiguity is not necessary for the perspective adopted in this book. Whatever the account above, US exports themselves are smaller with XDs than they are without. And that is reason enough to care, as this chapter argues. I will maintain that the ratio of exports to output is a much more important correlate of prosperity than the difference between exports and imports!

1. Bergsten and Cline (1987, especially 138–43) reason from this perspective. So does Litan (1991), although he also pays passing respect to the third view, that the impact is negative.

2. This discussion springs from current analytical thinking about international payments, which stresses the role of international assets trade as the dominant determinant of exchange rates and, hence, of trade in goods. Although we have become accustomed to viewing international borrowing as a means of filling gaps between exports and imports, in today's world this traditional perspective may be misleading. It may be more nearly correct to think of trade in goods and services as adjusting to gaps between capital exports and imports. When this is so, the nation's current-account deficit will mirror the capital-account surplus; for further discussion, see McCulloch and Richardson (1987).

ever, even this benefit is not unique to exports. Improved technology is another way of turning milk to cream.

Exports are important equivalently because the jobs they provide are on average more productive and remunerative than the jobs that would be available with a smaller export share in overall economic activity. Exports and "high value-added" jobs go together.[14]

Political Economy. Exports are important for political and diplomatic reasons. Export interests are often effective counterweights to insular special interests and thus helpful in supporting open-trade policies, as documented by Destler and Odell (1987). Export interests serve informally as "commercial diplomats," communicating US market, cultural, and political information to foreign interests.

14. Indicative of this are studies such as US Trade Representative (1992) that show that US workers in export-related jobs earn 17 percent more than the average US worker and that US workers in import-sensitive industries earn 16 percent less than average. See also Bregman, Fuss, and Regev (1991), who find a similar pattern in Israel.

Newer Answers from Microeconomics

Modern thinking about the current world trade environment suggests many new and less obvious reasons why exports may be important. Potential new benefits from exporting include fixed-cost economies, competitive intensity, diversification and self-insurance, informational and infrastructural externalities, and competitive "timbre."

Modern thinking also emphasizes two fundamental questions. The first fundamental question is whether some export sectors promise more of these new benefits than others do. If so, then concentrating export advantage in such sectors would be especially desirable, and XDs in such sectors would be especially costly. Some reasons for believing this to be the case will be apparent below. The second fundamental question, which is subsequently addressed, is whether these benefits can be achieved just as effectively by overseas affiliates of US firms as by US exports.

Fixed-Cost Economies. Exports are important when they allow fixed resource costs to be spread across a larger customer base. An open world market of 10 firms, each with its own research and development (R&D) laboratory, for example, conserves resources, compared with a world with 180 closed national markets, each with 10 firms and 10 R&D labs. The first world requires exports; the second need have none. In other words, exports mean low overhead.

Competitive Intensity. Fixed-cost economies notwithstanding, exports are important when they increase the density, and hence the intensity, of competition. An open world market of 1,800 firms (180 countries with 10 firms per country), each able to sell freely to any customer, has more intense competition than the segmented world of 1,800 firms divided into 180 national markets served by 10 firms each. The first world requires exports; the second need have none.

The qualitative density of competition matters, too, not merely the numerical density. An open world market of 1,800 finely differentiated varieties of a product comes closer to satisfying the precise specifications of industrial buyers and consumer preferences than a segmented world of national markets with 10 varieties available in each.[15]

---

15. Qualitative density, or the number of varieties available for any basic product group, is sometimes considered to be of minor importance. The attitude is that variety caters to the rich, whose preferences for BMWs relative to Mercedes ought not to be indulged by the society at large. But this attitude is both dubious on the face of it and misleading. Variety is not frivolous. More than two-thirds of US exports and half of US imports are made up of intermediate and producer goods, purchased by firms themselves for productive use and further processing. Qualitative density can make available "just the right lathe" or "the perfect truck for our route structure," increasing corporate productivity, not consumer utility.

Diversification and Self-Insurance. Exports are important when they facilitate diversification. Since business cycles are not synchronized across regions, a nation's firms enjoy more predictable and stable prosperity when exports allow them to be diversified than when the same average business volume is locally concentrated. A derivative benefit is that export promotion may even serve as an alternative to import protection. Recourse to "trade remedies"[16] that are contingent on "injury" can be less frequent in a world where exports even out an industry's business swings and injury from rival imports is consequently less frequent. From this vantage point, exports are a form of natural self-insurance for a firm and its workers against the vagaries of import competition. Exports conserve resources that would otherwise be expended in formal administrative procedures and trade barriers that proxy inefficiently for insurance.[17]

Informational and Infrastructural Externalities. Exports are important for their externalities.[18] For example, they can be effective channels by which information about foreign markets and customers is acquired and disseminated within the United States. Activities of seasoned exporters convey free yet valuable information to neophyte exporters, reducing their costs of "taking the plunge." Early exports enhance the economic viability of private export infrastructure: trade journals, advertisers, marketing consultants, and shippers and consolidators that specialize in markets abroad (see, for example, "More Small Firms Are Turning to Trade Intermediaries," *Wall Street Journal*, 2 February 1993, B2). Later exports enjoy lower costs "free" because of the existence of infrastructure that could not have covered its fixed costs without the early exports. These informational and infrastructural externalities are of less importance, of course, when whole export sectors become seasoned. But they may be still quite significant for the United States where exporting is still an exotic sideshow for many firms, especially those that are smaller and newer.

Exports can also be effective channels by which information about US products and services is disseminated to overseas buyers. So-called "follow-on" business involves both repeated sales and service by a firm

16. Trade remedies are temporary barriers to imports (safeguards, antidumping, and countervailing duties) that are contingent on demonstrations of injury from import competition.

17. Self-insurance also reduces so-called "moral hazard" inefficiency, in which formal insurance such as trade remedies causes firms to alter behavior in costly ways—for example, diverting corporate resources into bringing antidumping suits to harass foreign rivals.

18. Externalities are hard-to-price (and unpriced) benefits or costs that spill over from one economic activity to another. Pollution is a classic negative externality. Those described in the text are positive externalities: the value of information and infrastructure that one firm gains "free" because of the exporting activities of other firms.

that has made the initial export incursion, and ancillary overseas sales and service by its own suppliers and subcontractors, which inherit the relevant commercial connections and networks "free" or at greatly reduced cost.[19] Conversely, as we will see below, export unpredictability, that XDs often foment can create negative informational externalities by making all US exporters suspect as unreliable suppliers.

Competitive "Timbre." Exports are important as a barometer of a firm's competitive success and also as a catalyst. Successful exporting is winning one's share of the "away games" (a helpful sports metaphor). Authors know that their writing is influential when it is translated for foreign audiences. Restaurants know that their service is first-rate when they attract clientele from far as well as near. Producers know that their product is competitive when its export markets are as diverse and deep as its home markets. Actively seeking to achieve export success can sharpen incentives to innovate[20] and can tighten up a firm's internal organization, enhancing its internal efficiency. Nelson (1993, 16–17 and 24) summarizes the strong cross-national evidence (from elsewhere in the same book) for how export orientation provokes corporate innovation. Caves and Barton (1991, 71–72, 93–93), Nishimizu and Page (1991), and Tybout (1992, 205–06) summarize the more mixed cross-time evidence for how export orientation enhances internal corporate efficiency.[21]

So Are Some Export Patterns Better Than Others?

Several reasons are now apparent for believing that some sectors' exports might be better than others. If all else were the same between two sectors, exports would be more beneficial when they come from those sectors with large fixed costs, significant positive externalities, and numerous varieties of quality (detected in practice by strong product

19. See Krugman (1992) for the view that even broader "infrastructural externalities," involving suppliers of nontradeable intermediate goods as well as marketing and information, establish an empirically relevant case for policy promotion of scale-sensitive industries that depend intensely on them. Facilitating exports is, of course, one example of such policy promotion.

20. Modern methods of time-series econometrics, for example, have resuscitated the venerable correlation between exports and growth as a causal relationship in which exports drive growth (Marin 1992).

21. Caves and Barton find that an industrywide measure of internal efficiency ("X-efficiency") is actually lower for US industries when export orientation is higher. But they argue that there is further evidence that this is an anomaly due to aggregation: exporting firms within an industry do enhance their internal efficiency, as expected. Nonexporting firms end up further away from the efficient frontier that has been pushed out by the exporting firms; when exporting and nonexporting firms are added together, the industry as a whole looks further away from its efficient frontier, but precisely because exporting has raised the standard for internal efficiency.

differentiation and by simultaneous exports and imports). High-technology goods and services are generic examples, with large R&D costs, significant spillovers to successive generations of their own and related sectors, and numerous vintages and variants between obsolescence and the latest version.[22]

High-technology and other sectors with these characteristics are sometimes called "strategic." The economic analysis of strategic trade and industrial policy has developed rapidly in the past 20 years yet is still subject to fierce debate over its deepest fundamentals.[23] The results of the present study depend on the debate only for their intensity. The cost of using XDs to attain worthy objectives is even greater than I calculate here if the sectors that are especially burdened are strategic in the sense just described.

If the answer to the first fundamental question is yes, we should care about the sectoral composition of US exports, what about the second? Should we care if US multinationals shift from US sourcing to sourcing abroad?[24]

Are Sales from Overseas Affiliates Just as Good?

Overseas investment by US firms seems initially to be capable of realizing many of the benefits of exports that modern thinking emphasizes. US firms that sell from foreign affiliates can spread fixed costs, compete intensely, diversify, and self-insure. They can enjoy positive externalities and maintain internal fitness by foreign sourcing as well as they can by exporting from US shores. US shareholders in US multinational firms ultimately earn these newer benefits through dividends and capital gains. Since corporate shareholding is widely dispersed across American society and includes the pension funds and insurance companies that repre-

22. The semiconductor industry is just one example of such a sector, in which the United States is both an exporter of differentiated specialty chips and microprocessors and an importer of "commodified" dynamic random-access memory (DRAM) chips. Other examples include specialty and standardized steel, machine tools, and machinery and equipment.

23. For example, whether there are such "strategic" sectors in practice is a matter of considerable debate. If so, whether governments could identify them successfully is just as fiercely debated. The traditional economist's answer is "no," and is well-represented in Krueger (1990). A more sympathetic "yes" is rendered by Krugman (1992), Teece (1991), and Tyson (1992). See Richardson (1993) for a survey of this literature.

24. This study finds that XDs often cause such a shift in sourcing. Whether US investment abroad and US exports are positively or negatively related in general is a broader question with a more ambiguous answer. One of the more recent studies, by Hickok and Hung (1992), finds the correlation to be negative. Another, by Bergsten and Graham (forthcoming), finds it to be positive. One of the most thorough, by Bergsten, Horst, and Moran (1978, chapter 3) finds that early MNC investment in sales, marketing, and distribution facilities abroad enhances exports but that subsequent additional investment has no effect.

Table 1.7 Three scenarios: benefits from exporting[c] versus selling from abroad[b] and neither exporting nor selling from abroad[a]

Alternatives	"Us"	"Them"
The Insular Case[a]		
Market density (number of firms)	1	1
Facilities (number of sites)	1	1
Export shares	0	0
Investment Cross-Penetration[b]		
Market density (number of firms)	2	2
Facilities (number of sites)	2	2
Export shares	0	0
The Export Case[c]		
Market density (number of firms)	2	2
Facilities (number of sites)	1	1
Export shares	½	½

Evaluation:

a. Alternative 1: Suitable capacity, but monopoly and lack of variety.
b. Alternative 2: "Excess" capacity, but duopoly and variety.
c. Alternative 3: Suitable capacity, duopoly, and variety.

sent US workers at all levels of income, the newer benefits of either US exporting or selling from abroad seem widespread.[25]

But there are two possible reasons for preferring exports to selling from abroad: duplication and distribution.

Duplication. Selling from abroad can often involve costly and wasteful duplication of capacity merely to avoid XDs. Table 1.7 provides a simple illustration that captures the essence of the concern.[26] Alternative 1 describes wasteful self-sufficiency in a hypothetical sector. Fixed costs cannot be spread, competition is minimally intense, no supplier is diversified, and cross-border externalities and dynamic stimuli are absent. Alternative 3 describes the other extreme—pure (and symmetric) export dependence, in which all the newer benefits of exports can be realized.

Alternative 2 describes a halfway house that is often the consequence of XDs.[27] Firms invest in sites abroad to avoid XDs, without abandoning

25. Those outside the labor force or in positions without fringe benefits that depend on equities markets gain only indirectly, if at all, from exports or sales from overseas affiliates. Channels for any indirect gains are input/output linkages and transfers/tax revenues.

26. See Brainard (1993) for a fully developed model in the spirit of the illustration.

27. It can also be the result of unpredictable medium-term misalignment of and variability in real exchange rates. This study makes no attempt to size up the export effects of misguided macroeconomics, but such policies are often alleged to cause similar proliferation of facilities through investment cross-penetration, and hence the same potential for waste

sites at home. Though some of the newer benefits are realized—competitive intensity, external stimuli,—fixed costs cannot be spread. They are in fact possibly "paid twice" (or even more often), causing all countries to sacrifice scale economies of market size, which are increasingly viewed as significant sources of gains from geographical concentration and trade.[28]

Distribution. A second possible reason for preferring exports to sales from overseas affiliates is the distribution of income in the United States between internationally "mobile" US resources and what I will call "rooted" resources. US XDs divert mobile resources from US activity to overseas activity.[29] This diversion deprives rooted US resources, such as low-skilled labor, of services that enhance their productivity. Rooted resources gain more from US exports than from the same sales carried out from US affiliates abroad. And the same XDs may discourage exports from US-based affiliates of foreign firms, which also may prefer to invest and source from abroad.[30] Rooted resource owners especially ought to oppose XDs. Mobile resource owners, by contrast, can realize many of the same export benefits by investing or moving abroad.

Rooted Americans include low-skilled labor, high-skilled workers in nontradeable service sectors (basic health care, real estate, government, personal law, primary and secondary education, etc.), and owners of commercial land and other properties. All of them lose productivity[31] when US managers, researchers, engineers, and other mobile workers are transferred abroad, and when foreign counterparts stay away because

---

from excess capacity and excessive outlay for fixed cost. Export diversion from temporary, though medium-term, misalignment is, however, presumably milder than export diversion from indefinite XDs.

28. In addition to the sources cited in note 23 above, see Grossman and Helpman (1991), who demonstrate the point in a dynamic model of research and development, innovation, production, and trade.

29. John J. Murphy, president and chief executive officer of Dresser Industries, provides an especially clear illustration. In describing inadequate US official support for export financing, he says, "Within our own company, we have dealt with this problem [inadequate official export finance] by manufacturing products developed by our US divisions in European and Japanese factories that qualify for export financing, and these foreign factories typically export 70% to 90% of their production!" (personal correspondence to C. Fred Bergsten, chair, Competitiveness Policy Council).

30. Lipsey (1991a) and Graham and Krugman (1991, pp. 67–70), for example, show that foreign-owned firms in the United States are less export-oriented than US multinational parents, though they emphasize as explanations their smaller size, younger age, and different industry mix, rather than US XDs.

31. To be more precise, the rooted resources necessarily lose average productivity, but may or may not lose "marginal productivity." For many typical—but not all—production relationships (functions), they will lose both average and marginal productivity (for one standard treatment, see Nicholson 1989, 281–82).

foreign investors find the United States to be an inhospitable location for exports.[32] These movements may have an unfortunate shadow as well if the United States geographically becomes more exclusively populated by rooted resources. US comparative advantage, exports, and production will, if anything, then shift in the direction of services and in the direction of industries requiring low labor skills.[33]

There are two possible rationales for caring about these distributional XD effects and their shadows. One is the familiar assessment of who receives the gains—specifically that the United States might deem owners of rooted resources to be more disadvantaged than owners of mobile resources, even in the presence of taxes and transfer payments that aim to resolve such distributional concerns directly. The second rationale is political, almost philosophical—that "US interests" ought somehow to represent US geography more intensely than US global interests, to represent its residents more than its citizens, and to represent its rooted more than its mobile resources.[34]

Whether one accepts these distributional rationales or not, there are still reasons to worry about the cost of US XDs. Some, such as the sanctions and export controls described in the next chapter, constrain both exports and sales from US affiliates abroad. Others invite wasteful duplication by causing less of the first and more of the second. In any case, "we" may often seem to be our own commercial enemy. So it is important at the end of this chapter to reassert the important reasons why US XDs exist in the first place and to differentiate this study from mindless mercantilism.

Important Caveats and Distinctions

Obviously, this study argues that export competitiveness is not to be treated as lightly as the United States has in recent decades. But exports are hardly sacred. And XDs are usually not mere whim.

---

32. They need not lose either average or marginal productivity when US technology is licensed for foreign use, since typically its availability for US use will not be diminished by such licensing.

33. Cutting in the opposite direction is any decline in migration by low-skill workers into the United States, due to better opportunities in US and other transplants in their home countries.

34. These comparisons are, of course, also influenced by tax/transfer policies, especially toward Americans working abroad and foreign-source income of US multinationals. They are also influenced by US policy toward inward foreign investment. The general concern over defining US interests is most frequently associated with Robert Reich's 1990 article "Who is US?" But for a counterview, see Tyson (1991). The controversy has been an important concern of the Clinton administration in its first year.

"Standard of Living Matters More Than Exports." Though exports contribute to a nation's standard of living in the important ways discussed above, the fundamental determinants of material living standards are technology, resources, incentives, and the institutions that allow markets to function and that regulate them. XDs are costly not just if they deter exports, but if they inhibit technology, divert resources, blunt incentives, and burden commerce. Certain of the policies alleged to be XDs, and described in this book, may actually do all of these things, and thereby lower material living standards. But if they reduce exports and national output proportionately, without changing their ratio, we may leave them unmeasured in this study—not deemed unimportant, but just not pure XDs by the precise definition adopted in the following chapter.

"Man Doth Not Live By Bread Alone." Most XDs aim at worthy objectives that are hard to measure in material terms: national security, democratic integrity, a safe and sustainable environment. One can hardly complain about a trade-off that involves material sacrifice for a greater, yet nonmaterial gain. Hence XDs may often be warranted for their enhancement of broad welfare. Yet two questions need always be answered. Do XDs actually attain their nonmaterial objective, or do they end up failing, and thus serve merely as symbols of the longing for some greater good? And if they do attain their objective, are the benefits worth the material sacrifice? This study we will address parts, but not all, of each question. I will try to size up the effectiveness and the material sacrifice of XDs. This study will not, however, try to assess the value of nonmaterial objectives.

2

Characterizing US Export Disincentives: The Issues

What exactly are export disincentives? So far, I have described them vaguely. It is time to be more precise. Which export disincentives matter most, either quantitatively or because they foreclose access to the many benefits of exports described in the previous chapter?

This chapter begins to answer these questions. I start by defining an XD family, then make some distinctions among its members and illustrate them with personality profiles. Certain family members turn out to be more dangerous than others. Some family members are easily rendered harmless. How the whole family affects exports, as opposed to its members one by one, turns out to be a subtle issue.

Definitions and Taxonomy

Export disincentives are self-imposed policy deterrents to export trade, according to chapter 1. This characterization begs a number of important questions. One question is "relative to what?" Another is "why?" I will address the first question explicitly and the second implicitly, through illustrations of various XDs in this chapter and the next. I begin with a precise characterization of XDs, then describe how it can be broadened or narrowed to fit alternative circumstances and judgments.

Relative to What? A Double Comparison. One answer to the "relative to what" question is "relative to domestic sales." XDs are a form of trade policy; they make a distinction at the border. Sales to foreign customers are treated differently from sales to domestic customers. Policies that impose barriers to export sales that do not exist for domestic sales I will call "restrictive" XDs. Policies that deprive exporters of inducements to commerce that domestic sellers enjoy I will call "passive" XDs. The classic examples of restrictive and passive US XDs are, respectively, export controls and official promotion and financial support of exports, which will be described below.

Yet pure XDs are more than border policies. A second part of the answer to "relative to what?" is "relative to our trading partners' policies." A double relative—a double comparison—is necessary to characterize the purest XDs on which there is most agreement. US export controls would presumably not deter exports much if all countries had comparable controls that discriminated against their exports relative to their domestic sales. Nor would exports be deterred much by inequity in government commercial support for exports relative to domestic sales, as long as all governments practiced comparable inequity.[1] US export controls are an archetypical restrictive XD because, on the contrary, the United States is alleged to impose export controls that exceed those abroad. US export promotion/finance is an archetypical passive XD because, on the contrary, official US support is alleged to fall far short of official foreign support.

In this light, much of the sizing-up exercise is based on the following precise characterization: *XDs are policy choices that either deter exports or fail to encourage exports more, relative to domestic sales, than policy choices abroad do.*

For some purposes, a broader conception will be useful. For example, this study provides a range of estimates for reductions in US exports to Eastern bloc enemies as part of Cold War multilateral export controls—controls that reduced exports of the entire Western alliance.[2] To take another example, this study provides a range of estimates for the effects of certain US regulatory policies that are alleged to diminish US export competitiveness, even though these policies make no distinction at the border.

For other purposes, a narrower conception may be useful. For example, commentators who are skeptical of proactive government commer-

1. *World* exports would presumably be lower if all countries imposed export controls and neglected export promotion, but US shares of the smaller total would presumably be the same. This would still involve sacrificing benefits to the extent that US and world shares of exports in total output were lower, as discussed in chapter 1.

2. The broader conception is useful because controls that appear to be multilateral are often really unilateral, a result of one country's intransigence. Such has been true, for example, of multilateral controls that still exist on exports to Russia of fiber optics, which are harder for intelligence agencies to monitor than traditional telecommunication networks, and of most exports to Vietnam. In both cases, and many others, the United States has been the implicit "enforcer" of multilateralism, for reasons of national security in the first case, and in the second, to elicit maximal cooperation from Vietnam on remaining prisoner-of-war issues.

cial policy might want to focus on "restrictive" XDs only. In distinguishing restrictive from passive XDs, the norm that is chosen is, of course, all-important.[3]

In this study, however, what matters most is US border policies relative to those of other countries, not relative to a preferred norm. I have attempted to size up how much greater US exports would be if US policies emulated those of all or some of its rivals, not whether US policies retard US exports more or encourage them less. I have also attempted, in the case of multilateral export controls, to size up how much greater US exports would have been if controlling countries had mutually refrained from restricting exports relative to other suppliers abroad.

In other words, what matters most to this study is the rough size of US XDs relative to those abroad among all or a subset of trading partners, not whether they are restrictive or passive.[4]

This approach was compatible with the spirit of the experts' comments in our survey (see chapter 3). Most "knew an XD when they saw one" and could rank them by perceived importance. Precise definitions and distinctions were unnecessary. Just one or two asked whether we were studying only "sins of (policy) commission"—restrictive XDs—or "sins of omission," too!

Archetypical US XDs

In the last section, it was noted that export controls and inadequacies in official promotion and financial support of exports were the classic cases of XDs. They are archetypical for several reasons. They are some of the oldest and most quantitatively important US XDs. They illustrate the worthy strategic and other goals that US XDs usually aim to achieve, whose value this study does not attempt to assess. They are both restrictive and passive. And they mix demand-constricting and cost-inflicting influences, a further distinction described below—most of the examples both shrink the demand facing US exporters and raise their costs.

---

3. Among possible norms are the "free" market, or some hypothetical policy-managed market, or the real status quo. For example, a US XD that concerns some commentators is antitrust policy. One argument is that the United States still regulates research and development consortia too stringently, keeping in mind that R&D is a well-accepted source of US export competitiveness. Judged against a free-market norm with no policy, any US constraint against such consortia would be a restrictive XD. Judged against a pure antitrust norm in which the general policy rule bans all interfirm cooperation or collusion, any US constraint would be a passive XD, since US trading partners make more explicit antitrust exceptions for R&D than does the United States.

4. The calculations can be easily unpacked, however, in a variety of ways, for example, to focus on restrictive XDs only, as we will see in chapters 4 and 5.

Export Controls[5]

Exporting, unlike domestic sales in the United States, is a contingent right (National Academy of Sciences 1990, 99). The most important contingencies historically have concerned national security and foreign policy.[6] Since the advent of the Cold War in the late 1940s, the US government has restricted exports of goods, services, and technology with military or dual-use military and civilian applications to target countries that threaten its national security. It has also restricted exports strategically for reasons of foreign policy—for example, to express its strong disagreement with and to deter South African policies of apartheid. The most extreme form of these restrictions is an export embargo, a complete ban on sales to proscribed demanders.

US export controls have been implemented historically through licensing requirements and procedures administered variously—and sometimes simultaneously—by the US Departments of Commerce, Defense, Energy, and State. Exporting firms have been forced to create costly export licensing departments and procedures, described below and in box 2.1. The coverage and severity of these export controls has risen during crises, such as the Iranian hostage crisis and the Soviet invasion of Afghanistan in 1979, and waned during détente, such as in the early 1970s and late 1980s. During the middle 1980s, roughly half of all US manufactured exports required a validated license, some on a product- or technology-specific basis that could in extreme cases take years to process, much less obtain.[7] (Technically, all US exports require some license, though many are easy to acquire.[8])

---

5. The descriptive literature on US and multilateral export controls is vast and is only briefly summarized here. The more recent representatives include Bertsch and Elliot-Gower (1992), Heinz (1991), Kuttner (1990; 1991, chapter 6), MacDonald (1990), and National Academy of Sciences (1987a, 1987b, 1991, 1992).

6. A third contingency is "short (domestic) supply," which has sometimes justified export controls to preserve the domestic availability of strategic materials such as oil or to counter domestic inflation such as helped motivate the soybean embargo of 1973. See Bergsten (1974) for illustrations and a useful history. Short-supply controls are less relevant today than in the 1970s and often involve "offsets" that are described in the cases of logs and oil later in this chapter.

7. This is still sometimes true. During the early 1990s India was forced to wait three years for US approval of a single $10 million Cray Research Corporation supercomputer. The US government was concerned that the Cray might facilitate the nuclear weapons and missile programs that it has suspected India of advancing. In the meantime, for about the same $10 million cost, India managed to perfect its own low-end supercomputer (priced at $350,000 each). India is now marketing it both at home and in Britain, Canada, Germany, and Russia. The country canceled the still-unapproved Cray contract (*Washington Post*, 19 March 1993, C1).

8. One expert observed that, "In fact, when you take baggage on an international flight, you are actually doing so under a US general export license called 'G-Baggage,' even though you don't file any documents and probably didn't know your government technically had to 'license' you to pack your socks!"

Other countries, of course, have enforced similar export controls, so US exporters have not been disadvantaged in principle. But practice has often been otherwise, with the US exercising unique or tighter controls compared with export competitors.

Since 1949 the Western alliance has coordinated its national security controls through the Coordinating Committee on Multilateral Export Controls (known as COCOM), currently with 17 members. Foreign policy controls are also sometimes coordinated, as in the case of South African, Iraqi, and other sanctions (Hufbauer, Schott, and Elliott 1990). Arms controls, though not explicitly covered in this study, have also been coordinated. Their relevance here is that they, too, often cover "dual-use" products such as computers, software, telecommunications equipment, machine tools, industrial furnaces, and laboratory testing devices.[9]

US exporters have never been satisfied with multilateralism in practice, however. They have argued that the United States has acted unilaterally for merely symbolic reasons, as it did in the mid-1980s ban on US equipment for the Soviet gas pipeline in Europe. They have argued that the United States has had stricter enforcement than other countries and a slower, more cumbersome bureaucratic approval/denial procedure.[10] They have argued that competitive East Asian and Latin American suppliers have not joined the various export control regimes, thereby undermining their success but leaving US exporters to pay the commercial cost. They have argued that export controls make no sense unless all sources of foreign availability[11] come under the regime.[12]

---

9. Under the Arms Export Control Act, for example, the US Defense and State Departments until 1992 insisted on individual validated licenses on exports of almost any encryption software. Such software encodes data and messages to prevent unauthorized access and is used by many businesses as well as by governments. Yet travelers could carry encryption software out of the United States on a diskette, and it was also exported routinely by several European countries. US controls were finally loosened in mid-1992, and the US government developed its own encryption software in 1993 (readable only by US officials with legal authority to conduct a wiretap). But at least a portion of early-1990s sales by US firms, estimated at more than $2 billion, was presumably lost (*Wall Street Journal*, 22 July 1992, B2 and 19 April 1993, B5; *Washington Post*, 14 November 1991, B11).

10. See National Academy of Sciences (1987a, appendix C) for an extensive discussion of burdensome procedures in the mid-1980s.

11. US law in principle prohibits export controls for national security reasons when the product is available in foreign countries, but not for foreign policy reasons. Exporters must file a foreign-availability petition with the Department of Commerce, along with relevant documentation. Various rules of origin and quality comparability must be met, and approval is by no means automatic. In early 1993, for example, telecommunications exporters filed a petition in regard to high-speed fiber-optics transmission equipment, allegedly available from Israeli rivals, and computer exporters filed one in regard to mid-capacity machines that were allegedly being exported by Brazil, Israel, Korea, Hong Kong, and Taiwan (*Inside US Trade*, 11 June 1993, 3).

12. European exporters have never been satisfied with multilateralism in practice either, seeing COCOM procedures endorsed by the United States as ways of slowing them down

Box 2.1 Two cases of cost-inflicting US XDs

Each of the following illustrations obviously involves a mix of fixed and variable costs of XDs. But the first prominently features fixed costs and the second, variable costs. The first also illustrates how selective sectors can bear disproportionate burdens from generic policies.

The fixed costs of product liability. For many chemicals and pharmaceuticals, machine tools, aircraft, and other sophisticated products, a great deal of money is spent before the first unit is produced to procure insurance, retain legal counsel, and perfect designs that are as safe as makes economic sense. Changes in US judicial interpretation and implementation of product liability law over the past 30 years (Schuck 1991) have made compensatory and punitive damages for torts an increasingly large business cost.

But that cost is not fully shared by foreign rivals unless they have extensive stakes in the United States. Frank (1991, 123–24) provides a cogent summary:

> ...the present US liability system is far more advantageous to plaintiffs in both procedural and substantive law than that of any other country. Discovery rules are more generous, particularly in determining awards for noneconomic loss. The concept of punitive damages, commonly used in the United States, is completely absent in most countries. Also, among major industrial countries, only the United States permits contingent fees enabling a plaintiff to bring a suit without paying legal costs up front. In the great majority of countries, liability suits are decided by judges, not juries. As a result of these differences, it is easier to sue and receive higher awards and settlements in the US.

Estimates of the extra costs facing US business are very high, running from slightly less than 1 percent of national output to 2 percent (Sturgis 1989; Litan 1991; Christman 1992; *Wall Street Journal*, 16 October 1992, A1).

General aviation aircraft are often alleged to be a prime example of the massive costs of exposure to product liability litigation. In 1978 more than

During the past 10 years, distinctions between export controls for national security, foreign policy, and arms proliferation became even harder to make than usual. The Soviet empire disintegrated. Its former members began liberalizing and trying to integrate themselves with the world economy. And a growing list of countries became capable of producing nuclear, chemical, or biological weapons and the missiles to deliver them. Export controls have been reoriented as a result.

Some reorientation has been unilateral and defended as responsible leadership while multilateral negotiations continued. President Bush implemented the Enhanced Proliferation Control Initiative (EPCI) by executive order in August 1991 after nine months of public discussion. In order to slow the spread of production capability for nuclear and other weapons of mass destruction, EPCI imposed strict licensing

so US exporters can catch up! This illustrates how apparently multilateral controls may reflect US unilateral initiatives, discussed above.

14,000 single-engine aircraft were shipped in the United States, of which more than 2,800 were exported (worth $124 million), for an export-to-sales ratio of almost 20 percent. In 1990 shipments were down to 608, and exports were minimal. One of the major suppliers of such aircraft, Cessna, stopped production in 1986; another, Piper, after declaring bankruptcy, sold its remaining corporate assets to a Canadian buyer (*Aerospace Facts and Figures* 1989-90, Aerospace Industries Association of America; *Wall Street Journal*, 11 December 1991, A1).

The variable costs of corporate licensing departments. A major United States exporter of high-technology products in the early 1990s, with $14 billion in annual sales, of which $4 billion to $5 billion may be exports, employs more than 100 people in its export licensing department. These employees evaluate licensing needs on each sale; assure that each export customer is not proscribed as a threat to security, an arms proliferator, or other undesirable that would expose the company to fines and jail sentences; and document the firm's surveillance of its customers and their subsequent use of the product in case of challenge by US export control authorities.

Monthly lists of "denied" customers can run 170 pages, and cross-classified lists of parts and products by customer and destination, which the firm must maintain, would require 50,000 pages of text. No part, no matter how insignificant, can be exported without being cleared by this department.

The positions require considerable judgment and skill. Each of the 100 employees costs the company an average of $100,000 per year in payroll, benefits, and ancillary personnel costs. Other costs of maintaining the department include equipment, space, and periodic audits of customer use to ensure compliance (that cost typically is $10,000 per audit).

Overall costs of maintaining this department annually are in the tens of millions of dollars, "verging toward $100 million" for the firm described here, according to one source. Expressed as a percentage of its export costs, half of that inflated figure would exceed 1 percent. Estimates from chapter 4 would imply export losses for this firm of up to 0.8 percent, or $40 million.

requirements on goods, services, or technology that would aid countries seeking such capability.[13] Furthermore, US exporters were assigned responsibility for monitoring the ultimate destination and end use of all exports to ensure that the United States would meet the antiproliferation goals, with severe civil and criminal penalties for failing to do so. In essence, since the export of anything at all might be used by a proliferator (who might live in any country at all), or to advance proliferation, more US exporters were affected than ever by EPCI controls. An illustration of some of the increased costs of the EPCI are described in box 2.1. These costs are now largely borne by exporters themselves rather than by the US government's export control bureaucracy.

13. The US list of target countries suspected of pursuing biological weapons capability, for example, includes most Middle Eastern countries and Afghanistan, Bulgaria, China, Cuba, India, Myanmar, North Korea, Pakistan, Romania, South Africa, most of the former Soviet Union, Taiwan, and Vietnam (*International Trade Reporter*, 28 April 1993, 689).

Some reorientation efforts for export controls have, however, been multilateral. The COCOM countries have drastically pared their traditional list of proscribed goods, technologies, and communist target countries and have actually worked to enlist former targets of the controls to enforce COCOM procedures (US General Accounting Office 1992a, 2–5). The United States and 26 other members of the Nuclear Suppliers Group agreed in 1992 to coordinate export controls for 60 dual-use goods. In the mid-1980s the United States helped create both the Australia Group, which coordinates export controls for materials that could be used in chemical and biological weapons, and the Missile Technology Control Regime (MTCR), which coordinates export controls for goods and technology crucial to missiles that could carry weapons of mass destruction.

But implementation procedures for these multilateral agreements are still not clear.[14] So the United States has continued to refine its own export control commitments unilaterally as well as multilaterally.

In November 1992 President-elect Clinton said that preventing the proliferation of weapons of mass destruction would be one of his administration's highest priorities (*International Trade Reporter*, 18 November 1992, 1, 962), and an interagency group is working on export control regulations to that end. US exporters have contributed a detailed set of recommendations for thoroughly rewriting the Export Administration Act to minimize needless export deterrence, but at the same time concerns about proliferation seem to be mounting.[15] The potential for export deterrence is still strong.[16]

---

14. For example, approvals and denials of specific exports are at every nation's discretion. Although there is an obligation to notify other members, there is no secretariat (as for COCOM) to encourage parallelism of treatment (*Inside U.S. Trade*, 7 May 1993, 4). Nor is there multilateral monitoring and reporting of subsequent uses of exported products, including, for example, subsequent reexports.

15. The Export Administration Act (EAA) is the key law governing US export controls on products other than munitions and nuclear materials. The EAA of 1988 lapsed in 1990 for two years because of dissension over how to rewrite it. US export controls were maintained and modified in the interim under the powers granted to the president by the International Emergency Economic Powers Act. The EAA of 1988 was revived in the spring of 1993 to cover the one-year period during which US export controls are meant to be rewritten "from the ground up."

16. A mid-1992 survey of 42 large US exporters by the National Association of Manufacturers found that 30 to 40 percent of their exports still required a validated license, compared with roughly 50 percent in the mid-1980s. More than half of the respondents thought that the US export control system was no better or worse than it had been the previous year, before EPCI. On average, each devoted 24 employees and $1.3 million a year to export licensing and compliance (*International Trade Reporter*, 26 August 1992, 1, 494).

Official Export Promotion and Finance[17]

Inadequate official support of exports is a passive XD. It is alleged to deter potential exports, not to ban actual exports. The two most important facets of official export support are export finance and export promotion, which are usually justified by some sort of market failure that the government can ameliorate—for example, information about foreign customers that is less complete than for domestic customers, or commercial creditworthiness standards that are needlessly stricter on export loans than they are on domestic loans.[18]

Finance

Official export finance is aid in the form of credit, often required to arrange exports of expensive items. Such aid takes several forms: loans, guarantees, and insurance. Official agencies sometimes make loans directly to exporters or foreign buyers of exports and sometimes subsidize the cost or lengthen the maturity of export credit. Official agencies often guarantee the value of export-related loans provided by private lenders and often insure exporters against losses from failure of an importer of their products to obtain or service a loan.

All these forms of official financial support for exports can be translated into reduced interest rates on export credit. Subsidized loans reduce such interest rates directly; guarantees and insurance reduce such interest rates indirectly by decreasing the size of the risk premiums that must always be built into the terms of credit. In this chapter, and especially in chapter 4, we will see how official financial support reduces not only the cost of exporting but shifts out and steepens the demand for a country's exports. It is in that sense that inadequate official support for export finance can be seen as both a cost-inflicting XD and a demand-constricting XD.

The United States provides official support for export finance through a number of agencies. The US Export-Import Bank (Eximbank) is the oldest and most familiar, but there is much more general support provided by offices of the Departments of Agriculture and Defense, as well as by the Small Business Administration.

17. The descriptive literature on official export finance and promotion is vast and is only briefly summarized here. On export finance, Abraham et al. (1992), Jepma (1990), OECD (1990), and Ray (1986) are recent examples, and on export promotion, Cavusgil and Czinkota (1990), Morrison (1993), and US GAO (1992a and b). On cross-country comparisons of both finance and support, see Schultz et al. (1991) and Industry Commission of Australia (1991).

18. Whether these really are market failures, and whether government export support would be warranted even if they were, are controversial issues. See Morrison (1993) for a summary and evaluation.

Through Eximbank, the United States also manages its "war chest" facility, designed to preserve fair competition among US exporters and foreign rivals in developing-country markets for infrastructure equipment, capital goods, and technical services. Financial terms in such markets were increasingly subsidized by other governments during the 1980s as a form of foreign aid that was tied to purchases of the country's own exports. These subsidies are called "mixed credits," reflecting the combination of aid and finance. Though OECD governments agreed in 1991 to a set of multilateral rules meant to "level the playing field,"[19] US exporters find the rules vague, doubt the enforceability of them, and claim that up to $10 billion of projects in the process of being negotiated were "grandfathered" out of being covered by the agreement.

US exporters and many commentators find official US support for export finance to be generally meager compared with that of important rivals. The Competitiveness Policy Council's (1993b, 180) summary is representative: ". . . export credit programs . . . of the United States . . . support less than 5 percent of total US exports. In contrast, Japan's export credit programs support 49 percent of Japanese exports, while 11 percent of exports are supported in Italy, 10 percent in France, 8 percent in the U.K., and 6 percent in Germany."

It is in this sense that inadequate US export finance might be considered a passive XD.[20] But the experts surveyed in chapter 3 were not in full agreement on this characterization.

Promotion

Official export promotion is sometimes taken to include finance but otherwise encompasses an array of informational, networking, marketing, and consciousness-raising programs to facilitate a country's exports. The United States has a panoply of such programs, usually small and rarely coordinated across the various departments and agencies in which they are housed. The US General Accounting Office (1992b and c)

19. The rules banned such mixed credits to high-income countries and to middle-income countries as well unless alternative credit sources were unavailable. They also established ceilings for the maximum amount of finance subsidy that can be provided to customer countries.

20. A closely related issue is whether general US financial policies discourage export financing from private-sector financial intermediaries. Limitations on branch or universal banking, for example, are sometimes alleged to make US intermediaries too small or too ill-informed to finance exports at competitive rates; excessive capital requirements and surveillance legislated by the United States in 1991 are sometimes alleged to have put US intermediaries at a competitive disadvantage relative to global rivals, with indirect export-deterring effects; community reinvestment regulations are sometimes alleged to tilt US intermediaries away from lending even on a national scale, much less for international activities.

describes them in detail and provides cross-country comparisons. The US government appears to underspend several important rivals on export promotion:

Country	1990 export promotion spending per $1,000 of nonagricultural exports
France	$1.99
Italy	1.71
United Kingdom	1.62
United States	0.59
Germany	0.22

Whether inadequate official export promotion is a passive XD is a more controversial question than whether inadequate official export finance is. Both research into comparative export promotion programs[21] and case studies of Germany suggest that industry associations and private export "middleman" companies can often more effectively provide the export infrastructure that is the aim of official export promotion. Indeed, in chapters 3, 4, and 5 below we find almost no evidence that inadequacies of official US export promotion programs have deterred US exports at all.

Further Distinctions

Several distinctions that turned out to matter in sizing up XDs were not apparent at the outset of this project and are described in more detail later. One was the distinction between XDs that altered export demand and XDs that altered export cost. "Demand-constricting" XDs mattered more than "cost-inflicting" XDs. And within those categories, subdistinctions mattered as well. XDs that foreclosed markets mattered more than those that merely encumbered access; XDs that raised fixed costs seemed to matter more, and fatally so to a margin of firms forced out of the export business, than those that raised variable costs. XDs that raised export costs comparably for all sectors had weaker effects on any one sector than XDs that were sectorally targeted.

Demand-Constricting XDs

Demand-constricting XDs are those that shrink or block export demand or that raise burdens to satisfying it. The most extreme example is an

21. See, for example, Keesing's and Singer's (1992) summary of such programs in developing countries.

export embargo, a prohibition of export sales to a particular customer country. The most significant US export embargoes are foreign policy sanctions. Currently, for example, no US export sales are permitted to Libya or North Korea, and only very limited export sales to Cuba, Iraq, and Serbia. Reasons range from discouraging terrorism to deterring violations of human rights, and some are simply residues of the Cold War.

Less severe demand-constricting XDs include milder foreign policy sanctions,[22] product standards that are not internationally harmonized,[23] US policies that provoke foreign retaliation against US exports,[24] and US policies that raise a product's "transfer cost"—the gap or wedge between what an overseas buyer pays for it and what the US exporter receives.[25] Of the various transfer costs, the purest example is cross-border transportation (see box 2.2).

But the most relevant example for the XD project is official support for export finance of "big-ticket" sales. Official support can narrow the

---

22. For example, since 1977 US law has banned US firms from cooperating with the Arab League's long-standing secondary boycott of firms doing business with Israel. US antiboycott regulations expose firms to civil and criminal fines and to bans on export-licensing privileges in such cases, even if they merely supply inappropriate information to Arab League overseers of the boycott. Because of information provided, LA Gear agreed in 1992 to pay a $0.4 million civil penalty. Baxter International was recently fined $6.6 million in civil and criminal penalties as a result of a guilty plea and risks losing even domestic business as a result, including that of the US Defense Department and New York City. Because only France and the Netherlands have similar antiboycott regulations, US businesses have felt unfairly burdened by this otherwise worthy foreign policy goal; they have lost exports to Israel and to the Arab League. German businesses in fact claimed impending losses of $5 billion of exports when the German government moved in 1992 to develop its own antiboycott rules. The estimates that we develop in chapter 5, however, show no strong evidence of significant US underexporting to Arab League members (Hattis-Rolef 1985; Sarna 1986; *International Trade Reporter*, 31 March 1993, 532; *Wall Street Journal*, 3 May 1993, A4; 28 April 1993, A3; 26 March 1993, A1; 20 May 1992, B7).

23. The National Association of Manufacturers claimed in a 1990 publication (NAM 1990, 2) that failure of the United States to act on requests by nine developing countries to develop and integrate product standards had deterred US exports significantly—by $100 million to $300 million to Saudi Arabia and its Persian Gulf neighbors alone, to say nothing of China, Brazil, and India, which were also among the petitioners. Shortly thereafter, a pilot US-Saudi program commenced.

24. For example, "get-tough" policies toward the European Community on agriculture, toward "priority unfair traders" under a new Super 301, or toward China on specific human-rights progress.

25. Transfer costs, because they are a gap between the buyer's price and the seller's return, could be analyzed either from a cost-inflicting perspective or from a demand-constricting perspective. We prefer the latter because it helps to clarify the way XDs such as typical export finance subsidies affect the intensity of competition, measured by an index of the market power of US exporting firms. The intensity of competition, in turn, influences export price, volume, and value. More intense competition, other things being equal, lowers price and increases export volume and value.

Box 2.2 Transport costs as a demand-constricting XD: Oil

XDs on Alaskan North Slope oil shipped through the trans-Alaska pipeline illustrate how transportation costs can be a demand-constricting XD. Alaskan oil exports have been effectively embargoed since 1973, with statutory rigidification in the Export Administration Act (EAA) of 1979, recently reauthorized until mid-1994.

Supporters of the embargo have argued that it enhanced national security, that it supported (protected) US maritime interests, and that it slowed the depletion of a nonrenewable resource. Alaskans have responded that they faced a lower, less profitable demand curve for their oil sales because transportation costs per barrel of oil shipped to Japan are roughly $1.00 lower than those on Alaskan oil shipped to the US West Coast, and roughly $4.00 lower than those on Alaskan oil shipped to the US Gulf Coast. Alaskan senators slowed reauthorization of the EAA to obtain relief from the embargo (*Inside US Trade*, 19 March 1993, 2), and Alaska has even sued the federal government for $2.5 billion in damages because of this effect (*Wall Street Journal*, 4 May 1992, C9).

Although estimates of the exports deterred by this embargo ranged as high as $15 billion per year in 1983 when oil prices were $30 per barrel (de Hamel et al. 1993) and $7.3 billion per year in 1990 when oil prices were $18 per barrel (England-Joseph 1990), it is not clear today that an end to the embargo would encourage significant Alaskan exports. North Slope shipments to Gulf Coast ports are now not economical, and the $1 differential between transport costs to Japan and to the West Coast may not be enough to offset oil companies' implicit earnings on and option value of vessels and refineries that were built especially for West Coast shipments.

gap between the buyer's price and the seller's return by reducing the burden of the financing that the buyer must pay for but the seller will not receive. As chapter 4 will show, official support of export finance expands the export demand facing US sellers, and lack of such support constricts it.

Cost-Inflicting XDs

Cost-inflicting XDs are those that raise the cost of exporting.[26] The purest form raises the cost of exporting for US firms relative to foreign rivals and also relative to the cost of sales to US buyers.

One of the most important illustrations in the United States is the cost of maintaining specialized corporate departments to apply for export licenses, to monitor customer compliance with US export control regulations, to maintain records, and so on, as described in box 2.1. Such administrative costs would obviously not be incurred if a firm sold only

26. Some examples also constrict demand as well. In practice, XDs are mostly one or mostly the other, not purely one or the other.

domestically and are not borne by important US competitors such as newly industrializing economies, who have yet to subscribe fully to the various multilateral export control regimes. Furthermore, it is often alleged by US firms that such administrative costs are higher and more burdensome in the United States than virtually anywhere else in the world, even among countries that cooperate in export control regimes.[27]

Somewhat less pure forms of cost-inflicting XDs raise US exporting costs relative to foreign rivals or relative to domestic sales, but not necessarily both. An illustration of the first is the cost of maintaining product safety and insuring against possible liability for injury caused by a firm's product. US tort law and precedent are extraordinarily tough on producers and generous to plaintiffs, whether domestic or foreign, relative to that of the rest of the world. (This example is discussed in greater detail in box 2.1. Similar examples are discussed in chapter 3.) An illustration of costs raised relative to domestic sales is currency sovereignty, which leads to costly foreign-exchange market transactions, or lack of policy support for special insurance (e.g., against overseas war or political upheaval) or special marketing services (e.g., translation) attached to overseas sales.[28]

Fixed or Variable? Cost-inflicting XDs can raise either fixed or variable costs of exporting, and the export consequences of each vary, as described below. Maintaining specialized accounting procedures in the export divisions of a firm, as required by the Foreign Corrupt Practices Act, is largely a fixed cost—a cost that must be paid, and remains constant, whether one or one thousand units are shipped.[29] Meeting packaging and labeling standards on export sales is largely a variable cost—a cost that must be paid on every unit and that therefore varies, often proportionately, with the number of units sold.[30] Special product stan-

27. Recently, however, German export controls have been significantly tightened, including, for example, 15-year prison sentences for exporters of newly restricted products and overseas pursuit of German offenders by German intelligence agencies (American Institute for Contemporary German Studies 1992).

28. Such costs affect exporters around the world in varying degrees and are not treated in any detail in this study. US insurance support through the Overseas Private Investment Corporation (OPIC) was treated as an export promotion policy in an early study by Morici and Megna (1983, 80–82), but they were unable to determine its intensity relative to US trading-partner counterparts.

29. The Foreign Corrupt Practices Act, enacted in 1977 and refined in the Omnibus Trade and Competitiveness Act of 1988, requires these accounting procedures in order to establish a paper trail for detecting illegal payments. Since 1988, illegal payments under the act include bribes to foreign officials to influence a business decision but not payments to facilitate routine processing of a decision already made. Penalties for illegal payments include fines, jail terms, and ineligibility for US export licenses.

30. Such standards exist for exports of agricultural pesticides, as described in the next chapter, as well as for other goods.

dards required by the Department of Defense on some exports of computers and telecommunications equipment illustrate both fixed and variable costs. Design and software must be altered to disable certain proscribed functions and allow the US government to map and reconstruct certain operations by foreign users; these strictures impose fixed costs. Installation, maintenance, and supply of spare parts must often be performed only by authorized personnel (for example, from COCOM countries), and products must include software bugs and protection against upgrades; these strictures impose variable costs. It is shown in chapters 3 and 4 how fixed-cost-inflicting XDs are generally:

- more restrictive than variable-cost-inflicting XDs;
- more uneven in their effects on firms, causing some to disappear and causing surviving rivals to reclaim portions of their business lost to XDs;
- less able to be passed on to customers and suppliers and thereby "shared."

Generic or Selective? Cost-inflicting XDs can affect all export sectors comparably or some sectors more than others. I will call the first generic and the second selective.

An illustration of allegedly generic XDs are tax inequities that afflict every sector. One claim is that US costs are higher than those abroad because relatively heavy US income taxes cannot, by international convention, be rebated to the seller of exports,[31] whereas the relatively heavy value-added taxes in the rest of the world can be.

An illustration of selective XDs is the product liability burden, described above, which weighs especially heavily on producers of chemicals, pharmaceuticals, aircraft, and machine tools. Another illustration is the inadequate official export finance described above, which affects "big-ticket" exports purchased typically with long-term credit arrangements, but not exports purchased typically with cash or short-term credit.

We show in ensuing chapters how selective XDs have fairly clear and intuitive effects, but that it is hard to detect significant export deterrence from generic, across-the-board XDs, either in practice or in principle.[32]

National or Regional? Cost-inflicting XDs can affect all regions of a country comparably, or some regions more than others. The first is what

---

31. Nor can they can be charged to imports, according to the conventional interpretation of the General Agreement on Tariffs and Trade. See box 4.2 in chapter 4 for the surprising logic of this case and for a recounting of all cases of generic XDs that inflict variable-cost burdens.

32. In this sense, selective XDs have effects similar to selective subsidies, which are distortionary and countervailable under GATT conventions. But generic XDs are similar to "generally available" subsidies, which are not usually countervailable.

we usually have in mind, and when necessary, I will call them national XDs as opposed to regional XDs. National XDs have already been described. An illustration of a regional XD is unique state-by-state packaging and labeling requirements that have been alleged to make exports more costly in sectors such as pharmaceuticals.[33]

So What?

For purposes of sizing up US XDs, this is not merely an arid taxonomy. These distinctions make a difference. Three stand out: importance, competitive mechanism, and incidence.

The first difference was in importance. Demand-constricting XDs turned out to be quantitatively more potent than cost-inflicting XDs. There were two sources for this conclusion, detailed in chapters 4 and 5. One source is that the roughly measured intensity of US XDs was greater for demand restraints than for cost encumbrances. The second source is that the responsiveness of US exports to the former was judged proportionally greater than to the latter. That is, exports are for various reasons more sensitive to demand-constricting XDs than to cost-inflicting XDs, and (furthermore) more sensitive to fixed-cost XDs than to variable-cost XDs.[34]

The second difference was in competitive mechanism. This study steers away from the perfectly competitive assumptions on which economic analyses often rest and includes rudimentary aspects of real-world competition. Thus, for example, the mechanism that explains why fixed-cost XDs were judged more important than variable-cost XDs appeals to imperfect competition. Fixed-cost XDs raise artificial barriers to entry. Would-be entrants, who are almost necessarily small or new suppliers, may be deterred by XDs. As a result, the competitive efficiency and dynamism that entry and threat of entry provides may also be discouraged. Incumbent firms will typically be larger, fewer in number, better able to exploit market power in a distortionary way, prone to holding down exports, and possibly more sluggish in organizational and technological evolution. None of this augurs well for export competitiveness, but none of it characterizes variable-cost XDs either.

The third difference was in incidence. The most important US XDs ultimately turned out to be unfortunately selective. They had their largest impacts on high-technology and other sectors thought to be channels for the benefits of scale, intensity, diversification, and dynamism

33. Whether they really do is doubtful for reasons addressed in the next section of this chapter. Hence, such regional XDs are not treated in any detail in this study.

34. Chapter 4 shows how sensitivity "per unit" can be measured and discusses why it varies for various XDs.

described in chapter 1. However large their overall discouragement of exports, XDs are more worrisome if they penalize the particular US sectors in which US exports may be especially advantageous.

Summing Up XDs: Additionality and Avoidability

As we have seen, XDs matter both one-by-one and in their overall burdensomeness. Sizing up overall burdensomeness, however, involves more than a mere summation across isolated XDs. Past efforts to size up US XDs, summarized in chapter 4, have usually ignored this point.

XDs confronting only some product lines, firms, or industries, and those affecting only some sources or destinations, often get offset by compensating exports of other products, firms, or industries from other sources or to other destinations. With such offsets, apparent XDs are never as severe as they seem to overall export competitiveness, nor should their estimated effects be blithely added together.

A different sort of offset occurs when US XDs induce multinationals to sell from overseas affiliates rather than exporting from the United States. With this offset, US exports may indeed be lower, but sales by US-controlled mobile resources may not. As we discussed in chapter 1, US sales from affiliates abroad are better than nothing, though possibly not as "good" as the continental exports they replace.

The following types of substitution, or XD avoidance, seemed to be the most important in this study.

Product Line Substitution within the Firm

XDs in one product line may encourage exports of another product line. The US telecommunications industry provides an interesting illustration of this and other offsets and is described in more detail below. When the US judiciary implemented the breakup of the former Bell Telephone system into American Telephone and Telegraph (AT&T) and seven regional firms (the regional Bell operating companies, or RBOCs), it placed a number of restrictions on RBOC business activities, most significantly that they were not to engage in US manufacturing.

This clearly inhibited their ability to export telecommunications equipment, and they have fiercely attacked such strictures ever since as an XD. The telecommunications industry as a whole, however, involves both services and equipment prominently. As might be expected, RBOCs have become aggressive US exporters of telecommunications services. At least some of their losses from equipment XDs may be offset by increased services exported. As discussed further in a following section, the offset may not have been complete and may have been disadvantageous even if complete.

Sourcing Substitution within the Firm

XDs for exports from one source (e.g., the United States or one of its states) may encourage exports from another source (e.g., overseas affiliates of US firms, or another of its states). Tables 1.3 and 1.4 provide a broad indication that as US geographical export competitiveness has declined over the years, the export competitiveness of worldwide resources controlled by the United States has remained strong. Anecdotal indicators of this kind of substitution were rife in the surveys and interviews documented in chapter 3.

It is even more likely that sourcing substitution within a firm offsets regional XDs. Multiregional US firms confronted with an XD in one place simply shift export sourcing to another. (Resources are, of course, relatively mobile across regions within a nation.) US exports overall may decline only a little, if at all. A classic illustration of this kind of offset is provided by the US prohibition of log exports from public lands, discussed below.

Interfirm Substitution within an Industry

XDs faced by one set of firms may encourage exports by another set of firms from the same industry. In the telecommunications case, AT&T has moved from almost no exports to a position as a major exporter of telecommunications equipment since being separated from the RBOCs in 1984. The barriers that were very clearly XDs for RBOCs may have been export enhancers for AT&T. It is admittedly not clear that the offset was perfect, but it is also possible that US exports of telecommunications equipment were actually larger with the RBOC XDs than without. This could, for example, be the consequence of strong scale or learning economies enjoyed by AT&T.

Destination Substitution within Firms and Industries

XDs on sales to one destination (e.g., grain to the Soviet Union) may encourage exports to another (e.g., grain to China). Standard economic intuition suggests that US XDs that restrict exports to a subset of customers—say, a set of sanctioned or security-threatening countries—may have little effect if any on overall US export competitiveness. Standard intuition observes that US rivals will now have relatively greater competitive opportunities in the restricted markets, and US suppliers will have incentives to compete even more intensely in nonrestricted markets. US export shares will rise in the latter markets and fall in the former markets, and rival suppliers' shares will move in the opposite direction. Neither US nor rival suppliers need lose worldwide export share.

One of the striking aspects of this study, however, is the absence of this substitution. There were no anecdotes to this effect, nor any supporting evidence in the previous sizing-up studies summarized in chapter 4, nor in the new studies described in chapter 5.[35] In fact, chapter 4 contains a discussion of why such offsets are not a likely feature of the most important demand-constricting US XDs toward high-technology exports, and why these XDs are therefore especially powerful export deterrents. The broadest explanation is that standard intuition is based on perfectly competitive industries and firms, whereas US XDs seem especially to afflict high-technology industries with imperfectly competitive industries and firms.

Foreign-Domestic Substitution within an Industry

XDs may encourage domestic market attentiveness and displace competitive import substitutes.[36] This is a particular variation of the previously discussed substitution and will fail in imperfectly competitive industries for exactly the same reasons given in chapter 4. But even if it occurs, this particular substitution leaves the ratio of exports to national output lower and may therefore sacrifice many of the benefits of a larger ratio described in chapter 1.

Sectoral Substitution across Industries

XDs in one industry may encourage exports by other industries. In the long run, selective XDs may have only a small effect on a country's overall ratio of exports to national output. Resources that would have been employed in restricted sectors will be deployed to other sectors. Exports will be smaller in the former sectors but larger in the latter than they would have been without XDs. The decline in restricted-sector exports will be an overstatement of the degree to which XDs deter overall exports.

Once again, the issue of export structure lurks close to the surface. The substitution of some sectors' exports for others can be treated with

---

35. This is not to deny historical instances. Richard N. Cooper observes that in 1980, Argentina failed to fulfill grain sales contracts to Italy in order to ship grain to the Soviet Union, which was willing to pay a premium after being embargoed by the United States. US grain sales to Italy subsequently rose.

36. For example, in the case of the US ban on Alaskan oil exports described in box 2.2, commentators such as England-Joseph (1990) understood that US imports would rise in response to any loosening of the ban.

nonchalance if on balance any dollar's worth of exports has the same value to a society's living standards. This is the traditional economic perspective. A dollar is a dollar is a dollar, and an export is an export is an export. In a traditional view, XDs may alter the quantitative outcomes of trade patterns according to comparative advantage but not the qualitative thrust of the case for free trade.

Newer views, reflected in chapter 1's discussion of why exports are important, are less sure and less dogmatic. There are reasons to be concerned about XDs that offset exports in structurally or strategically important sectors with exports from other sectors.[37] Overall exports may be the same, but the US gains from trade will be smaller. According to these views, selective XDs that do not change aggregate exports can still be costly to the US economy.

Additionality and Offsets: Some Illustrations

Logs from US Public Lands

Exports of unprocessed logs from federally owned forests in the Northwest United States have been banned since 1973, and in 1990 a federal law (recently declared unconstitutional) extended the ban to state-owned forests. But it is not clear that these embargoes have deterred overall US exports much, nor even US log exports.[38]

There are many objectives behind these bans, and they have varied in importance over the years: making logs cheaper in order to protect domestic sawmills and preserve sawmill jobs; raising log costs to Japan in order to encourage it to purchase more processed wood and wood products, against which it has high barriers; and preserving the habitat of the endangered Northern spotted owl.

But log exports are not prohibited from privately owned lands, which account for 90 percent of forest land in the Southeast United States, though only 50 percent in the Northwest. Weyerhauser and other multiregional lumber companies have increasingly shifted activities toward the Southeast (roughly 45 percent of the tree harvest in 1991) and away from the Northwest (roughly 20 percent). Single-region companies such as the Plum Creek Timber Company, a spinoff of Burlington Northern, have in the past few years aggressively increased tree harvesting (and

37. By the same logic, of course, XDs in *other* sectors may be less problematic if they encourage exports from favored sectors.

38. This material is based on various articles from the *Wall Street Journal* (5 May 1993, A13; 24 June 1992, A1; 9 July 1991, A17; 18 June 1990, A1; 12 June 1990, A21) and from *The Economist* (9 November 1991, 26).

presumably exporting) from privately owned forests in the Northwest. So log exports have increased from southeastern and private lands to offset their decline from northwestern and public lands.

It is very doubtful that this clear regional XD could possibly be a significant national XD.

US Telecommunications Deregulation

Among the prominent US XDs, according to some experts, was mindless US regulation and deregulation. Telecommunications provided the most frequently alleged illustration, especially the court-supervised breakup of the Bell System in 1984 into AT&T and seven regional Bell operating companies (RBOCs).[39] But it is not clear that the 1984 changes have deterred overall US exports, nor even US telecommunications exports very much.

The principal objective of the breakup was to stimulate domestic competition and innovation, thought to be sluggish for several reasons. Local telephone service was thought to be a natural monopoly and consequently was regulated. But local affiliates of the integrated Bell System bought virtually all of their equipment from Western Electric, another Bell affiliate, at prices the US government thought to be excessive and at quality it thought to be dubious. Bell could use the implicit excess profits to subsidize long-distance and other telecommunications services and thereby preclude competitive entry and innovation. It could also preclude competitive entry and innovation in its equipment business because it owned the local service providers and ultimately could resolve that their suppliers should be Bell itself!

So went the government's antitrust theory. So went its practice, too. After 10 years of litigation, AT&T proposed, and the government accepted, a divestiture of the RBOCs from the rest of the Bell system, striking at the heart of the perceived problem by forcing their relationship to be arm's-length. To solve the problem and yet preserve the economies of scale that were admittedly present in telecommunications, each RBOC maintained its regulated monopoly over local service and was banned from long-distance and certain other services and from equipment manufacture.

Many commentators have attacked this reasoning and the subsequent "solution." One of the most vocal attacks is that the United States was hardly an insular, closed market. Indeed, imports of telecommunications

39. This material is based on Areeda (1992); *The Economist*: 12 February 1991, 70–71; 27 April 1991, 77; 5 October 1991, Special Survey; Hausman (1991); the *Wall Street Journal*: 4 October 1991, Special Report, R1–R16; 20 November 1991, B2; 22 January 1992, B4; 14 May 1992, A3; the US International Trade Commission (1991); and on discussions with industry representatives.

equipment surged as the RBOCs were now free to buy on the most competitive terms.

But the RBOCs and others claimed that US telecommunications exports were undermined also. They could not manufacture equipment for export competitively, they claimed, because world rivals could spread the enormous fixed costs[40] of innovation across a worldwide market, while the RBOCs could spread them only across the non-US market. The RBOCs could neither engage in joint ventures with each other nor enjoy the advantage of experimental manufacturing innovation "close to home" with customers they knew well, nor could they easily exploit synergies between US-based manufacturing research and services research. So they claimed.

These narrow XD effects, however, ignore two important offsets. One is product line substitution. RBOCs were forced by lack of a better alternative to become aggressive producers—and exporters—of telecommunications services. And they have. The following list tallies some of the more important RBOC overseas investments in privatized systems, mobile phones, data transmission, paging services, and cable television. Many of these services require ancillary US exports, though not necessarily from the RBOCs, and all generate repatriable revenue, which is in essence the valuation of the services exported.

- Ameritech: extensive European investments, New Zealand
- Bell Atlantic: extensive European investments, Argentina, New Zealand
- Bell South: extensive European investments, Argentina, Australia
- NYNEX: extensive European investments, Japan, Thailand
- Pacific Telesis: extensive European investments, Thailand
- Southwestern Bell: Britain, Mexico
- US West: extensive European investments

The second offset is interfirm substitution. AT&T became a more imposing exporter of equipment and services[41] than if the RBOCs had been rivals in exporting. AT&T may even have become a more imposing equipment exporter than eight US firms would have been collectively, if it was better able to realize economies of learning and scale. AT&T's equipment exports in fact have risen from around 8 percent of sales in

40. Hausman (1991, 70), for example, estimates the development costs of digital central office switches to be $1.5 billion to $2 billion per switch.

41. More than 60 percent of AT&T's overall sales come from services and less than 40 percent from equipment, according to *The Economist*, 27 April 1991, 77.

1984 toward a current 25 percent and are forecast at 50 percent by the year 2000.[42]

These offsets to the XD effects of restrictions on RBOC business may be small or large. The overall data on US telecommunications exports in table 2.1 suggests strong, growing US export competitiveness in both equipment and services. Exports of both have risen more rapidly than domestic sales in the past five years, and although the export intensity of equipment sales is almost twice that of services, the sales base of services is almost two and a half times that of equipment.

These trends are consistent with the belief that "offsets" are so large that the effects of alleged regulatory XDs on overall US telecommunications exports are really quite small.

---

42. Some of the dramatic surge is due to AT&T's acquisition of NCR. By comparison with AT&T, Bell Atlantic, one of the RBOCs, hopes to attain only 10 percent of its revenue from international operations by 1994 (*Wall Street Journal*, 4 October 1991, R5).

Table 2.1 US export trends in telecommunications equipment and services, 1986–92

Equipment							
	Exports (HTS)[a]		Exports (SIC)[b]		Shipments[b]		Exports as a share of shipments
Year	Billions of dollars	Growth (%)	Billions of dollars	Growth (%)	Billions of dollars	Growth (%)	
1986	2.7	8.7	n.a.	n.a.	n.a.	n.a.	n.a.
1987	3.0	13.2	n.a.	n.a.	65.9	n.a.	n.a.
1988	3.8	25.3	n.a.	n.a.	69.4	5.4	n.a.
1989	5.1	32.3	7.2	n.a.	67.0	−3.5	.107
1990	6.3	24.7	8.5	18.1	69.6	3.9	.122
1991	6.7	5.4	9.0	5.9	69.7	0.2	.129
1992	n.a.	n.a.	9.6	6.7	n.a.	n.a.	n.a.

Services					
	International operating revenue[c]		Domestic operating revenue[c]		International as a share of domestic revenue
Year	Billions of dollars	Growth (%)	Billions of dollars	Growth (%)	
1988	5.8	n.a.	141.3	n.a.	.041
1989	6.8	17.2	149.1	5.6	.046
1990	8.3	21.6	154.4	3.5	.054
1991	9.9	19.6	161.1	4.3	.061
1992	11.7	7.7	170.0	5.5	.069

n.a. = not applicable

a. Harmonized Trade System classification categories from US Department of Commerce (1992a, 8517 through 8544, but also including communications satellites and parts (8802503000 and 8803903000) and optical fibers, bundles, and cables (900110000).

b. Standard Industrial Classification categories from US Department of Commerce (1992b), chapters 29 and 30: SIC 3661, 3663, 3669, and 3812. 1992 data are a forecast, with exports of 3661 assumed to grow at the same rate as exports in other categories. 1991 data are an estimate.

c. Standard Industrial Classification categories from US Department of Commerce (1992b, chapter 28: SIC 4812, 4813, and 4822). 1992 data are a forecast, and 1991 data are an estimate.

3

The Commentators' Catalog of US Export Disincentives

Export disincentives are not always easy to identify, characterize, or assess, as we saw in the last chapter. The first task of the sizing-up project involved surveying those who knew them best. What came to mind when we said "US export disincentives?" Which ones seemed strongest, most insidious, most neglected? This chapter summarizes their answers.

One notable generalization is how well perceptions of *relative* severity lined up with subsequent rankings in the quantitative results. Export controls and sanctions topped almost everyone's list, and they do in the sizing-up experiments of chapters 4 and 5 as well.

Perceptions of *quantitative* severity, however, provided another interesting generalization. Relative to the sizing-up experiments, informed commentators understated the severity of the most severe XDs (in terms of dollars of deterred exports) and overstated the severity of the least. Controls and sanctions were even more significant XDs according to our experiments than according to our experts. Taxes and regulatory burdens, though, were thought to be more significant XDs by our experts than any of our experiments suggest.

The early phases of the project involved interviews, informal surveys, and brainstorming meetings with experts on exports. The sample included representatives of trade and consulting groups, corporate representatives, journalists, and past and present administration officials and congressional staff. The selection was admittedly not scientific but still attempted to be comprehensive. Among corporate commentators, however, both small exporters and services exporters were probably under-represented in numerical terms. Out of these meetings came consensus, controversy, and some curious neglect.

Consensus XDs

Consensus characterized the XDs that have turned out in this project to be both the most important and the most innocuous. Virtually everyone agreed that US export controls for national security, foreign policy, or antiproliferation were important XDs. And virtually everyone agreed that US bans on exports of grain to the Soviet Union or of logs from public lands were particularly pure exemplars of narrow XDs but also unimportant in their effects on overall US exports. They usually cited the many channels of avoidance and substitution described in the previous chapter.

Stories of export sales lost or delayed due to controls were abundant. Some had taken on mythic proportions.[1] Some drove home the uncomfortable parallels between export control regimes and a command economy ("Moscow on the Potomac"). A few stories continued to unfold during the entire life of the sizing-up project. One of these was the sale of commercial aircraft to Iran. Commercial aircraft are a dual-use good to the extent that they can be used for military transport and surveillance. Some commentators made a strong case for withholding sales[2] on the grounds that the Iranian government is carrying out an elaborate weapons program and that it supports global terrorist movements. In fact, the US Commerce Department turned down a sale of 16 Boeing jets to Iran in August 1992. Iran appealed through the US judicial system, and the case is pending. In this particular case, as well as a similar one about to occur in China, more than 20 percent of the components of rival Airbus models were US-manufactured. So both Boeing and its Airbus competitors fell under the jurisdiction of US export controls.

What other commentators feared, however, was that Airbus might begin "designing out" US components so as to avoid the reach of US controls. A move to certify Rolls-Royce engines for Airbus models had begun quite late in the life of the aircraft concerned, and at substantial cost, as an alternative to standard GE/Snecma engines. And Honeywell had expressed concern in 1990 that it would lose its avionics contract for the Airbus A-320 because of similar US export controls toward Eastern

---

1. See, for example, "Kachajian's Rebellion: The Story of How One Small Manufacturer Spent Six Years Fighting to Save His Business from the Deadening Hand of Export Controls—and Won. Sort of," *Inc.*, October 1986, 92–98, and "Kachajian's Revenge," *Inc.*, August 1987, 13.

2. See, for example, an article by Kenneth R. Timmerman in the *Wall Street Journal*, 21 April 1993, A14. Other information for this case comes from the *Wall Street Journal* 9 April 1993, A7; and 1 October 1992, B4.

Europe (testimony of Charles R. Hough, director of trade administration for Honeywell Inc., before the Subcommittee on International Finance and Monetary Policy, US Senate Banking, Housing, and Urban Affairs Committee, 28 March 1990). These commentators asked rhetorically how the short-run gains in national security could justify the possibly indefinite losses in economic security.

Several commentators stressed the unpredictability of foreign policy sanctions, even relative to national security and antiproliferation controls. When long-term contracts had to be broken unexpectedly, there were not only uninsured losses to write off, but the loss of reputation as a reliable supplier and hence of future contracts. One commentator said that his company, a defense contractor and exporter of dual-use equipment, chose not even to consider doing business with countries such as India. While India is not a target of any current sanctions, the company viewed the risk of future sanctions to be high enough that the contingent liabilities were unacceptable.

There was a "mixed" consensus on the alleged inadequacies of official support for export finance. The corporate experts agreed that deficient support was a large export deterrent because the lack of Eximbank commitments deprived them of a source of leverage and flexibility. But the consensus of the government experts was that the effect of Eximbank support was only modest and probably concentrated on inadequacies in deploying "mixed credits," discussed in chapter 2. Government commentators doubted that Eximbank's loan guarantee program and direct loans were significantly less generous overall than others, although corporate commentators cited case after case in support of their contention. Government commentators did agree that loans and loan guarantees were unavailable in some cases in which buyers were targeted by foreign policy sanctions and national security concerns. Such coverage inadequacies could completely foreclose markets. Corporate commentators seemed to view Eximbank commitments in a broader way than the government commentators, taking account of the competitive value of an overall seal of approval, of the opportunity to build a reputation for creditworthiness and other positive traits, of facilitation of leasing and fee-for-service arrangements that were often part of the terms of sale, and of the option value that financial support can have as one of the last aspects of a sale that can be adjusted flexibly and independently.

Inadequate US export promotion was mentioned by some commentators in tandem with inadequate US export finance. Here the alignment was different. Those who mentioned it typically represented government agencies or small business; it was never mentioned by any representatives of large firms.

A near-unanimous pattern in our surveys was that globally integrated firms were easily able to substitute foreign-affiliate supply for US supply in response to both licensing requirements and official export finance. Firms were circumspect about the first kind of substitution but very open about the second.[3] For example, numerous (but unnamed) US oil-exploration and production companies were said to have established offshore operations to facilitate sales of technical data and engineering services, otherwise severely encumbered by US national security controls.[4] And a major US arms producer claimed to have sourced a large Turkish order from two European affiliates rather than from the United States because official support for the financing aspects was much more generous from the two European locations; had its affiliates not existed, went the testimony, the Turkish order would have been lost to British competition.

One recurrent lament was the loss of follow-on business from XDs. Manufacturers of aircraft and their engines, telecommunications equipment, and power plants emphasized that any single export sale can generate not just its own revenue, but subsequent sales and revenue from spare parts, maintenance, interlinking products, successive generations of the same product, and so on. One expert from the National Association of Manufacturers estimated annual follow-on business to be typically 15 percent of an original large order, according to the group's members. XDs that inhibit one year's sales or one customer's purchase or one product's export prospects were thought to deter future sales or other customers or related products. A forward-looking version of the same point was that XDs often prevent the establishment of an "installed base" of equipment, or strangle an existing installed base. Either makes sales impossible that depend on or service an installed base. Such sales losses may often cumulate over many years.

The economics of this lament is that XDs do more than the obvious initial damage when firms produce joint products, including successive generations of similar products, and when their competitiveness is determined not just by price and quality, but by dependability, flexibility, diversity, and modernity of product line, and contingent capability to supply. These sorts of characteristics play important roles in the economics of imperfect competition and of recurrent relationship. They have no

---

3. Rarely were taxes, regulation, or any other alleged XD mentioned as provoking this kind of substitution, with one exception. This pattern is consistent with these XDs being less certain and weaker XDs, as discussed below. The one exception was the case of computer makers shifting laptop production abroad in response to antidumping duties on display screens, discussed below in box 3.1.

4. Such anecdotes, though numerous, were always oblique and anonymous, for reasons that are obvious in the case of national security. The defense in every case for sourcing from affiliates was that national security was undiminished because foreign rivals would have done the business if US affiliates had not. This is the classic "foreign availability" attack against US export controls described in chapter 2.

role in the usual models of perfect competition in which products are homogeneous and unrelated and in which no costs are attached to entry and exit from any market, whether chosen or forced.

Controversial XDs

Unlike the uniform expert opinion on export controls and finance, opinions on taxes and regulatory XDs were varied, diffuse, and sometimes contradictory. Some commentators decried the uncompetitive US tax structure, others answered straightforwardly that taxes were of secondary significance. Many judgments ran along the lines of "regulatory burdens diminish competitiveness." But some of the more vocal experts argued that *de*regulatory initiatives burdened competitiveness, especially in telecommunications and in financial services.

On taxes, our respondents provided about as many illustrations of admittedly favorable treatment—for example, the treatment of foreign-source income[5]—as they did of tax-based XDs. Mentioned most often as potential XDs were alleged inequities in border tax adjustment (specifically US inability to rebate direct taxes on exports and charge them to imports) and in personal taxation of Americans living abroad to facilitate US business. The first is discussed implicitly below and explicitly in box 4.2. The second was never pressed very hard as an XD, perhaps because it was clear that, for normal operations, foreign nationals could represent US firms abroad and exports about as well as Americans. Both the Tax Reform Act of 1986 and US state taxation practices were mentioned occasionally but quizzically or without conviction.[6]

The clearest agreement among our commentators on the importance of regulatory XDs came in those cases that most clearly matched our definition of XDs from chapter 2. Both the Foreign Corrupt Practices Act and US antiboycott laws (see chapter 2, footnotes 22 and 29) impose regulatory mandates on US exporters that are not faced either by foreign rivals or by domestic rivals with strictly domestic business. Both require special accounting procedures to track financial or other information that would compromise US commercial integrity or its foreign policy

5. Hufbauer and van Rooij (1992, 127), for example, claim that accommodating US procedures for taxing foreign-source income (e.g., tax concessions for income from Foreign Sales Corporations) stimulated US exports in 1990 by $25.6 billion, compared with what they would have been without such accommodation. Other countries accommodate foreign-source income to about the same degree on average, according to the study so that there are no strong grounds for labeling this as a US XD.

6. See US International Trade Commission (1986) and Gravelle (1987) for calculations of quite small effects on US international competitiveness of actual and proposed tax reforms of the mid-1980s.

opposition to the Arab League's boycott of Israel. Both expose companies to contingent costs in the fines specified for violation, even inadvertent violation. And our experts emphasized the severe costs of uncertainty and lost business stemming from other aspects of both laws that seemed vindictive, not just punitive.

One violator of the Foreign Corrupt Practices Act, for example, lost not only the right to receive US export licenses, but even the ability to sell to innocent US exporters. They could not even receive licenses for products that embodied the violator's components. Baxter International's admitted antiboycott violations provided another example. In addition to fines, it confronted both a two-year loss of all rights to receive licenses for export to Saudi Arabia and Syria and a possible indefinite loss of $125 million per year of strictly domestic US Defense Department business.[7]

The vindictive flavor of these regulatory XDs also characterizes penalties for violation of export control law. One commentator argued that the threat of penalties actually functioned to constrict demand as well as to inflict extra cost because companies decided internally to embargo high-risk customers and products.[8] Of course, when the benefits of these regulations outweigh the costs, this apparent vindictiveness is a desirable deterrent.

There was less agreement among our experts on the importance of US antitrust policy as an XD. US law makes several border distinctions. Some are actually export incentives, shielding qualifying exporters from the full weight of antitrust obligations. The Webb-Pomerene Act of 1918 exempts from US antitrust any association whose sole business is exporting.[9] The Export Trading Company Act of 1982 allows the Commerce and Justice Departments to grant "antitrust preclearance" to associations of firms for export activities such as establishment of export prices, territorial restrictions on exports, refusals to deal, joint bids, and exchanges of information and technology.[10]

---

7. The grounds would be that Baxter's offense was a felony (*Wall Street Journal*, 22 April 1993, B8; *International Trade Reporter*, 31 March 1993, 532).

8. Possible sanctions against India, mentioned earlier, are a case in point. Unlike any of its trading partners, the United States imposes a 10-year denial of all exporting or importing privileges on any party convicted and sentenced to prison for a criminal violation of export control laws (National Academy of Sciences 1991, 99).

9. Though relief from antitrust for such Webb-Pomerene cartels could in principle lead them to restrain exports monopolistically, Dick (1991) estimates that joint marketing economies allowed 16 cartels on average to sell 15 percent more volume at 7.6 percent lower prices between 1919 and 1970.

10. The act also removes the threat of triple, though not single, damages that might be assessed against the export association for US parties injured by domestic spillovers from export conduct.

Though our export experts generally felt very unsatisfied with the bureaucratic hurdles and uncertainties necessary to use either of these routes for insulating their export activities from US antitrust, they were able to document counterbalancing disincentives only anecdotally. Anecdotes concerned uncertainties of enforcement, slow processing of merger and acquisition inquiries, and insufficient weight to the merger's potential contribution to the firm's joint global competitiveness (for examples, see Competitiveness Policy Council 1993b, 187–88). There was also some endorsement of recent US legislation that has given production joint ventures the same favorable antitrust treatment as research joint ventures received in the mid-1980s, essentially removing the threat of treble damages for registered joint ventures and leaving them liable only for single damages. But economic reasoning suggests agnosticism on whether more production joint ventures among self-interested incumbent exporters would really boost US exports[11] and also suggests fewer potential exports from would-be entrants that the joint venture deterred. In sum, our survey of experts did not suggest that US antitrust was a very significant XD.

Expert opinion varied widely on other types of taxes and regulation. For example, there was only rare reference to taxes or regulatory mandates that raised costs for all US business, whether export-oriented or not. The ratio of taxes to aggregate output, labor-relations law, and occupational safety and health standards were almost never mentioned as US XDs. Nor were mandated benefits or workplace discrimination laws, though family-leave legislation was being considered at the time of our surveys,[12] and the Americans With Disabilities Act and the 1991 Civil Rights Act had just recently been passed. Among other explanations of the low profile of these policies among XD candidates, one stands out. In addition to being shared across all sectors, workplace regulations may often end up being "shared" with workers, who are willing to accept somewhat lower wages and salaries in return for greater safety, security, and fringe benefits (box 4.2).[13] Similar "burden sharing" with

11. Economic reasoning suggests there would be smaller sales from a given group of firms that collude to some degree than from the same group when their opportunities for collusion are restricted.

12. President Clinton signed the family and medical leave bill in February 1993 and is likely to propose health care reform that will raise corporate spending on employee health benefits.

13. Grossman and Krueger (1992), 24–28, for example, find only a very small and imprecise (possibly zero) relationship between worker compensation costs (proxied by injury rates) and the ratio across industries of US imports from Mexico to total shipments of the US industry. They find an inverse cross-industry relationship between such costs and US assembly operations in Mexico.

suppliers and customers may weaken the XD effect of many other across-the-board taxes and regulations.

Process-related environmental standards were mentioned more often as XDs but were seen to have two faces. They clearly raised current costs, but they also created new technologies, equipment, intermediate products, skills, and experience that themselves have market value, often in export markets.[14] Perceived regulatory burdens in this case are never actualized. They are in essence shared with, or even fully shifted to, customers who desire the "benefits of the burdens."

Process-related standards had still another pair of faces. They often divided an industry into surviving firms and sacrificial firms. The latter paid the ultimate price; regulation made a product line, or sometimes the whole firm, no longer viable. But the survivors were often able to reclaim viability by increasing their shares of the (admittedly smaller) overall market and were the heirs to any favorable effects on technologies, equipment, and experience—including exports of such products.[15] Process standards thus often hastened a sort of industrial triage: some ailing firms were allowed to die so that others could be nursed back toward full health.[16] However much such regulations discourage exports, they may also encourage exports to the extent that large firms have higher propensities to export than small firms. On the other hand, as discussed above and in chapter 1, exports may be lower when competition becomes less intense because firms exit, and the small firms that are often victims may be some of the most innovative and rapidly growing (if currently tiny) exporters.

Product safety standards and product-related environmental regulations were even more prominently mentioned as US XDs, especially for selected products. One pharmaceuticals company sourced exports of a

14. A US representative of one large, diversified firm said, for example, that meeting environmental standards turned out to be a "brighter constraint" than the firm originally thought. The firm developed extensive contacts with East European counterparts that were interested in the techniques, and what started as an environmental burden turned out to be also a market development device.

15. See, for example, an account of how federal regulations on pollutants from diesel engines turned Cummins Engine, Caterpillar, and Detroit Diesel into exporters to European truck and engine makers, (*Wall Street Journal*, 15 December 1992, B5). See also an article describing the way environmental standards for wood-burning stoves caused a decline in the number of stove suppliers from 300 to 36 survivors, which then prospered (". . . How an Industry's Disaster Can Be Turned to a Firm's Advantage," *Wall Street Journal*, 16 January 1991, B2).

16. One commentator emphasized that large corporations value the scale economies created by research and development, which is necessary to satisfy Food and Drug Administration (FDA) clearance regulations. He believed competition could be less intense if regulatory fixed costs drove marginal rivals out of business. Winter (1990) shows indeed how small firms are affected more than large firms as a result.

drug for river blindness from its French affiliate because US exports would have required approval by the Food and Drug Administration (FDA), even though river blindness does not occur in the United States. US producers of agricultural pesticides for export only must still meet requirements for labeling and customer disclaimer when the products have not been registered for US use by the Environmental Protection Agency.[17] The FDA approval requirement acts like a regulatory embargo and the pesticide labeling like a cost-inflicting XD. Both show, however, how XDs often aim at worthy objectives, in these cases the health and safety of overseas populations.

US product liability laws and procedures, discussed in box 2.1, were mentioned as US XDs about as often as product standards were.

Neglected XDs

Several possible XDs were mentioned only occasionally but thought to be important by those who mentioned them. One was import barriers (MBs) that can function as XDs. Another was inadequate US public infrastructure.

There were several ways that MBs were perceived to be XDs. In principle, they too, like regulation, can raise costs. Well over half of total US imports are industrial supplies and materials or capital equipment such as machine tools; an unknown percentage of manufacturing import categories are components and semifinished, rather than finished, goods. Two US import barriers were mentioned by respondents as possible XDs. A few thought US steel protection had raised user costs significantly in the mid-1980s, and a larger number mentioned the infamous antidumping duties on flat-panel displays as a disincentive to US computer exports. Both are described in box 3.1.

Retaliation is an even clearer, though historically less important "MB as XD" that came up in several discussions. In 1983 China sharply reduced purchases of US wheat and other agricultural products in retaliation for US tightening of quotas on Chinese textiles and apparel.[18] More signifi-

---

17. See *International Trade Reporter*, 24 February 1993, 301–02. Concerns that US agricultural imports might carry residues of such pesticides—the so-called "circle of poison"—have recently led to legislative proposals to ban exports entirely for certain pesticides.

18. See Destler and Odell (1987, 16 and 42–43). The retaliation ended quickly after US exporter pressure succeeded in softening the quotas slightly. Destler and Odell (1987, 48–49) also provide several related explanations for why MBs might be rarely mentioned as XDs. US exporters are ambivalent about criticizing US policies that aid other industries, even supplier industries. Sectoral logrolling and assurance of supply matter: the time may come when the exporters will want to ask for US government support, and they will want to minimize opposition; and within limits, maintaining stable and secure relationships with domestic suppliers may be a kind of insurance for which the premium is higher input prices.

Box 3.1 Import barriers as XDs

Steel protection. The US International Trade Commission has attempted in two reports (USITC 1989, 1985) to estimate the effects of US import protection for steel in the 1980s on US user industries. Its approach includes estimates of the export-deterring effects of such protection.[1] The estimated effects are, however, fairly small:

Year	Reduction in US exports
1983	$0.19 billion
1984	$0.40 billion
1985	$0.26 billion
1986	$0.67 billion
1987	$0.70 billion
1988	$0.10 billion

One reason for the small size of the estimates is that, besides construction machinery and equipment, large US steel users (motor vehicles, construction) tend not to be exporters (Destler and Odell 1987, 49, 192–93). Another reason is that US steel protection essentially vanished in the late 1980s. Voluntary export restraints ceased to be filled as the dollar's exchange value fell and as technologically advanced US "mini-mills" increased their share of US steel sales above import shares.[2] More recent initiatives for US steel protection, which employ antidumping and countervailing-duty remedies, might have had more severe export-deterring effects. After falling in 1991 and 1992, spot steel prices rose 15 percent in early 1993 coincident with preliminary assessments of antidumping and countervailing duties (*Wall Street Journal*, 9 March 1993, A3). Many of these assessments, however, were made irrelevant by the US International Trade Commission's failure to find injury in mid-1993.

Displays and computers. One of the more bizarre—but also significant—illustrations of an MB as XD is the US antidumping duties levied in 1991 on active-matrix liquid crystal displays (AMLCDs) from Japan. Such displays are the flat screens that laptop computers use, accounting for 30 to 50 percent of these computers' cost. Early in 1991 the US Commerce Department found such screens being sold in US markets at less than fair value, and later in the year the US International Trade Commission approved duties of 63 percent against the AMLCDs, with lower duties against lower-quality displays for larger computers and other uses.

US manufacturers of laptops had no formal right or standing to challenge the antidumping duties during the government's consideration of the case; no user industry ever has such rights under current practice. But laptop manufacturers were major US exporters, unlike AMLCD producers, of which there was only one US firm, Optical Imaging Systems (OIS), which supplied less than 5 percent of US needs.[3] Several laptop manufacturers promptly announced that because of the ruling they were shifting production in this $4 billion to $6 billion global industry from the United States to other locations.[4] Toshiba shifted production from Irvine, California, to Japan; Apple Computer moved planned production from Fountain, Colorado, to Cork, Ireland; other laptop manufacturers threatened the same kind of export diversion.

But in late 1992, OIS mysteriously asked the Commerce Department to review the antidumping duty decision, with the aim of reversing it, on the grounds that "circumstances" had changed. On 21 June 1993, Commerce revoked the duties, despite opposition from the other original co-petitioners of OIS, who may yet appeal the decision. If they do not, all antidumping duties will be refunded, dating from Commerce's very first preliminary determination decision in early 1991. This XD will be not only eliminated, but expunged from history![5] (From *International Trade Reporter*, 10 February 1993, 223; *The Economist*, 1 February 1992, 79–80; *Wall Street Journal*, 21 January 1993, B8; 22 October 1992, B10; 12 August 1992, A10; 5 November 1991, B5; 26 September 1991, B2; 16 August 1991, B3.)

---

1. USITC first calculated increased prices of imported steel from the import restraints, adjusted for exchange rate movements, then calculated the implied increase in user-industry costs employing the US input-output table. User-industry cost increases were then assumed to be reflected point for point in prices, making these industries less competitive against imports and in export markets. Forgone exports were estimated using a set of user-industry price elasticities of export demand. These methods are very similar to those used by Christman (1992) and by Bayard and Rousslang (1980) in studies of other cost-inflicting XDs (see chapter 4, especially table 4.1).

2. While all were binding in 1985, in 1988 only Mexico's VER was fully filled (USITC 1989).

3. OIS had been one of six or seven firms that had jointly brought the antidumping petition. The others made lower-quality, "passive matrix" screens not used in laptops.

4. Forecasts of the global laptop market in the year 2000 range above $50 billion; forecasts of the global market in the year 2000 for liquid crystal displays—AMLCDs and close substitutes—range as high as $16 billion. Defenders of the antidumping duties maintain that US firms had competitive potential and export possibilities in new-technology displays that would have been nourished by the import protection. Motorola and In Focus Systems, in particular, have embarked on a joint venture to produce the next generation of displays, at allegedly one-quarter the price of AMLCDs, by 1995.

5. A similar and potentially larger MB as XD was the 1992–93 antidumping suit against South Korean dynamic random-access memory chips. US prices of all such chips rose 20 percent when the petition was filed, and preliminary duties of 87 percent were assessed. But the subsequent duties assessed ranged only from 1 to 7 percent, not much of an XD for the many US exports that embody DRAMs (*Wall Street Journal*, 12 March 1993, A5; 17 March 1993, A10).

cant for the future might be Chinese retaliation against much larger US exports, of both manufactures and agricultural goods, if the United States were to refuse to continue to extend most-favored nation treatment in its annual review of China's trade and human rights record. The Aerospace Industries Association claims, for example, that $2.2 billion of US aerospace exports to China would have been at risk in 1992 and that the amount for 1993 and beyond would run even higher. AT&T, General Electric, Boeing, TRW, Honeywell, and Motorola claimed that $6.5 billion a year of exports were at risk between 1993 and 2010, in a 1993 letter to President Clinton.

A less certain but arguable influence is the way that overall US import barriers might cause a stronger dollar than otherwise would have been the case and/or other price adjustments that diminish US exports (see the description of the "zero" option in box 1.1). Estimates of the degree to which a country's average implicit tax on imports causes wage, price, and exchange-rate adjustments that tax exports range from 0.4 to 0.7 percent export tax per 1 percent import tax [*World Development Report* (1987, 80) synthesizing estimates from Clements and Sjaastad (1984) and Greenaway and Milner (1987)]. Using these estimates as rough guides to volume effects, along with the recent calculations by Hufbauer et al. (forthcoming) that US imports are 1 to 3 percent lower due to "special" (that is, especially high) import protection,[19] one could claim that from $2 billion to $12 billion of US exports were deterred by these barriers. However accurate that may be, only academic experts mentioned it as a possibility.

Forgone exports may be the opportunity cost of import barriers. To the extent that import concessions can still be used to induce export market access from trading partners, any import barriers imply lost export opportunities. Chapter 1 argued that between two economies that were otherwise similar, the one with both higher exports and imports will be more prosperous.

Though inadequate public infrastructure is often alleged to be an XD by infrastructure experts,[20] our export experts rarely mentioned it. When they did, their illustrations were very narrow. One said that his firm's exports were inhibited by diversion of US customs resources from Mexi-

19. The 1 percent figure assumes protection-induced dollar appreciation; the 3 percent figure does not.

20. Hulten (1991, 42) quotes David Aschauer, one of the chief proponents of higher public investment, as saying, "A root cause of the decline in the competitiveness of the United States in the international economy may be found in the low rate at which our country has chosen to add to its stock of highways, port facilities, airports, and other facilities that aid in the production and distribution of goods and services." Hulten is a skeptic on these issues. See Aschauer (1989, 1990), Holtz-Eakin (1989a and b, 1991), Hulten and Schwab (1991), Munnell (1990a, b, and c), and Tatom (1991a and b).

can border clearance to drug interdiction in the middle of every night. The firm exported modem assemblies to its Mexican border affiliate, which processed them and reexported them to Japan. Nightly border closure to the firm's trucks raised their inventory costs and impeded the application of just-in-time inventory management.

Finally, several other possible XDs were rarely mentioned and not thought to be important by those who did. Among these were US nonadherence to metric measurement, US law that requires food aid to be carried by US ships, and unique state and local taxes or regulatory mandates.[21]

21. See the discussion of sourcing substitution in chapter 2 for one explanation of why these may be unimportant XDs.

4

Estimates and Issues from Numerical Approaches

The XD commentators surveyed in chapter 3 cited not only personal, corporate, and government experience, but also scattered quantitative calculations for selected XDs.

Only a few commentators offered opinions on how reliable these quantitative calculations were, either relative to other calculations or with respect to their likely range or their sensitivity to changes in methods or assumptions. Some are, to be generous, opaque. Many have been generated in charged atmospheres—for instance, at critical turning points in the legislation or administrative practice underlying an XD. A few have in fact seemed to acquire mantra-like qualities. Repetition enhanced these calculations' power to persuade and converted the uninformed to truly concerned believers as they heard the same numbers so often from so many authoritative sources.

This chapter begins with estimates previous researchers have made, then constructs a generic framework for improving on typical calculations, and implements it illustratively for export finance support.

The generic framework has several virtues. It imposes an economically logical structure on XD calculations. It allows XD calculations to be sensitized to details of industry structure and other assumptions, thereby allowing a researcher to define a meaningful "range" of variability for an estimate. And it characterizes various XDs in ways that permit them to be compared with each other, making it possible to say something about their relative quantitative strength.

The most surprising single finding of this chapter is that the generic framework yields conclusions that were not immediately apparent. In

fact, these conclusions run parallel to the expert opinions in chapter 3, the scattered earlier quantitative calculations, and the econometric experiments in chapter 5.

Two conclusions are notable. Demand-constricting XDs (such as embargoes) are more potent than cost-inflicting XDs (such as regulatory burdens). And XDs that inflict fixed costs on firms (such as legal/administrative support for export licensing departments) are more potent than those that inflict variable costs (such as product standards).

Numerical Estimates from Previous Studies

Our chapter 3 commentators frequently buttressed their illustrations by referencing quantitative testimony. The testimony ranged from surveys of exporters, to scaling exercises, to simulations based on statistical procedures. Some of the most important references are characterized briefly in table 4.1. There are several notable traits of these quantitative XD predecessors and one important conclusion from them.

In some cases, such as Nollen's (1987) survey of losers from the 1982 Soviet pipeline embargo, the quantitative claims of participants were taken at face value. In other cases, such as Preeg's (1989) expansion of US Export-Import Bank (1989), surveys were not only taken at face value but scaled up to represent the full population of potential losers and losses from US XDs.

Studies that scale up statistical results, or convert estimates of XD costs into forgone exports using estimated export equations, avoid the surveys' possible problem of strategic, self-interested response. Such scaling studies, though arguably more objective, remain vulnerable, of course, to untrustworthy data and misleading assumptions. Examples are Christman (1992), Bayard and Rousslang (1980), and National Academy of Sciences (1987a, b). Indeed, the third of these produced an estimate which, though cautiously presented in the actual study, subsequently acquired an authority that far exceeded its own claims. It is discussed in box 4.1.[1]

Yet for all their fragility, the quantitative estimates of table 4.1 generate a surprising conclusion. Their relative ranking of various US XDs corresponds remarkably closely to the impressions of chapter 3's experts, to the slightly tighter approach to sizing up US XDs that is presented in the next section of chapter 4, and to the still more demanding statistical approaches of chapter 5. Embargoes, sanctions, and export controls have relatively large estimated impacts on US exports. Cost-inflicting regula-

---

1. Box 4.1 also discusses briefly the mysterious disappearance of draft copies of the only other attempt to size up the most important set of US XDs for their simultaneous effect on US exports, the report of the US Export Disincentives Task Force (1980).

tions regarding the environment and worker safety have relatively small estimated impacts. Inadequate support for export finance is somewhere in between, with modest effects.

Generic Order-of-Magnitude Estimates from Numerical Simulations

Overview

In the spirit of early quantitative estimates, but at the next level of sophistication, certain general results can be established from simulations of a baseline industry structure and its reaction to numerically stylized XDs. The advantage of this approach over the previous one is that the numerical reasoning is disciplined by the maximizing logic of an economic model. The underlying credo is that "smart" firms "ought" to act like this and ought to be the only survivors of rivalry with less-smart firms. Industries ought to be made up of smart firms.

The model, however, is a discipline, not a straitjacket. It can be implemented to reflect any of a number of alternative aspects of real industrial structure and any given aspect can have different quantitative weight from industry to industry. Numerical inputs can (and will) differ from industry to industry and will in all cases come from real data.

The general method is outlined in three diagrams below, and described in detail in appendix A. It is implemented below in a general way for three standard types of XDs: embargoes and export controls, inadequate export finance, and tax or regulatory burdens to variable and fixed costs. Simulated effects of each XD are quantified in four different regimes: with dense or sparse competition, and among incumbent firms only or allowing for exit and free entry. Then in the next subsection the method is implemented more specifically for US export finance.

What is remarkable about the exercise is that not all its conclusions are obvious. There are apparently things to learn from these generic simulations that seem to stand up well next to the more informed testimony of experts in chapter 3 and the more sophisticated statistical attempts to size up XDs in chapter 5. Among the most important conclusions are the following.

Embargoes and export controls are particularly strong XDs, especially for high-tech goods. They choke off exports without allowing US resident firms the same options to diffuse their effects that other types of XDs allow. In particular, reorientation of exports toward uncontrolled markets is not generally an option; rival suppliers maintain or increase market shares in uncontrolled markets as well as completely displacing US suppliers in controlled markets. The counterintuitiveness of this result is discussed below.

Table 4.1 Estimated export losses from selected previous survey and numerical approaches

Source of estimate by type of study	Year relevant	Range of estimated loss	1991 dollar equivalent[a]	Comments
Survey				
1982 embargo of suppliers to Soviet gas pipeline (Nollen 1987).	1982–87	$2.1–$2.6 billion over six years	$2.4–$2.9 billion over six years	Survey of large suppliers of bulldozers, pipelayers, and turbine rotors for lost business through canceled contracts (virtually all the estimated loss) and lost follow-on sales and service, net of business reclaimed.
Exports lost through absence of US mixed credit/tied aid program (US Export-Import Bank 1989).	1985–88	$0.4–$0.8 billion annually	$0.5–$0.9 billion annually	Survey of firms representing 50–100 percent of export business in 5 industries especially affected: telecommunications equipment, computers electric power generating equipment, transportation equipment, earthmoving equipment.
Numerical scaling, general				
Sanctions and export controls toward COMECON, N. Korea, Vietnam, Cuba, S. Africa, Angola, Cambodia, Libya, Iran, Nicaragua, Panama (Hufbauer et al. 1990).	1987	$7.0 billion	$7.8 billion	Export shortfall from assuming that in the absence of US export controls and sanctions, US export shares in each controlled country would be equal to export share of the rest of the OECD.

Exports lost through absence of US mixed credit/tied aid program (Preeg 1989).	1989	$2.4–$4.8 billion	$2.5–$4.9 billion	Scaling up of numerical calculations from US Export-Import Bank (1989) study above to reflect unrepresented firms, industries, and practices (e.g., not bidding a mixed credit project) and to reflect trend growth in practices over 1985–88.
Cost-raising effects of transactions to cope with and deter product liability (Christman 1992).	1991	$2.4 billion	$2.4 billion	Product liability transactions costs assumed to be reflected point for point in export price, volume effect calculated by aggregate US export demand elasticity, value effect implied by price and volume effect.
Cost-raising effects of compliance with 1976 environmental regulations and those for occupational safety and health (Bayard and Rousslang 1980).	1976	$0.0–$1.4 billion inclusive of import effects and dependent on exchange-rate system ($0.0 billion under floating rates)	$0.0–$2.5 billion inclusive of import effects and dependent on exchange-rate system ($0.0 billion under floating rates)	Compliance costs assumed to be reflected point for point in prices of exports and import substitutes, volume effects calculated from disaggregated export and import price elasticities, value effects implied by price and volume effects.
Numerical scaling of econometric estimates				
Unilateral export controls (National Academy of Sciences 1987b).	1985	$7.3 billion ($9.3 billion)[b] Range[c] $1.3–$13.6 billion	$8.3 billion ($10.6 billion)[b] Range[c] $1.4–$15.4 billion	Time-series regression applied to exports of analytic instruments; during 1984 such instruments were subject to temporary de-control; exports were 7 to 12 percent higher

Table 4.1 Estimated export losses from selected previous survey and numerical approaches Continued

Source of estimate by type of study	Year relevant	Range of estimated loss	1991 dollar equivalent[a]	Comments
				than regression predicted before and after. Result was scaled up to cover all controlled exports by scaling factors that differed by destination's risk of diversion and criticality of good or technology.
Unknown numerical technique				
US Export Disincentives Task Force (1980), summarized in Morici and Megna (1983, 88–89).	1978	$5.0–$10.0 billion	$8.0–$16.1 billion	Unknown methods or coverage. US Export Disincentives Task Force report never included in Annexes to US President's Export Council (1980), Vol. II, or discussed in text section on export disincentives, Vol. I, pp. 87–95. Original unpublished report cannot be located.

a. Dollar figures scaled to 1991 by implicit price deflator for exports of goods and services. *Source: Economic Report of the President 1992,* table B-3, p. 303, and US Department of Commerce, Bureau of Economic Analysis Press Release 92-49.

b. Figures in parentheses reflect unrelated adjustments for administrative costs, R&D, and lost profits.

c. Range was calculated in the following way: minimum value came from taking the smallest regression coefficient and subtracting one standard error; maximum value came from taking the largest regression coefficient and adding one standard error.

Demand-constricting XDs, such as export controls and inadequate export finance, have stronger effects on US exports than cost-inflicting XDs such as tax and regulatory burdens. One reason is that regulatory costs can in some measure be passed on to buyers, suppliers, or workers,[2] while disincentives such as inadequate export finance cannot be passed on as readily. A second reason is that most demand-constricting XDs increase the intensity of the competition facing the typical US exporter and thereby amplify the negative effect on export revenues.[3]

Fixed-cost-inflicting XDs are generally more restrictive than variable-cost-inflicting XDs; more uneven in their effects on firms, causing some to disappear and survivors to reclaim portions of their business lost in XDs; and less able to be passed on to buyers, suppliers, and workers.

When XDs are assumed to provoke exit of firms from export activities, the demise of the exiting firms moderates the losses of surviving firms. Indeed, some measures of export success, such as market share, are larger for each surviving firm with the export disincentive than without it. Political economy makes this conclusion important. Incumbent firms (survivors of XDs) have mixed feelings about abolishing XDs. They may benefit on balance, but new entrants bleed away some of the gains. Incumbents' lobbying to abolish XDs is modulated and lobbying by potential new entrants is weakened by their provisional incipience.[4] Interfirm fairness may also make this conclusion important, for example, if the marginal firms are small or otherwise disadvantaged.

These four conclusions seem fairly insensitive to the density of competition, measured by the number of firms producing an "American variety." More precisely, there are only small differences between the calculated effects of generic XDs when there are four US rivals and the effects when there are ten.[5]

Three Diagrams for Three XDs

Figures 4.1, 4.2, and 4.3 depict the effects of embargoes, export finance, and tax and regulatory burdens, respectively, on the demand and cost

---

2. The degree to which they are passed on to buyers or workers and the corresponding degree to which they are borne by supplier firms is called the "incidence" of XDs (see box 4.2). Though this may create distributional problems of determining who fairly bears the burden of XDs, it also vitiates their quantitative effect on costs and hence on exports.

3. XDs differ in this regard from import barriers such as quotas, which reduce the intensity of the competition among US firms competing with imports.

4. In the extreme, new entrants who would gain from abolishing XDs are essentially disenfranchised.

5. This may be a result of the particular form of imperfect competition assumed in these exercises (i.e., Cournot competition, as described in appendix A). Or it may be a more general empirical regularity, as suggested, for example, in empirical research by Bresnahan

Box 4.1 A mantra and a mystery

The mantra. The National Academy of Sciences Report (1987a,b) on national security export controls was one of the most quantitative, carefully documented, and influential of the many comparable studies on these particular US XDs. Out of it came conclusions that have been absorbed into the received wisdom of informed commentators: the observation that almost half of the dollar value of manufactured exports in the late 1980s required a validated export license (compared with 30 to 40 percent today); the especially large share of US exports that were lost to markets in Western allies (because of the unreliability of US suppliers) rather than to markets in East-bloc adversaries. The conclusions powerfully supported the argument that US national security controls had large commercial costs relative to their strategic benefits and were an important influence on revisions to the Export Administration Act of 1988 and on parts of the Omnibus Trade and Competitiveness Act of 1988.

No conclusion of the NAS study was more influential than the estimate that US national security controls caused US suppliers to lose $9.3 billion of 1985 export business—roughly 3 percent of total exports and more than 6 percent of net exports in 1985. The number was cited by nearly every person surveyed in chapter 3 and has been reiterated in nearly every serious discussion of US XDs since 1987. One commentator claimed that the number "galvanized" all the impressive illustrative and anecdotal evidence for anticompetitive XDs that was contained elsewhere in the NAS report.

It is not very well-known that this number was a controversial 11th-hour addition,[1] nor that a range of sensible variation around it would run from as little as $1.3 billion to as much as $13.6 billion.[2] That is not, of course, to invite dismissal of the estimate—at one end of the range of variation it suggested all the more reason to worry about this particular US XD. But it is instructive to see how magnetic and catalytic a single estimate from a reputable source can be and how much the policy community craves one.

The mystery. Comprehensive sizing-up computations very similar to those of the present study were undertaken as background for President Jimmy Carter's Export Council. It issued its report in 1980 without alluding to the quantitative estimates prepared by its own US Export Disincentives Task Force (1980). The only reference to those numbers is their total range, $5 billion to

curves facing a typical US exporter. The exporter is assumed to have some degree of market power. Appendix A embeds these figures in a model of the imperfectly competitive industry as a whole (not just a typical firm) in a world trading environment with different varieties of the same product competing against the American version.

Figure 4.1 depicts the effects of a 25 percent export embargo. One out of every four customers of the typical American firm is deemed an enemy, a proliferator, a security risk, or a target of sanctions. The firm's

and Reiss (1991, 978), who find in an econometric study of 202 geographical markets for professional services that ". . . almost all variation in competitive conduct occurs with the entry of the second and third firm. Surprisingly, once a market has between three and five firms, the next entrant has little effect on competitive conduct."

$10 billion of forgone exports in 1978, reported by Morici and Megna (1983, 88–89). Many members of the task force, contacted for the present study, remember having participated in the earlier sizing-up exercise. None remembered its conclusions, coverage, or methods. Though several tried, none could put their hands on the manuscript draft of the elusive 1980 task force report, not even an inveterate pack rat![3] XDs seem to have deterred more than exports.

---

1. What follows is based on interviews with informed sources.

2. The foundations for the scaling that produced the $9.3 billion were two coefficients in a statistical regression that "explained" US exports of analytic instruments with variables measuring industrial production, weighted exchange rates, and export controls. There were two export control variables. One was a "phase-out" variable, the other a "phase-back-in" variable. The first took successive quarterly values of 0.25, 1.00, and 0.25 during a period when controls on analytic instruments were temporarily phased out. It had a positive coefficient that predicted exports of analytic instruments that were 7 percent higher than before the controls were lifted. The second variable took successive quarterly values of 0.50 and 1.00 during the phase-back-in period and had a negative coefficient that predicted exports of analytic equipment that were 12 percent lower than during the phase-out period. The 7-percent-higher, 12-percent-lower comparisons were "averaged" to a 10 percent estimated impact of the controls. The resulting export effect for analytic instruments was scaled up to cover all exports by sophisticated scaling factors that differed according to the destination's risk of diversion and the criticality of goods and technology (relative to analytic instruments). The low and high estimates of table 4.1 were calculated, respectively, by scaling 9.3 down by 7/10 × (first coefficient − one standard error), and by scaling 9.3 up by 12/10 × (second coefficient + one standard error).

3. Informed sources allege that leaks had become so severe that numbered draft copies were collected after each meeting of the task force and that the calculations in the final draft were discredited by a conflict of interest on the part of a prominent member. In fact, two other sizing-up studies from the same period could not be located by their authors, one of Eximbank financing, the other of the Foreign Corrupt Practices Act.

---

forgone demand must be met by foreign rivals. The heavy demand curve D_{s1} represents the curve facing the export seller after the embargo; the light demand curve D_{s0} represents the relevant curve without any XDs. The most natural location of D_{s1} is three-quarters of the distance horizontally between D_{s0} and the vertical axis, because only three-quarters of potential export demand is "legal" at every price.[6] The curves labeled mr_0 (pre-embargo) and mr_1 (post-embargo) are the firm's perceived marginal

6. Alternatively, one might view D_{s0} as the horizontal summation of the demand curves of four buyer countries. If the four customer countries had identical demands and one was "banned," the curve that horizontally sums the remaining three is precisely D_{s1} (see appendix A).

Figure 4.1 Effects of embargoing 25 percent of a typical firm's export customers

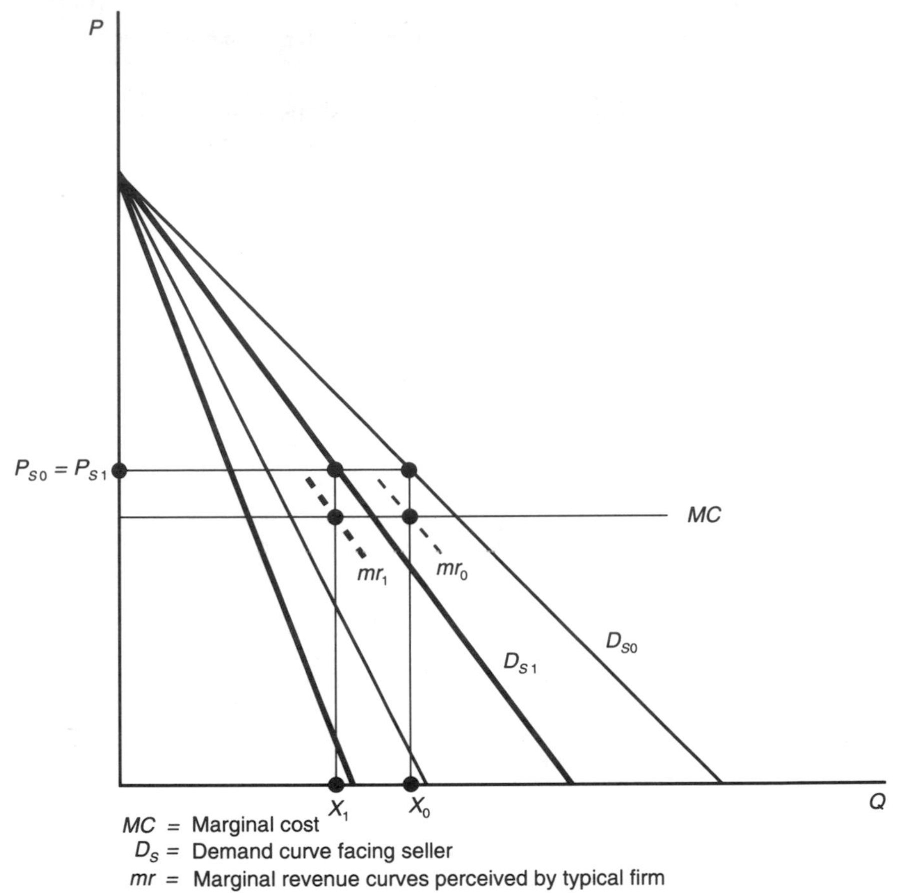

A 25 percent embargo eliminates one out of every four export customers at every price. This pivots the exporter's demand curve inward and also the marginal revenue it perceives given the exports of domestic rivals under Cournot competition and prices of foreign varieties (see appendix A). The elasticity of the demand curve remains the same at every price.

revenue curves, described in appendix A. They are "perceived" curves because they account for how the typical firm thinks its rival US exporters will respond to the embargo. The typical firm will expect to maximize profits at the export volume for which perceived marginal revenue is equal to marginal cost, assumed constant and equal to variable cost and depicted by the curve labeled MC. The firm will price at the height of D_{s1} above its optimal export volume.

As pictured, the 25 percent export embargo causes, for the typical exporter: no change in export price, a 25 percent decline in export volume and value, and a decline in profits that depends on average costs, which

Figure 4.2 Effects of 10 percent rise in export buyer's outlays due to finance costs

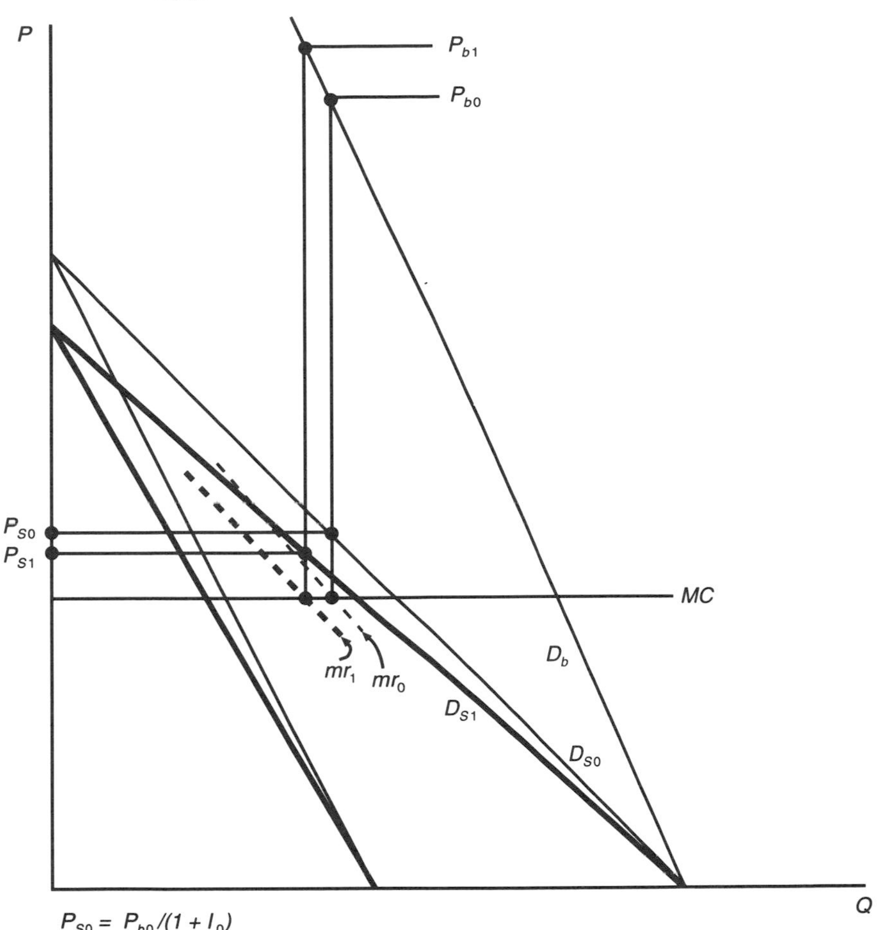

$P_{S0} = P_{b0}/(1 + I_0)$
$P_{S1} = P_{b1}/(1 + I_1)$
I_0, I_1 = Ratio of total (financing inclusive) price to cash-on-the-line price
MC = Marginal cost
D_b = Demand curve facing buyer
DS = Demand curves facing seller
mr = Marginal revenue curves perceived by typical firm

A rise in financing costs—a wedge between what a buyer pays for an export and what a seller receives—shifts down the demand price earned by the seller for any given price faced by the buyer. The price faced by the buyer rises 10 percent. The seller's demand curve pivots in a way that increases its elasticity and shifts the firm's perceived marginal revenue curve inward under Cournot competition (see appendix A).

Figure 4.3 Effects of higher variable costs on a typical exporting firm

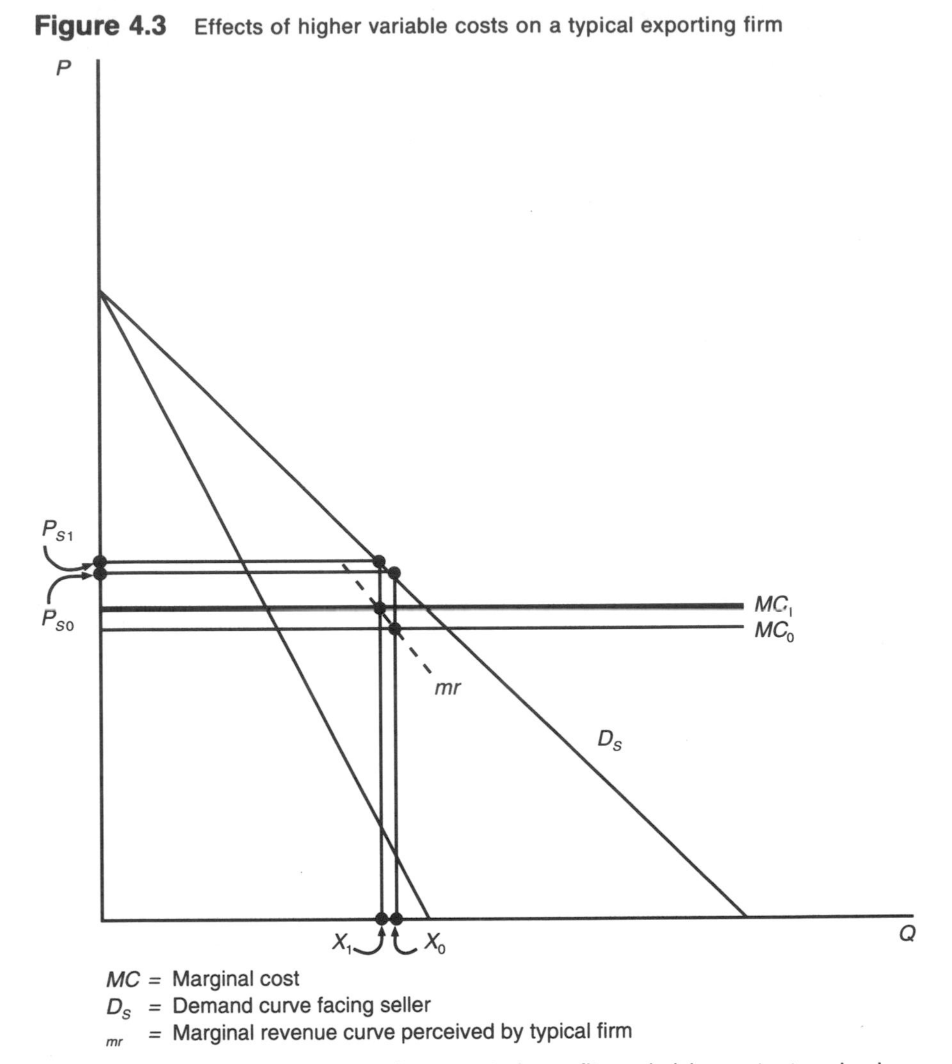

MC = Marginal cost
D_S = Demand curve facing seller
mr = Marginal revenue curve perceived by typical firm

A rise in (variable) costs moves the exporter's profit-maximizing output and price choices along the fixed demand curve.

are not pictured. Since the exporter is typical, the same results hold for aggregate US exports, as long as no existing exporters leave the industry.

These are somewhat surprising results that hold up reasonably robustly even in the more complex calibration experiment described below and in appendix A. The results violate the intuition that somehow US exporters ought to be able to compete *more* intensely in uncontrolled markets because they have been embargoed in sanctioned markets, reallocating sales to make up in the former at least some of what they lose in the latter. But the intuition is wrong in the case depicted because the embargo does not pressure US suppliers to reduce price anywhere, and gives them no advantage over foreign rivals in any market. The embargo would pressure them to lower price if the typical firm's marginal cost curve was rising with export volume instead of flat. But in many industries, especially the high-technology industries that are the principal targets of US export controls, typical firms may face marginal cost curves that are flat or even falling with export volume because of learning-by-doing effects and sometimes because of economies of scope.

In this instance, embargoes force firms back up their marginal cost curves, even in uncontrolled markets. The result is that firms become less (not more) price competitive in uncontrolled markets, as well as in controlled markets. They lose market share everywhere. There is a perverse XD "multiplier" that makes a dollar's worth of primary export deterrence do more than a dollar's worth of ultimate export destruction.[7] For example, if the marginal cost curve in figure 4.1 had been drawn to depict costs roughly 50 percent higher for the first units produced, then linearly declining to its initial equilibrium level, the 25 percent export embargo would have caused export volume to be roughly 40 percent lower.[8] The perverse XD multiplier would be approximately 1.6.

Figure 4.2 depicts the effects of reducing subsidies to export finance on "big-ticket" items such as telecommunications infrastructure for a developing country eligible for mixed credits. The specific scale[9] is chosen to illustrate a shrinkage of export finance subsidies such that the overall cost of US exports to foreign buyers, inclusive of interest, rises 10 percent.

One revealing feature of this experiment is "leverage": that is, how small the interest-rate subsidy can be that creates a 10 percent change in price to the buyer. Consider a big ticket item costing, say, $11 million, with $1 million down and $10 million financed over 30 years. US truth-in-lending forms for mortgages, if applied to this export transaction, would show "total payments" equal to $27.4 million at 8 percent financing and $24.9 million at 7 percent financing—an almost 10 percent difference in overall payments by the buyer for a mere 1-percentage-point

7. See Krugman (1984) for a discussion of this same regime, in which import protection serves as a form of export promotion. Finally, note that price could also either rise or fall if the demand curve facing the seller was not linear. All these generalizations are familiar features of the simple microeconomics of seller optimization.

8. Economics of scope or from learning are notoriously hard to measure, however, and marginal costs are no easier. That is why antitrust and regulatory economists in practice adopt proxies instead of trying to measure marginal costs, and why the analysis of this chapter assumes constant marginal costs on average.

9. A version of the diagram with a less accentuated vertical scale could depict export subsidies more generally, or any ad valorem wedge between the price a buyer pays and the price a seller receives.

difference in interest rate. A 10 percent price advantage is large indeed when considering alternative suppliers.

In Figure 4.2 the demand curve D_b represents the curve facing buyers of a typical US firm's exports, with price P_b reflecting both costs of the item and financing costs. The D_s curves face the sellers, with the gap between D_b and D_s representing financing costs and revenue to an intermediary. The heavy demand curve D_{s1} represents the schedule of revenue received by the seller without export finance subsidies; the light demand curve D_{s0} represents the schedule of revenue with export finance subsidies (of about 1 percentage point to the interest rate in the example above).

Alternatively, one might think of the two D_s curves differing because intermediaries' spreads have risen, due to lack of official loan guarantees or insurance, or due to increases in insurance premiums on deposits or other regulation, or even because the financial environment has become riskier, say because of shortcomings in prudential regulation.[10] The curves labeled mr_0, mr_1, and MC all have the same interpretations as they did in figure 4.1.

As pictured, the reduction in export finance subsidies causes, for the typical exporter: a decline in price, a decline in export volume and value, and a decline in profits, dependent on average costs (not pictured). In addition, it causes an increase in the intensity of competition, as measured by the elasticity of demand facing the firm at any price (which is higher), and this in turn accentuates these effects.

What is perhaps most surprising in this generic experiment is magnitude. A seemingly small (1 percentage point) interest subsidy (or wedge) has considerable leverage over the price facing buyers and sellers, in part because of capitalization, but in part because of its effect on the intensity of competition perceived by the typical seller.

In contrast, figure 4.3 shows how the effects of tax or regulatory cost burdens may be quantitatively small, muted by the ability of sellers to pass them along in part to buyers, suppliers, or workers. This shiftability of cost burdens is discussed further in box 4.2. Figure 4.3 depicts burdens to variable costs only. The heavy and light MC curves depict marginal operating costs[11] with and without regulations that require diversion of firm resources. Other curves have the interpretations given above. The case of taxes or regulations that raise fixed costs is covered in the tables below and in appendix A.[12]

---

10. See chapter 2 for a brief discussion of these possibilities.

11. With flat marginal cost curves, variable and marginal costs are identical.

12. Taxes that raise fixed costs or that are levied on (excess) profits have no effect except profit reduction when there are stable incumbent firms and no free entry; these same taxes cause exit and reduced density of competition when there is free entry, just as regulatory burdens to fixed costs do.

As pictured, the rise in variable costs, for the typical exporter, causes a rise in price received, a decline in export volume and a smaller decline in value (the demand curve is necessarily elastic), and a decline in profits, dependent on average costs (not pictured).

Three Counterfactual Experiments for Three XDs

Tables 4.2 through 4.5 record the estimated effects of four generic XDs under four "regimes," using a calibrated version of the framework sketched above. The algebraic model and calibration procedure are described in appendix A.

The four XDs are a 25 percent US export embargo, a 10 percent elevation of US export prices due to relatively small financing subsidies, variable export costs that are 2 percent higher than they would be otherwise, and fixed costs that are 20 percent higher than otherwise due to various tax or regulatory burdens.

The four regimes capture a relatively strong (four-firm) and a relatively mild (ten-firm) US oligopoly, for a stable set of incumbent firms and for free entry and exit. US firms are assumed to supply a homogeneous product that competes with sales of differentiated foreign goods. The (realistic) assumption that US-resident firms supply one-sixth of world exports is important for the calculations, as are assumed demand curve parameters[13] and the share of fixed costs assumed in base-case total costs. This share is almost 20 percent in the four-firm regime, but roughly 10 percent in the ten-firm regime. In this latter case, the 2 percent rise in marginal export costs and the 20 percent rise in fixed costs have similar magnitude (they each cause total costs to rise by somewhat less than 2 percent)[14] and can be quantitatively compared for their severity as export disincentives. Other numerical data involved in the calibration is unimportant, since calculations are recorded as percentages.

The proper way to interpret the entries in tables 4.2 through 4.5 is by comparison to the XD "shocks" and always in relative terms. Thus, for example, in table 4.2, the 25 percent estimated decline in export value caused by the 25 percent export embargo is large—1 percent for every 1 percent, eye for eye and tooth for tooth—relative to the "small" 0.4 percent decline in export value caused by the 2 percent rise in marginal regulatory costs, or only one-fifth of a percent for every 1 percent. And

---

13. Assumed demand parameters imply overall market own-price elasticities from roughly −1 to −2, but closer to the first than to the second, and cross-price elasticities close to 0.50. Corresponding perceived elasticities, assuming Cournot behavior for each firm, are of course much higher.

14. Both administrative costs of export control and product liability costs have been estimated to be 2 percent. See box 2.1.

Box 4.2 Shifting XDs, or taxes, and burden bearing

One of the oldest fallacies in economic commentary is that the immediate bearer of a tax also bears the ultimate burden of the tax. The corresponding fallacy for XDs is that the immediate burden bearer is also the ultimate burden bearer.

The intuition behind this fallacy is compellingly simple, but wrong. In reality, taxes and XDs can often be shifted backward to suppliers and forward to customers. Their ultimate burdens can be shared widely. The shares of various parties in the burden define the so-called "incidence" of a tax.

Many XDs could be used to illustrate. One that is often mentioned relates to taxes. It is an asymmetry in tax conventions between the United States and much of the rest of the world. US taxes are predominantly direct taxes on incomes of workers and owners of capital. Elsewhere in the world there is much greater reliance on indirect taxes: excise taxes, sales taxes, and especially value-added taxes. According to international conventions covering border tax adjustments, a country can charge its own indirect taxes to imports and rebate them on its exports. The United States cannot do the same for its direct taxes.

At first blush, this seems unfair and burdensome. It seems to put both US exports and import substitutes at a competitive disadvantage. It seems that US firms face higher costs because the US labor and capital resources they buy are taxed directly. US firms (purchasers of primary US inputs) bear the tax, and, it seems, they bear the burden. Rest-of-world (say, European) rivals, by contrast, seem to bear no burden because their primary inputs are not taxed. Their costs seem to be lower and their competitiveness higher.

But this simple intuition is simply wrong. In reality, European workers will observe that their cost of living is higher because European indirect taxes get added to and embodied in the prices of local goods that they buy. Sensible European workers will demand correspondingly higher wages. European firms as employers will face higher costs because employee demands for take-home wages are higher (in contrast to US firms, who face higher costs because the

this conclusion, that generic export embargoes reduce export revenue more significantly than generic cost shocks is quantitatively even more striking in the free-entry regimes (tables 4.3 and 4.5) compared with the no-entry regimes (tables 4.2 and 4.4).

Or, for another example, in table 4.5, the 1.1 percent estimated decline in export value caused by the 20 percent rise in regulatory fixed costs is large relative to the near-zero decline caused by the 2 percent rise in regulatory marginal costs. The fixed-cost XD also causes significantly greater pressure for firms to exit from exporting entirely, relative to the marginal-cost XD. These are notable conclusions because each XD causes total costs to rise by the same degree, somewhat less than 2 percent. Fixed-cost XDs are relatively more severe (per dollar) than marginal-cost XDs.

gross wage they pay before deductions exceeds the take-home wage received by their workers by the amount of the direct income tax).

In fact, if European and American workers are similar and aim to receive similar real wages, and if government services, overall tax rates, and other basic conditions are similar, then European and US firms will face similar payroll costs. There will be no cost advantage or disadvantage for either region. Of course, European take-home wages will be higher than American, but so will European commodity prices. The conventional border tax adjustment by which Europe will charge its indirect taxes to imports from the United States and rebate its indirect taxes on exports to the United States merely restores price similarity between European and American goods, in both Europe and America. It provides no competitiveness advantage. And this conclusion is as true for fixed exchange rates as for floating; it does not depend on an exchange rate adjustment that "washes out" the border tax adjustment.[1]

The general lesson is that many XDs, especially those that are cost-focused and especially those that affect many sectors at once, can be shifted and avoided.[2] Chapter 5 will discuss the surprising lack of evidence that US exports suffer from either heavy environmental regulation costs or taxes (see also Feldstein and Krugman 1990; Tait 1991).

---

1. See also Bruce Bartlett, "Not VAT Again," *Wall Street Journal*, 16 April 1993, A14. Bartlett also cites a Brookings Institution study of the VAT in Europe that finds "no evidence that it had any material impact on the balance of trade."

2. For a parallel, Gruber (1992) finds that mandated maternity benefits in Illinois, New Jersey, and New York were fully absorbed by negotiated wage acceptances that were lower than they would have been in the absence of the mandate. In this case, a regulatory mandate was estimated to leave firms' variable costs at their former level, with no anticompetitive effects. For a general discussion of how mandated benefits do not necessarily raise variable costs by the cost of the benefit being mandated, see Summers (1989).

Or, for a third example, there are only small differences in the estimated effects of the various XDs when competition is denser (tables 4.4 and 4.5) than when it is more oligopolistic (tables 4.2 and 4.3). Thus the conclusions above are not much affected by the intensity of competition.

All these conclusions size up one type of XD relative to another. One should not doubt these "relative, comparative" conclusions just because one doubts the realism of a 25 percent export embargo or a rise in regulatory costs of 2 percent.

Thus, these experiments support the conclusions laid out earlier. Demand-constricting XDs such as embargoes, sanctions, export controls, and lack of financial support can be assumed to deter exports more strongly than cost-focused XDs such as taxes or environmental or worker

Table 4.2 Effects of generic export disincentives on four-firm oligopoly with no free entry (percentages)

	25% US export embargo	10% higher US export cost due to relatively smaller finance subsidies	2% increase in US marginal[a] cost of exports due to regulation
Export price			
US	0	−3.6	+1.3
Competitors	0	+0[c]	+0
Export volume per firm			
US	−25	−8.2	−1.6
Competitors	+5	+0.1	+0.1
Export profits per firm			
US[b]	−25	−26	−3.3
Competitors[d]	+4.9	+1	+0.2
Total export volume			
US	−25	−8.2	−1.6
Competitors	+5	+0.1	+0.1
Total export value			
US	−25	−12.5	−0.4
Competitors	+5	+0.1	+0.1

a. In the case of no entry, regulatory shocks to fixed costs were not simulated; they would have caused nothing but dollar-for-dollar changes in calculated profits.
b. Calculated based on initial profit level of 4,840 units.
c. 0 = zero percent; +0 = positive change smaller than 0.05 percent; −0 = negative change smaller than 0.05 percent.
d. Calculated based on initial profit level of 4,153 units.

safety regulation, especially when these burden variable instead of fixed costs. Firms forced by XDs to exit from export activity are, of course, fatally deterred, but their surviving rivals gain back some of the XD losses from the demise of the exiting firms.

These results seem robust to the density of competition, measured by the number of US rivals that a typical exporter has. They also seem to be reflected in results from the more sophisticated statistical approaches to sizing up XDs, described in chapter 5.

A Notoriously Inscrutable[15] Illustration: Officially Supported Export Credits

Allegations that official US export finance is inadequate compared with that offered by important rivals provide a useful illustration of how

15. Export finance is a difficult area in which to estimate degrees of support or disincentive, precluding most of the statistical approaches pursued for other policies in chapter 5.

Table 4.3 Effects of generic export disincentives on four-firm oligopoly with free entry (percentages)

	25% US export embargo	10% higher US export cost due to relatively smaller finance subsidies	2% increase in US marginal cost of exports due to regulation	20% increase in US fixed cost of exports due to regulation
Export price				
US	+2.5	−1.0	+1.6	+1.8
Competitors	−0.4	0	0	0
Export volume per firm				
US	−12.5	+5.0	+0[a]	+9.0
Competitors	+2.5	0	0	0
Number of firms exporting				
US[b]	−15.9	−16.5	−2.0	−11.3
Competitors[b]	+3.0	+1.0	+0.1	+0.2
Total export volume				
US	−26.4	−12.3	−2.1	−3.2
Competitors	+5.6	+1.0	+0.1	+0.2
Total export value				
US	−24.6	−13.2	−0	−1.6
Competitors	+5.1	+1.0	+0.1	+0.2

a. 0 = zero percent; +0 = positive change smaller than 0.05 percent; −0 = negative change smaller than 0.05 percent.

b. Estimated changes in the number of US firms exporting are subject to the "integer problem." That is, for example, in table 4.5, the "problem" that while −10.6 percent may signal the departure of one of the 10 firms assumed, −1.8 percent signals the nonsensical departure of a fraction of a firm. It is more revealing, however, not to think of this as a problem. A figure of −1.8 percent suggests that no firms depart, but that excess profits of the original 10 firms are reduced commensurately. Each of the 10 firms is calibrated in the base case to earn excess profits that are halfway between zero and the level that would cause an 11th competitor to enter.

to apply the insights from these generic simulations in a somewhat more realistic setting. The method applies the scaled response from the generic simulations to comparative data from a recent authoritative study.

The Industry Commission of Australia monograph (1991) on cross-country comparisons of export enhancement policies includes a chapter on export finance. One table provides comparative data on the share of a country's total exports covered by official credit support; another provides comparative data on the concessionary interest rate component in such official support.[16] Table 4.6 distills these data for the United

16. Industry Commission of Australia (1991, table 5.3, p. 52, and table 5.4, p. 53). Table 5.3 data are for 1988; table 5.4 data are for 1990. The original source of table 5.4 is the US Export-Import Bank (1991).

Table 4.4 Effects of generic export disincentives on 10-firm oligopoly with no free entry (percentages)

	25% US export embargo	10% higher US export cost due to relatively smaller finance subsidies	2% increase in US marginal[a] cost of exports due to regulation
Export price			
US	0	−2.0	+1.6
Competitors	0	+0[c]	+0
Export volume per firm			
US	−25	−8.1	−1.6
Competitors	+5	+0.1	+0.1
Export profits per firm			
US[b]	−25	−26	−3.3
Competitors[d]	+5	+1.5	+0.3
Total export volume			
US	−25	−8.1	−1.6
Competitors	+5	+0.1	+0.1
Total export value			
US	−25	−10.0	−0
Competitors	+5	+0.1	+0.1

a. In the case of no entry, regulatory shocks to fixed costs were not simulated; they would have caused nothing but dollar-for-dollar changes in calculated profits.

b. Calculated based on initial profit level of 1,089 units.

c. 0 = zero percent; +0 = positive change smaller than 0.05 percent; −0 = negative change smaller than 0.05 percent.

d. Calculated based on initial profit level of 1,001 units.

States and for an aggregate[17] of six important trading partners: Canada, France, Italy, Germany, Japan, and the United Kingdom.[18]

Using this distillation, one way of characterizing the "inadequacy" of US policy toward export finance is to say that (on average) it covers 1.6 percent fewer exports with 1.35 percent less generous terms than policies in major trading rivals. The less generous financing terms translate into as much as a 13.2 percent price disadvantage for US exports financed by long-term (10-year) credits and a maximal grace period, and a 6.4 percent price disadvantage for US exports financed by comparable medium-term (5-year) credits. With no grace period, the respective price

17. The aggregate figures are weighted averages, using officially supported exports as weights. France, the most activist official export financier, has a weight of 0.39 in the aggregate.

18. Concession levels are based on a market norm defined as the rate of interest on medium- or long-term government bonds plus 1 percent.

Table 4.5 Effects of generic export disincentives on Ten-firm oligopoly with free entry (percentages)

	25% US export embargo	10% higher US export cost due to relatively smaller finance subsidies	2% increase in US marginal cost of exports due to regulation	20% increase in US fixed cost of exports due to regulation
Export price				
US	+1.4	−0.5	+1.8	+1.0
Competitors	−0.2	0	0	0
Export volume per firm				
US	−12.5	+5.0	+0[a]	+9.6
Competitors	+2.5	0	0	0
Number of firms exporting				
US[b]	−14.0	−14.6	−1.8	−10.6
Competitors[b]	+2.8	+0.9	+0.2	+0.1
Total export volume				
US	−24.8	−10.4	−1.8	−2.0
Competitors	+5.3	+0.9	+0.2	+0.1
Total export value				
US	−23.7	−10.9	−0	−1.1
Competitors	+5.1	+0.9	+0.2	+0.1

a. 0 = zero percent; +0 = positive change smaller than 0.05 percent; −0 = negative change smaller than 0.05 percent.

b. Estimated changes in the number of US firms exporting are subject to the "integer problem." That is, for example, in table 4.5, the "problem" that while −10.6 percent may signal the departure of one of the 10 firms assumed, −1.8 percent signals the nonsensical departure of a fraction of a firm. It is more revealing, however, not to think of this as a problem. A figure of −1.8 percent suggests that no firms depart, but that excess profits of the original 10 firms are reduced commensurately. Each of the 10 firms is calibrated in the base case to earn excess profits that are halfway between zero and the level that would cause an 11th competitor to enter.

Table 4.6 US and key trading partners: comparison of official support for export finance (percentages)

	Exports covered	Interest-rate concession	
		medium-term	long-term
United States	2.5	0.0	1.1
Major rivals	4.1	1.4	2.4
Difference/disincentive	−1.6	−1.4	−1.3

Source: Industry Commission of Australia (1991, tables 5.3 and 5.4, pp. 52–53).

disadvantages are roughly half as large.[19] From tables 4.2 through 4.5, the largest and smallest percentage responses of US export values to a 10 percent price gap were 13.2 and 10.0 percent, respectively. Thus a range of scaled export responses to price gaps from the distillation above runs from (1.32)(−0.132) to (1.00)(−0.032). The appropriate choice of an estimate within the range depends on relative shares of medium- and long-term credits; the grace period allowed; the intensity of exporter competition, reflected in the price elasticity of demand; and whether or not entry is possible to the exporting industry.

Applying this range to 2.5 percent of US merchandise exports in 1991, equal to $10.7 billion, yields forgone exports in a range from $1.86 billion to $0.3 billion.

If it is then argued that US export disincentives include lower coverage of exports than that of important trading partners,[20] then the range will be scaled up by the quotient of the coverage ratios: 4.1 over 2.5, yielding forgone exports in a range from $3.05 billion to $0.5 billion.

Avoidability, Additionality, and the Numerical Approaches

One final advantage of the numerical approaches is their ability to take account of at least some offsets to XDs due to various substitution margins. Thus, for example, since the simple model explicitly includes multiple firms and multiple customer destinations, both interfirm substitution and destination substitution are taken into account in sizing up the generic XDs.[21] Indeed, the model's structure is what leads to the important conclusions that there is no destination offset to XDs in many high-technology sectors and that XDs can drive a wedge between firms forced out of business and incumbent survivors.

The model is too simple, of course, to incorporate multiple product lines, sourcing, or sectors. So cautions about additionality and avoidability still remain. But so does the overall conclusion of this chapter: simple simulation models can teach us a lot about sizing up XDs.

---

19. The technique for deriving these price disadvantages is similar to that described in the section above, except for the consideration of grace periods. The market rates assumed in the calculation were 8 percent, reduced by official support to 6.65 percent.

20. The 4.1 percent coverage ratio for major trading partners is largely due to France, with coverage of 7.3 percent of its exports. Otherwise US coverage is roughly comparable to that of its rivals.

21. See the discussion of these offsets in chapter 2.

5

Estimates and Issues from Econometric Approaches

The key to sizing up XDs is to solve the counterfactual conundrum. What would exports be if a disincentive did not constrain them?

This chapter examines two statistical approaches to answering this question. Each establishes a norm against which to judge distorted exports. The first approach examines any difference between recorded exports and the norm for the residual effect of hard-to-pin-down demand-constricting XDs such as national security controls, foreign policy sanctions, and antiboycott regulation. The second approach allows an estimate of how the norm for exports itself shifts with changes in export promotion, infrastructure, taxes, and regulatory expenditure, all candidates for cost-inflicting XDs.

The two approaches have quite different implications for US XDs. The first suggests larger departures from the export norm for demand-constricting XDs than most commentators have considered. The second suggests smaller sensitivity of the export norm to cost-inflicting XDs than most commentators have feared.

Each approach is described briefly below and in more detail in appendices B and C.

The Approaches in General and Antecedents

Each approach in general rests on the proposition that a statistical regression, described below, is a form of averaging or norm setting. A regression from this point of view is merely a typical relationship between a variable to be "explained"—in our case, exports—and its possible determinants, including any measurable potential XDs.

To be more specific, exports (X) can be considered to be made up of two pieces:

$$\text{Total } X = \text{Typical } X + \text{Unusual } X,$$

The typical portion can be related to a set of measurable determinants (D_i) that help "explain" typical exports:

$$\text{Typical } X = b_o + b_1 D_1 + \ldots + b_n D_n.$$

The equations together pose a relationship that is called a regression. When data on exports and their determinants are examined in order to infer the values of the various *b* coefficients, the resulting regression is called the "estimated regression."

Each b_i is a constant that expresses the way exports and the respective determinant vary with each other, given the values of the other determinants. A negative value of the *b* attached to a *D* measuring regulatory costs, for example, implies an inverse relationship—that is, higher regulatory costs typically correspond to lower exports, given the values of the other determinants.

The "unusual" portion of exports (lumped into one term in the equation called the "error term") is then made up of whatever exports cannot be explained by the measured determinants. It includes exports due to random anomalies, mismeasurement, determinants that have not been conceived or considered among the explicit *D*s, and hard-to-measure determinants that have been therefore omitted from the *D*s—such as, in our case, various XDs.

Among previous attempts to size up US XDs, only the National Academy of Sciences (1987b), described at the beginning of chapter 4, has used methods similar to those in this chapter.

Approach No. 1: Demand-Constricting XDs and US Export Variation across Trading Partners

The first approach is well-suited to country-focused, demand-constricting XDs such as foreign-policy sanctions. It rests on inferring their effects from "unusual" or "unexplained" US export variation across its trading partners. This approach is described in greater detail in appendix B.

The first step in the approach is to determine the norm for exports—that is, what would be the usual variation in US exports across its trading partners. Although there are several contenders, one commands consensual attention: the "gravity model" of cross-country variation in trade. It has in fact been widely used in a recent series of admittedly inconclusive attempts to decide whether Japan imports less manufactures than the norm, and if so, how much less (Balassa 1986; Balassa and Noland 1988; Bergsten and Cline 1987; Lawrence 1987; Noland 1993; Saxonhouse 1986). It has also been used to size up the trade effects of regional integration and intellectual property protection.[1]

A simple version of the gravity model suggests that US exports to trading partner j depend on j 's size, wealth, and proximity.

$$\begin{aligned}[\text{Typical } X_{j,US}] = {} & b_0 + b_1 \,[\text{Income per person}]_j \\ & + b_2 \,[\text{Population}]_j \\ & + b_3 \,[\text{Resistance}]_{j,US} \\ & + b_4 \,[\text{Income per person}]_{US} \\ & + b_5 \,[\text{Population}]_{US'}\end{aligned}$$

where square brackets around a variable denote a particular rescaling of its natural units of measure.[2] The structure, based on an analogy to gravity's determinants in physical science, has been shown to track typical exports between countries quite closely.[3] Incomes per person and population combine to create a positive force for trade, much as physical density and volume multiply to create mass. Economic intensity, reflected in high standards of living, and the size of a country, measured by its population, both encourage trade. Thus b_1, b_2, b_4, and b_5 are all found typically to be positive. By contrast, b_3 is typically found to be negative, because "resistance" factors can vitiate the gravity-like forces encouraging trade. An obviously important resistance factor is distance, with countries further apart from each other trading less, given the other determinants. Other possible resistance factors include dissimilarity of language, culture, and political system.[4]

This equation was statistically estimated in several ways. The initial and foundational set of estimates used a cross-section of 130 US trading partners in 1989 to establish the norm against which to compare actual

---

1. See Frankel (1992), Frankel and Wei (1992), Hamilton and Winters (1992), and Wang and Winters (1991) for applications to regional integration, and Maskus and Eby Konan (1991) for intellectual-property applications.

2. The particular rescaling is a logarithmic transformation.

3. It tracks both aggregate and disaggregate exports, with a reinterpretation of the coefficients first explained by Bergstrand (1989). It also tracks typical imports quite closely, as well as the sum of exports plus imports. See appendix B for a discussion of its consistency with other economic models for establishing export norms, including the one used later in this chapter.

4. A nation's average policy barriers to trade and the average of its trading partners' barriers are reflected in the "intercept" coefficient b_0 ; high barriers imply low b_0, low barriers imply high b_0. When the equation is applied to disaggregated commodity groups rather than aggregate exports, then two commodity groups that differed in their comparative advantage, other things the same, would also have different b_0; b_0 would be larger for the group with comparative advantage, smaller for the group with comparative disadvantage. See appendix B.

US exports.[5] Supplementary estimates employed a cross-section over 66 to 67 US trading partners, in both 1989 and 1991, for which comparable OECD data could be obtained for major rivals. Our discussion concentrates on the first set of 1989 estimates because the 130-trading-partner sample is richer. The 1991 estimates are summarized more briefly. They generated similar qualitative and quantitative conclusions, a surprising and important result in light of the radical reform in all Cold War rivals and the ensuing liberalization of multilateral COCOM controls in 1991.

For aggregate US exports, the following are the ranges of estimates for the various b coefficients in the 1989 base estimation.[6]

$$
\begin{aligned}
\text{Estimated } b_0 &= 11.04 \text{ to } 11.39 \\
\text{Estimated } b_1 &= 1.33 \text{ to } 1.36 \\
\text{Estimated } b_2 &= 0.77 \text{ to } 0.79 \\
\text{Estimated } b_3 &= -0.99 \text{ to } -1.04
\end{aligned}
$$

Because of the rescaling denoted by the square brackets, b_1, b_2, and b_3 are actually estimated elasticities, which establish covariation in percentages. Here, for example, they imply that US exports in 1989 were estimated to be typically 1.3 percent larger for every percent that one trading partner's standard of living was higher than another's; 0.8 percent higher for every percent that one trading partner's population was larger than another's; and 1 percent lower for every percent that one trading partner was more distant than another.[7]

With these estimates, "typical" US exports to any particular trading partner can be estimated by inserting into the equation the trading partner's income per person, its population, and its distance from the United States. The difference between this estimated normal value and actual US exports is "unusual" exports—those due to any omitted considerations, among which, of course, are US XDs toward particular trading partners.

---

5. Data from Summers and Heston's (1988) definitive study were employed to measure income per person. This high-quality measure was not available for most of the early research on gravity models. See appendix B.

6. Estimates of b_4 and b_5 cannot be isolated using US data alone, because US income per capita and population stay at the same 1989 values across all trading partners in the observation set. There is no variation in them against which to compare the variation in exports. But the average influence of US income per person and population on exports is not left out; it is in fact absorbed into the estimate of b_0, the intercept coefficient.

7. Each estimated coefficient has a range of statistical variation described by its standard error. The respective ranges for standard errors of b_1, b_2, and b_3 are 0.100 to 0.104, 0.075 to 0.075, and 0.243 to 0.249. By normal statistical standards, the estimated coefficients are quite "tight." But appendix B gives reasons for caution in applying the normal standards. The range of R squares for the whole regression was 0.71 to 0.73, suggesting that variation in typical exports accounted for 71 to 73 percent of the total variation in US exports across its trading partners; 27 to 29 percent was unusual variation in exports, not explained by the determinants considered.

The second and most important step in this approach is to disentangle XDs from the myriad other candidates for the "rest of the story" to "explain the unexplained" residual exports. Since all candidates for explaining the residuals are unmeasured or unmeasurable determinants, this is less an exercise in formal statistics and more a forensic task—courtroom weighing of the circumstantial evidence in favor of and against each candidate.[8]

Some of the "unusual exports" themselves are displayed in tables 5.1, 5.2, and 5.3. Those displayed are for a subsample of US trading partners in 1989, including 15 US trading partners that deviate the most from the norm, in dollars of underexports. The United States exported much less to these 15 "top" countries than the regression norm predicted. Of these 15, the USSR, its East European allies, and China are presented in table 5.1; Iran appears in table 5.2; and a complement of Western European and other trading partners appears in table 5.3.

The results are provocative for a number of reasons. The first is the heavy representation of countries that were the targets of US sanctions and national security controls in 1989. This concentration is even more striking if the export shortfalls are expressed as percentages of actual or typical exports. Then all Western European countries drop out of the top 15 (or 20) underimporters and are replaced by sanctioned countries from table 5.2 and by African trading partners.

Second, the size of the estimated export shortfalls is provocatively large—as much as $10 billion or more for the Soviet Union alone. Naturally, there are many possible explanations: for example, explicit and implicit barriers to US exports caused by trading-partner policy; differences in language, culture, and social and political systems that make "resistance" higher than mere distance implies; random reasons for a large shortfall; measurement error (see box 5.1).

Yet several features add credence to the hypothesis that US policy itself accounts for a significant share of the shortfall. The results are far more concentrated on Cold War rivals and targets of sanctions than would have been the case if overseas trade barriers, cultural differences, political systems, and randomness had been the sole determinants of atypically low US exports. Many other trading partners with high barriers and distant political and cultural systems have less conspicuous shortfalls.

Furthermore, the right side of table 5.1 reveals disproportionately large US export shortfalls in SIC 28 and 35-38 to the Soviet Union, Bulgaria, the former East Germany, and Romania. These high-technology commodity

8. In fact, this approach is also frequently used in courtroom discrimination cases, where the question is whether compensation differs between groups residually, after taking into account as many economic determinants of compensation as possible. See, for example, the detailed interchange in Dempster (1988).

Table 5.1 Soviet Union, China, and Eastern Europe: shortfall in US exports compared with gravity model prediction, 1989 (millions of dollars)

	All merchandise		SIC 28, 35–38[c]	
Country	1989 exports	Range of est. shortfall[a]	1989 exports	Range of est. shortfall[a]
Soviet Union	4,252	9,522–14,046	582	7,260–10,379
Mainland China	5,728	5,107–10,729[b]	3,260	2,795–6,184[b]
German Democratic Republic	94	2,961–3,649	38	1,546–1,903
Czechoslovakia	54	2,653–2,702	29	1,353–1,353[b]
Poland	376	1,726–2,613	251	735–1,214
Hungary	122	1,257–1,282[b]	99	550–581[b]
Romania	153	734–1,371	12	373–698
Bulgaria	177	735–783	22	404–420
Total	10,954	24,695–37,175	4,294	15,016–22,732
Subtotal attributable to export controls		4,500–19,990[d]		4,500–12,200[e]
Minimal subtotal attributable to unilateral controls		1,700–8,600[f]		1,040–5,200[d]

SIC = Standard Industrial Classification

a. Except where indicated, the first number of the range is drawn from Summers and Heston 1980 real GDP per person employed, updated to 1988, and the second is from Summers and Heston 1985 real GDP per person employed. See Appendix B.

b. First number of range is drawn from Summers and Heston 1985 real GDP per person data; second number is from Summers and Heston 1980 data.

c. Includes chemicals, industrial machinery, electronic/electrical equipment, transportation equipment, instruments, and related products.

d. See text.

e. Maximum to the left, scaled by total, above.

f. Range to the right, scaled by total, above.

Table 5.2 Other countries subject to foreign policy sanctions: shortfall in US exports compared with gravity model prediction, 1989 (millions of dollars)

Target country	Date sanctions began	Export commodity coverage	Est. 1987 effect[a]	1989 exports	Est. 1989 shortfall[b]
Iran	1979	Chemicals Aircraft Arms Controlled technology Scuba gear	857	59	1,282–1,798
Nicaragua	1981	Embargo	100	2	223–323
Syria	1986	Crime control equipment Military equipment Controlled technology Chemicals Helicopters Aircraft Agricultural goods[c]	n.a.	91	233–329
Cuba	1960	Embargo	432	3	174–180[d]
Libya	1978	Embargo	341	0	216–245
North Korea	1950	Embargo	99	0	157–169
Myanmar	1988	Military equipment	n.a.	4	82
Vietnam	1954	Embargo	46	11	13
Total				169	2,381–3,139
Angola	1986	None[e]	35	98	23
Sudan	1989	None[f]	n.a.	81	5–(13)
Somalia	1988	None[f]	n.a.	21	(7)–(10)
Ethiopia	1976	None[f]	n.a.	69	(20)–(21)[d]

Table 5.2 Other countries subject to foreign policy sanctions: shortfall in US exports compared with gravity model prediction, 1989 (millions of dollars) Continued

Target country	Date sanctions began	Export commodity coverage	Est. 1987 effect[a]	1989 exports	Est. 1989 shortfall[b]
Suriname	1982	None[f]	n.a.	139	(49)–(53)[d]
Guatemala	1977	None[f]	n.a.	662	(105)–(106)
Haiti	1987	None[f]	n.a.	471	(353)–(364)[d]
Panama	1987	None[f]	109	729	(386)–(407)[d]
Chile	1973	None[f]	n.a.	1,411	(489)–(686)
South Africa	1962	Arms	329	1,619	(536)–(554)[d]
		Oil			
	1985	Computer hardware, software			
		Nuclear goods			
		Some controlled technology			

n.a. = not available or not applicable.

a. Estimated 1987 effects are from Hufbauer, Schott, and Elliott (1990, 81).

b. Except where otherwise noted, the first number in the range is based on Summers and Heston 1980 real GDP per person employed, updated to 1988, and the second number is Summers and Heston 1985 real GDP per person employed. For entries with only one number, Summers and Heston 1985 data cited. See appendix B. Parentheses denote positive residuals, i.e., unusually large exports rather than shortfalls.

c. Subsidies for the purchase of agricultural goods were rescinded.

d. The first number in the range is drawn from Summers and Heston's data on 1985 real GDP per person employed, and the second from their 1980 data, updated in 1988.

e. Aid, loans withheld.

f. Aid, loans withheld, US assets frozen.

Table 5.3 Other trading partners with large shortfalls in US exports compared with gravity model prediction, 1989 (millions of dollars)

Trading partner	1989 exports	Range of estimated 1989 export shortfall[a]
Norway	1,036	1,254–1,406
Austria	873	999–1,099[b]
Denmark	1,052	921–1,043[b]
Finland	969	575–585[b]
France	11,585	306–791
Italy	6,929	183–876
Spain	4,691	316–733
Argentina	1,037	368–483
Brazil	4,799	447–673
Oman	168	91–224

a. Except where indicated, the first number of the range is drawn from Summers and Heston 1985 real GDP per person employed, and the second is from Summers and Heston 1980 real GDP per person employed, updated to 1988. See appendix B.
b. First number of range is drawn from Summers and Heston 1980 real GDP per person data; second number is drawn from Summers and Heston 1985 data.

groups are those for which the vast majority of US national security export controls pertained in the late 1980s,[9] and these particular countries (with the addition of Czechoslovakia) were in the most tightly controlled group (National Academy of Sciences 1987a, 80–85).

A very conservative sizing-up rule that looks only at the degree to which these commodity-group shortfalls exceeded other commodity groups' shortfalls to these countries and takes this alone to be the estimated effect of national security export controls still produces a fairly large $4.5 billion to $5.2 billion range of forgone exports to these four countries. That sizing-up rule in essence would deny that such US XDs had any role in US export shortfalls except in the very tightest security categories to the most tightly controlled countries. It can thus serve as a hypercautious base for the range of estimates.

A less conservative approach might use trading partners such as Austria and Finland (table 5.3) to establish "shortfall benchmarks" due to culture and political system alone, and then might identify the excess of table 5.1 shortfalls above Austria's or Finland's as the estimated effect

9. These categories are chemicals and allied products (28); electrical and electronic machinery, equipment and supplies (36); other (nonelectrical) machinery (35); transport equipment (37); and scientific and professional instruments, photographic and optical goods, watches and clocks (38). Many commodities in these fairly aggregated groups required minimal or no export controls, of course. For uncontrolled commodities, "unusual" or residual exports should average out to be zero, leaving the aggregated group residuals still subject to the influence of controls on national security–sensitive subcategories.

Box 5.1 Effect of mismeasured Eastern-bloc GDP

Possible mismeasurement of Soviet per capita income is only a moderating explanation and leaves intact the main point: the size of the estimated table 5.1 shortfalls is still large. The Heston and Summers data on per capita income has been criticized for overstating Soviet GDP. The joint study of the Soviet Union's economy by the International Monetary Fund, World Bank, OECD, and European Bank for Reconstruction and Development (1990), *The Economy of the USSR*, sets 1989 Soviet per capita GDP at $1,780 instead of the Heston-Summers figures of $5,126 to $6,266. (The same study sets $2,465 as the average figure for Bulgaria, Czechoslovakia, Hungary, East Germany, Poland, and Romania, instead of the higher Heston-Summers counterparts.)

These lower values of per capita income were substituted for the Heston-Summers values, and the regression was reestimated on the OECD data described below for both 1989 and 1991. The substitution indeed reduced estimated export shortfalls because expected normal US exports are lower to countries with lower standards of living. But it also raised the estimated US shortfall to China, whose per capita income was left at the Heston-Summers level ($2,444 to $3,316). The following columns show a matched comparison of entries that employ the Heston-Summers figures with the counterparts that employ lower per capita income in the Soviet Union and Eastern Europe for both 1989 and 1991. The differences between 1991 and 1989 results are discussed later in the text.

	OECD data counterpart to table 5.1 shortfall		Shortfall with lower Soviet, East European income	
Country	**1989**	**1991**	**1989**	**1991**
USSR	7.4	13.5	(0.4)	1.5
China	3.4	6.5	7.9	13.4
GDR	n.a.	n.a.	n.a.	n.a.
Czechoslovakia	2.3	2.9	0.8	0.8
Poland	3.0	3.0	1.1	1.3
Hungary	1.3	1.5	0.5	0.4
Romania	1.5	1.8	0.8	0.9
Bulgaria	0.9	1.1	0.3	0.4
Total	19.8	30.3	11.0	18.7

Summed estimated US export shortfalls in 1989 fall from $19.8 billion to $11.0 billion, still a large number in light of the ranges of variation given in table 5.1.

These conclusions remain qualitatively the same for the most tightly controlled industrial categories, as defined below. The summed estimated shortfalls for them fall from $7.0 billion to $4.2 billion in the 1989 data, with estimated shortfalls to China growing from essentially zero to $2.1 billion. These conclusions also characterize the 1991 regressions and British, French, German, and Japanese counterparts to the US regressions. Whatever upward bias in estimated shortfalls that is created by overstating Soviet and Eastern European income is partially reversed through a resulting downward bias in estimated shortfalls of exports to China.

of national security controls and Cold War sanctions. This produces estimates of $6 billion to $10 billion of lost US exports using Austria as a benchmark and $11 billion to $19 billion of lost US exports using Finland as a benchmark.[10] Other candidates for benchmarks might include Brazil and India, especially when evaluating shortfalls for the Soviet Union and China, because they are similarly large countries whose development strategies prized self-sufficiency. But US exports to Brazil were only slightly below the norm, and US exports to India were actually above normal. Employing Brazil as a benchmark leaves $21 billion to $31 billion of US export shortfalls from table 5.1 still unexplained, and employing India as a benchmark leaves the whole $25 billion to $37 billion still unexplained.[11]

One might argue that, strictly speaking, US XDs should be distinguished from multilateral COCOM XDs and that US export controls should not take all the blame. A large part of the national security component in the table 5.1 entries certainly is due to export controls negotiated between the United States and the Western alliance. But the United States has been accused of bullying its COCOM partners into accepting stricter controls than they otherwise would have chosen, as described in chapter 2, and also of unilateral controls and enforcement that exceed those of its COCOM partners.[12]

To examine the possible differences between multilateral and unilateral XDs, a second set of similar regressions were run over 66 or 67 common partners in 1989 (and 1991) for the United States, Britain, France, Germany, and Japan, all of which were COCOM allies.[13] Export shortfalls

10. Finland in 1989 was subject to the same favorable US licensing procedures as US COCOM allies; Austria did not obtain this treatment until mid-1990 (*Wall Street Journal*, 17 August 1990, A12). Total US exports to Austria in 1989 fell short of their typical value according to table 5.3 by roughly 54 percent. The figure for Finland was roughly 37 percent. But according to table 5.1, total US exports to the eight countries represented fell short of their typical value by 69 to 77 percent, depending on which end of the "shortfall range" is selected. The figures in the text are the dollar equivalents of the difference between 69 or 77 percent shortfalls and 37 or 54 percent shortfalls.

11. Total US exports to Brazil in 1989 fell short of their typical value according to table 5.3 by 9 to 12 percent.

12. Cooney (1991, 27–28), for example, makes such an accusation after observing that the United States share in 1989 of OECD exports of manufactures to Eastern Europe and the Soviet Union was only 3 to 4 percent, compared with 20 percent US shares of overall OECD exports of all products to all destinations. (Cooney blames export finance XDs as well as export controls and US sluggishness in awarding MFN status.) Our methods, unlike Cooney's, disentangle the effects of proximity (US exports are low because other OECD suppliers are closer) from XDs and other sources of low export shares.

13. In this case, the US regressions were rerun over the much smaller subset of trading partners using the same data source as those for Britain, France, Germany, and Japan (OECD, *Foreign Trade by Commodities*, various issues). Germany's regressions were for 1988. All others were for 1989, as in table 5.1. Regressions were run for aggregate exports and

as a percentage of hypothesized "typical" exports are tallied below for the five exporting countries vis-à-vis the importers of table 5.1.[14]

	Overall export shortfalls to COCOM-targeted countries in table 5.1 in 1989 (percent)	Export shortfalls to COCOM-targeted countries in table 5.1 in 1989 for SITC 7-78, 87, 88[15] (percent)
United States	63.7	72.4
United Kingdom	74.9	71.3
France	66.8	60.8
Federal Republic of Germany	62.1	67.2
Average, Europe	65.2	66.9
Japan	70.8	80.5

Leaving Japan aside,[16] the United States appears to bear no disproportionate share of overall export shortfalls in 1989, but it does appear to bear a disproportionate share of exports of SITC 7-78, 87, and 88—precisely the high-technology categories most sensitive to national security concerns. In these categories, if the United States had experienced the average shortfall of Britain, France, and Germany (66.9 percent, weighted by hypothetical typical exports), its 1989 exports of these categories to table 5.1 countries would have been $1.04 billion higher. This measure might be a very conservative lower bound for the lost exports from unilateral US national security controls—controls that go beyond COCOM strictures either in practice or in principle.[17] A higher estimate

a group of controlled categories, as described below. Residuals for the aggregate category were generally smaller than their counterparts in table 5.1, which represent summations of residuals from two-digit SIC categories. See appendix B for why this is to be expected.

14. The German Democratic Republic is not represented in these regressions on OECD data.

15. Machinery and transport equipment except for road vehicles plus professional, scientific, and controlling instruments plus photographic apparatus, optical goods, watches and clocks–a rough concordance to the SIC-based categories on the right side of table 5.1, on which security-based export controls fell especially heavily.

16. The results for Japan suggest that Japanese export shortfalls were even more pronounced than the US shortfalls. An informed source, however, claims that the "word had been out" for a long time among COCOM experts that Japan scrupulously observed the letter of the COCOM controls but not the spirit, through lax policing of transshipment of Japanese products through third countries. To the degree this occurred, Japanese shortfalls in the table above are overstated and should not be used to evaluate US experience.

17. The National Academy of Sciences (1987a) report claimed that most US exports forgone due to national security controls were forgone West-West export sales ($5.9 billion out

of lost US exports from unilateral controls would be in order to the extent that unilateral US controls applied to European affiliates of US firms[18] and to the extent that the United States unilaterally coerced its COCOM allies into multilateral controls that they would not otherwise have implemented. For example, suppose that US power to coerce Germany vanished by 1991, after reunification. (Indeed, Germany has been the most public opponent of US caution in liberalizing COCOM controls since 1991.) Then the difference between US and German 1991 high-technology shortfalls (81.1 percent − 58.3 percent; see below) could be taken to be a better measure of lost US exports from "unilateral" controls. US exports in 1989 to countries in table 5.1 would have been $4.3 billion lower, with a scaled range based on table 5.1 figures of from $3.4 billion to $5.2 billion.[19]

An estimation of shortfalls in exports to Iraq provides some sad further credence to the XD-centered interpretation. During 1989 the United States aggressively promoted Iraqi purchases of US agricultural exports while maintaining sanctions against other exports.[20] US exports of agricultural products were much higher than the norm would have sug-

of $9.3 billion) to allies that found US extraterritorial export controls too onerous and unpredictable. We find little evidence for that from comparing US shortfalls in "neutral" countries—that is, not members of COCOM—to the shortfalls of British, French, and German exporters. Nor do we find evidence of US export shortfalls in British, French, or German markets. Finally, in the fashion of Ruder (1991), we estimate gravity equations like those in the text that explicitly ask whether US exports to COCOM trading partners are abnormally low. The coefficient on the dummy variable that provides the answer to this question is large, positive, and quite precise (that is, significantly different from zero according to the usual boundaries of statistical confidence). So, if anything, we find US exports abnormally high to COCOM trading partners. Ruder's estimated coefficient on a similar variable was large and negative, but quite imprecise (not significantly different from zero).

18. A higher estimate would also be in order to the extent that a portion of US unilateral controls affected all US trading partners, European or not—whether allied, controlled, or neutral. Extraterritorial controls applied to exports from all offshore affiliates of US firms and from any offshore firm using significant US components in its exports. Any such US XD that was quantitatively "common" to all trading partners would be included in the estimated intercept b_0, and could not be reclaimed or "teased out" using the present methods.

19. And the range could be made still higher by correcting for the effect of unilateral US controls on US affiliates in Germany, or by scaling up for the perverse multiplier effects described in chapter 4. The same qualitative conclusions regarding unilateral relative to multilateral controls hold when IMF, World Bank, and EBRD data are used as described in box 5.1, only with more modest quantitative magnitudes, as summarized in that box.

20. The United States reportedly provided Iraq with $5 billion in export credit guarantees for agricultural purchases from 1983 through 1989 (*Wall Street Journal*; 15 February 1991, A14; 18 March 1991, A16). And though it also authorized $1.5 billion in exports of commercial aircraft, computers, and other controlled manufactures, the Iraqis were able to complete only $0.5 billion of the authorized purchases (*Wall Street Journal*, 12 March 1991, A20).

gested, by $850 million, but US exports of nonagricultural products were lower than the norm, a shortfall of $247 million. Thus, their export shortfall is outweighed in the aggregate by the US export surplus to Iraq in crops and food.

Estimated US export shortfalls from table 5.2 are also among the largest from the regression approach and appear to reflect US sanctions for reasons of foreign policy. Several aspects are notable besides their absolute size. First, their size relative to the table 5.1 shortfalls is not large. This suggests that foreign policy XDs, though quantitatively important in 1989, were less important than national security XDs. Second, the size of various table 5.2 entries relative to each other makes sense from an XD perspective. The shortfalls of countries in the top of the table, facing US embargoes and explicit export restrictions, are larger than those of countries in the bottom of the table, facing restrictions on aid and loans but not on US exports.[21] Iran's share of the US export shortfall from 1989 sanctions is large, averaging more than $1.5 billion; Vietnam's share seems surprisingly small, especially given the recent furor over the commercial gains to removing sanctions. Its small size is due to poverty and distance. The level of per-person GDP used to establish the export norm was very low,[22] and it is one of the most distant destinations for US exports.[23] Third, the table 5.2 entries line up very roughly with estimated US export shortfalls in 1987 from Hufbauer, Schott, and Elliott (1990, 81).[24]

But would these results for 1989 really characterize US trade in the mid-1990s? Changes in the world order have been truly revolutionary, and export controls for national security purposes especially have been liberalized in response, as described in chapter 2. The answer is surprising, at least with respect to 1991, the most recent year for which OECD data are available over the same 66 or 67 trading partners above, and

---

21. In fact, for most of these countries US exports are larger than expected, including South Africa, which did face explicit commodity export barriers.

22. The World Bank's *World Development Report* places Vietnam in a category where $300 per person seemed a reasonable estimate of annual real income in 1989. If instead Vietnam had been assigned the real income of Cuba ($790), the second poorest sanctioned country, then the estimated US export shortfall to Vietnam would have risen to around $80 million. This is still a small number.

23. Some of the US pressure for removing sanctions on Vietnam may come from US firms with affiliates in the fast-growing Asian market rather than from pure US exporters. Then removing sanctions might indeed stimulate US business modestly, but not US exports.

24. The same sort of calculation that underlies tables 5.1 and 5.2 would permit an answer to whether US exports to Arab League boycotters of Israel were unduly low due to US antiboycott strictures. For Oman and Syria (subject also to sanctions), the answer is yes; for Saudi Arabia and the United Arab Emirates, the answer is no. On balance, it is hard to detect any overall effect of antiboycott regulation on US exports in 1989.

the year during which the most radical paring of COCOM restrictions took place. Export shortfalls as a percentage of hypothesized "typical" exports are tallied below for the more recent year:

	Overall export shortfalls to COCOM-targeted countries in table 5.1 in 1991 (percent)	Export shortfalls to COCOM-targeted countries in table 5.1 in 1991 for SITC 7-78, 87, 88[25] (percent)
United States	73.6	81.1
United Kingdom	81.3	80.0
France	76.0	73.4
Federal Republic of Germany	63.1	58.3
Average, Europe	68.0	63.8
Japan	74.0	84.5

Two conclusions are striking. On average, US export shortfalls to countries listed in table 5.1 are larger in 1991 than in 1989, both overall and in high-technology categories. But German shortfalls are significantly smaller in those high-tech categories.[26] Some of the anomalous US results are due to strong aggregate US export growth between 1989 and 1991 to most of its trading partners, much stronger than to sanctioned countries and those that pose security risks. This means that typical US exports rose strongly between 1989 and 1991, especially in high-technology categories. It seems equally likely that the US has been slow to liberalize or rationalize its export controls, so that forgone exports and corresponding burdens on US competitiveness have been growing strongly too.

In sum, there are many reasons not to dismiss the main message of tables 5.1 through 5.2 too quickly—that demand-constricting, country-focused sanctions and export controls may create sizable export shortfalls. One reason is that most of the foreign policy sanctions summarized in table 5.2 remain in place (except South Africa), along with sanctions toward Iraq and Haiti that were not present in 1989. US controls on exports to Iran, Iraq, and China are in some ways even tighter than in 1989 because of the sharp shift toward legal penalties and licensing to deter proliferation. Sanctions and controls on exports to China may be poised to jump if its eligibility for most-favored-nation treatment is not renewed in 1994 and/or if it retaliates against US pressures on human

25. See footnote 15.

26. The GDR is not included in either these regressions or their 1989 counterparts, but is included in table 5.1. The same qualitative conclusions regarding 1991 over 1989 hold when IMF, World Bank, and EBRD data are used, only with more modest quantitative magnitudes, as summarized in box 5.1.

rights and proliferation issues.[27] Those countries most likely to be removed soon from sanctions (possibly Vietnam) had little detectable effect anyway, according to the table. A second and more important reason is that export controls have been drastically tightened for antiproliferation purposes. Thirty to forty percent of US manufactures exports still require a validated license, versus 50 percent in the mid-1980s. The identities of the negative outliers in such regressions across trading partners may thus change, and the estimated shortfalls for some may indeed diminish, but shortfalls for others will rise. In addition to China, large US trading partners such as Brazil are under the scrutiny of antiproliferation officials.

Approach No. 2: Cost-Inflicting XDs across 50 States

The second approach is well-suited to cost-inflicting XDs. It attempts to detect the US export effects of several alleged XDs that are somewhat more measurable than export controls, such as burdensome taxation and regulatory costs, or inadequate export promotion and "public capital." The question is whether US states with more of these burdens have smaller exports than other states do, either overall or in selected product categories. Four variants of these alleged XDs can be measured across the 50 US states and the District of Columbia: state taxation of earned and unearned income, statewide spending on pollution abatement, state export promotion and related budgetary outlay, and state and locally owned infrastructure such as streets and schools. Indicators of competitiveness such as technological endowments and average educational attainment can also be measured at this level. This approach is described in greater detail in appendix C.

The first step in the approach is to determine the norm for exports—that is, what would be the usual variation in US exports across US subregions. The second step is then to determine whether XDs and other policies help explain unusual variation in US exports across subregions, where unusual variation is what is left over after the normal determinants have been taken into account.

In determining the norm for exports in the first step, there are again several contenders, of which generalizations of the "factor endowments" model have dominated professional discussion for some time.[28] The

27. See the discussion of US import barriers as potential XDs in chapter 3.

28. A resurgent contender to the generalized factor endowments model is the "economies of scale" model, first outlined by Adam Smith. Some versions suggest that a region's luck, technological dynamism, or wise government policy can turn it into an exporter of goods for which it realizes economies of large-scale production earlier than rivals—without regard to factor endowments. For similar reasons, it could import goods in which it was at a scale disadvantage, without regard to factor endowments. Other versions of scale-based

generalized factor endowments perspective suggests that a region will typically export those goods and services that embody inputs with which it is abundantly endowed by world standards. In the generalized approach, inputs include natural resources, distinctive skills and technologies, and the services of labor, capital, and land. Conversely, a region will typically import goods and services that embody its relatively scarce inputs.

A simple-to-understand version of the factor endowments model, pioneered empirically by Leamer (1984), suggests that for every produced good, region *i* 's

$$\text{typical exports} = b_0 + b_1 E_{1i} + \ldots + b_m E_{mi},$$

where the intercept coefficient, b_0, includes the region's imports of the good, as shown in appendix C, and where each E represents the difference between the region's and the world's relative endowments of one of m factors.[29] Each E can in fact be interpreted as the amount of an endowment implicitly embodied in an export ("b units" of the endowment, to be exact) and shipped away to foreign buyers as commodities. The equation as a whole implies that each good exported is in fact merely a summation of its embodied factors. Thus, for example, high-technology exports might be largely made up of embodied services of scientists and research and development. For a cross-section of regions, exports of high-technology goods should be highest from regions having relatively abundant researchers and laboratories. Such exports should be correspondingly quite low from regions having abundant farm land or unskilled work forces. Thus, in the cross-section regression for regions with high-technology exports, the b coefficients on endowments of researchers and laboratories ought to be positive, and the b coefficients on farm land and unskilled workers may well be negative.[30]

---

trade, however, still allow factor endowments to play a foundational role (e.g., Markusen and Svensson 1990 from the theoretical literature and Murrell 1990, Tobey 1990, or Smith 1992a and b from the empirical literature).

29. More precisely, if E_{ji} represents region *i* 's endowment of factor *j*,

$$\begin{aligned}(\text{typical exports of a good})/Y_i &= b_o \\ &+ b_1 (E_{1i}/Y_i - E_{1w}/Y_w) \\ &+ \ldots \\ &+ b_m (E_{mi}/Y_i - E_{mw}/Y_w),\end{aligned}$$

where each of the determinants in parentheses represents the region's abundance (if positive) or scarcity (if negative) of various factor endowments relative to the rest of the world's (w) endowment of the same factor. Endowments are scaled by gross regional product (Y) according to the theory, and that, of course, makes meaningful each comparison of a region's endowments to its rest-of-world counterpart. Relative size, or scale, of a region obviously plays no role here in the composition of what it exports.

30. Abundant farmland and unskilled workers would give a region comparative disadvantage in high-tech exports in this case. A similar regression for exports of farm products or simple manufactures, however, would presumably have positive coefficients on endow-

This equation was statistically estimated in several variants. The most important variant provided estimates for the top 12 US exports by two-digit Standard Industrial Classification (SIC) in 1989;[31] these exports represented more than three-quarters of all US exports, and the estimates used a cross-section of 50 US states and the District of Columbia.[32] It was also estimated for exports of all durable manufactures, all nondurable manufactures, and total manufactures. As discussed below, for most of the 12 commodity groups and the three aggregates, the estimation establishes a reasonably reliable norm for how 15 "natural" US factor endowments determine typical US exports.

For purposes of studying XDs, however, the second step of the approach asks the interesting question. Do various "policy endowments" have any additional covariation with US exports, once natural factor endowments are taken into account? For example, does a measure of export promotion relative to world standards have reliable, positive *b* coefficients for most goods, since it is an alleged export inducer (a "good" policy endowment, from a narrow export perspective alone)? Or, conversely, does any measure of regulatory or tax burdens have reliable, negative *b* coefficients for most goods, since they are allegedly XDs?

For these purposes, there are two great advantages to a cross-section of US international export data across 51 states. One advantage is that there is indeed state-to-state variation in the intensity of several alleged XDs, so that we can examine the way in which state exports covary with them. The second advantage is that the coefficients on natural and policy endowments can be estimated with US data alone. The researcher need not observe world counterparts.[33] To estimate whether US regulation discourages US exports across subregions, one need not know whether it is more burdensome than regulation abroad or less.

---

ments of farm land and unskilled workers and possibly negative coefficients on researchers and laboratories.

31. The equation was also estimated for 1987, 1988, and for a larger set of exports than the top 12 yet a smaller set of explanatory variables, pooled over 1987, 1988, and 1989. When the data were pooled, the overall explanatory power of the regression was significantly sharpened, as was the precision of the estimated coefficients. See note 34.

32. The state export data, including only international exports, and not state-to-state exports are described in detail in appendix C. They seem to have acquired an undeserved reputation for unreliability. Categories for crops, forest/fisheries products, and minerals are indeed afflicted by "consolidation bias." This is the error introduced by measuring exports at the point of consolidation, where they can be clearly identified as destined for an export market, often a port or other location different from the location of production. We have not found consolidation bias to be a serious problem for manufactured exports, however (see appendix C).

33. Because the data do not include state-to-state exports (see Appendix C). The overseas counterpart policies, and indeed all the overseas endowments labeled *w* in the model (see footnote 29), have the same value for each US state in the cross section. Because their

The equation actually estimated for each particular good is

$$\begin{aligned}(\text{typical US state } i\text{'s exports of a good})/Y_i = {} & b_0' \\ & + b_1 (E_{1i}/Y_i) \\ & + \ldots \\ & + b_m (E_{mi}/Y_i) \\ & + b_{1p} (P_{1i}/Y_i) \\ & + b_{2p} (P_{2i}/Y_i) \\ & + b_{3p} (P_{3i}/Y_i) \\ & + \ldots,\end{aligned}$$

where b_0' differs from b_0 by including the effects of all the world endowments, where E_{ji} represents region i's endowment of factor j, where Y_i represents its GNP, and where P stands for policy "endowments."

The most significant[34] first-step coefficients for the 15 "natural" factor endowments appear in appendix C, table C.1. These show sensible patterns and typically explain one-third to one-half of the variation across states in international exports of each SIC group. Thus, states with large endowments of patenting activity[35] tend to have large exports of manufactures (except paper products) and especially large exports of instruments, machinery, and transport equipment. States with large endowments of structural capital[36] tend to have large exports of several manufacturing groups, especially transport equipment. States with large endowments of professional and technical workers tend to have especially large exports of electronics and electrical equipment.[37] States with large endowments of administrative workers probably produce services more intensively than other states and hence produce and export fewer manu-

---

measured value is the same constant for every state, their influence is naturally incorporated into the influence of other constant factors included in coefficient b_0.

34. Smith (1992a) obtains even tighter and more reasonable results in a series of cross-state regressions pooled across 1987, 1988, and 1989 for each of the two-digit SIC categories of manufactured exports, not just the top 12, and using only capital, labor, and patents endowments (no resource endowments).

35. The variable measuring patenting activity measures current patents issued, not patent stocks. Experiments with patent-stock variables, constructed by cumulating annual patent issues to state residents over multiple-year intervals and discounting by several sensible rates showed a surprising result. The patent-stock variables almost never outperformed current patent issues in the various regressions. Current patent issues therefore may be proxying for something else—for example, technological initiative and ferment. Smith (1993) decomposes the patent variable into industry-specific and generic components to detect interindustry externalities and examines the explanatory power of adding adjacent regions' patents to detect interregional externalities.

36. Structural capital is a cumulated stock of private nonresidential construction by state, designed to reflect a state's immobile capital endowment, the only type that belongs in this sort of regression (Leamer 1984, 22–23).

37. The negative coefficient on chemicals, though, seems anomalous.

factures. Other natural endowments enter with signs that are mostly sensible, and only occasionally suspicious.[38]

More important for this project are the second-step coefficients from adding selected "policy endowments" and state-by-state measures of XDs to these regressions. If they have important influences (beyond the influences of the natural endowments), then they, too, should help explain cross-state variation in US exports. Five variables in particular were added, as described in more detail in appendix C:

- state government budgets for promotion of state exports and investment by foreigners;[39]
- various "environmental taxes," measured by spending on pollution abatement by manufacturing firms resident in each state divided by their primary input costs (value added);[40]
- state and local stocks of infrastructure, or "public capital"—typically the value of roads, utilities, land, and schools owned by state and local government;[41]
- state and federal tax rates on earned income;
- state and federal tax rates on unearned income—that is, capital gains.

Aspects of each of these have been alleged to put US firms at a cost disadvantage relative to international competitors, as discussed in earlier chapters. Inadequate government export promotion and infrastructure and burdensome regulation and taxation are on the list of XDs mentioned by at least some informed commentators. But it is significant that these

38. For example, the explanatory power of physical resources is strong in resource-based exports and inconsequential for manufactures in the higher SIC groups. But some of the signs on their estimated *b* coefficients are peculiar.

39. The raw data contained a number of gaps and anomalies. An attempt to remove them by running "auxiliary regressions" is described in appendix C.

40. The discussion below of the results in table 5.4 centers on the most defensible of the various measures—an unweighted arithmetic average of 19 ratios of pollution abatement expenditure on operating costs to value added, one ratio for each of the 19 manufacturing industries in the two-digit Standard Industrial Classification (SIC). Across industries for all states together, petroleum products (SIC 29) had the highest ratio, 11 percent; primary metal products (SIC 33) the second highest, 4 percent; and printing (SIC 27) the lowest, 0.2 percent. Across states for all industries together, Wyoming, New Jersey, and Louisiana had the highest average, and Connecticut, Kansas, and Oregon the lowest. Alternative measures and the effect of using them (all of which produced results very similar to those in table 5.4) are described in appendix C.

41. Roughly 35 percent of the average state value of public capital represents streets and highways. Approximately 20 percent is educational structures, and another 20 percent is sewerage and capital of local utilities. The remainder is miscellaneous buildings and land.

were almost never at the top of our surveyed experts' lists, and there was some controversy over whether they really were XDs.

Even in that light, the results of adding these alleged XDs to the cross-state regressions are surprisingly weak. Table 5.4 summarizes their estimated *b* coefficients, given the influence of the natural endowments.[42] Several features are striking.

- Export promotion seems almost entirely unrelated to exports.
- Pollution abatement spending as a ratio of primary input costs seems, on average, to be *positively* related to exports.
- Exports of transport equipment are positively related to public infrastructure, but not many other categories are in any strong way.
- High tax rates are related to low exports of certain goods but appear unrelated to exports of overall manufactures, durables, or nondurables.

Several of these results deserve further discussion.

Export promotion. We saw in chapter 3 that inadequate export promotion was rarely mentioned as an important XD, and chapters 2 and 4 discussed why it might not be expected to have strong effects. It is a generic XD, not sectorally targeted, and if anything inflicts potentially higher costs than otherwise on US exporters. But such costs are shiftable. In this light it may be less surprising that export (and investment[43]) promotion seems to have almost no significant effect on exports and sometimes even negative effects.[44]

---

42. Coefficients were estimated for all natural and policy endowments in all industry groups. The estimated coefficients on natural endowments from table C.1 are hardly changed at all when the five additional policy endowments are added to the regression. For the estimated coefficients on policy endowments, only those that could be pinned down relatively precisely in a statistical sense are shown in table 5.4. Those coefficients marked with a single asterisk were one to two times as large as their statistical standard error, a measure of dispersion for the estimated coefficient itself. Those marked with a double asterisk were more than two times as large as their standard error. Blanks in the table thus represent imprecisely estimated coefficients—coefficients that were so small relative to their respective standard errors that sign reversals or zero values could not be ruled out using standard statistical criteria.

43. Foreign direct investment (FDI) by itself does seem to affect exports, if entered as an explanatory variable. States that host more FDI than others have more exports of crops, food, paper, chemicals, and other nondurables. They also seem to have less exports of machinery and other durables.

44. One of our experts expressed no surprise at the poor performance of the export promotion variable, claiming that the state budget and employment data on which we relied were terrible even relative to the normally terrible quality of most data. Appendix C describes some ways in which it was "improved" for our purposes without, however, changing the result.

Table 5.4 Effects of US state policy variables on state exports, 1989 (export changes in thousands of dollars)

SIC group		Export promotion (thousands of 1988 dollars)	Environmental cost ("tax" rate)	Public capital (thousands of 1982 dollars)	Tax, earned income[a] (personal tax rate)	Tax, capital gains[a] (personal tax rate)
01	Crops		1,992**		n.e.	n.e.
20	Food		603*		−3,270*	
24	Lumber	220*		37.6**		
26	Paper		206**			
28	Chemicals		1,049**			
30	Rubber		84**		952*	222.3*
33	Primary metal			16.9**	−1,644*	−509.5*
34	Fabricated metal	−54*				
35	Machinery	−219*	−518*	−38.7*		
36	Electronics		1,700*		−4,300**	−1,195.0*
37	Transport			203.1**		
38	Instruments		−295**		−1,856*	−557.4*
ND	Nondurables		n.e.			
D	Durables		n.e.	225.1**		
T	Total manufactures		n.e.	219.2**		

* = estimate is one to two times standard error.

** = estimate is more than two times standard error.

n.e. = not estimated

SIC = Standard Industrial Classification

Nondurables = SIC 20–23, 26–31

Durables = SIC 24–25, 32–36

Total manufactures = Nondurables plus durables.

a. These regressions were run on 1987 data, the latest year for which earned income tax rates were available.

Column Headings:

Export promotion = state "international budget" appropriated, fiscal 1988, in some cases estimated by an auxiliary cross-state regression of international budget on number of state office staff and number of foreign offices.

Environmental cost = simple average in each state of 19 manufacturing industry ratios of (i) pollution abatement operating cost expenditure to (ii) industry value added within the state. *Source* of (i): US Department of Commerce, *Pollution Abatement Costs and Expenditures, 1988,* except where not reported because of small size or to maintain confidentiality. In those cases, the ratio of (i) to (ii) was set equal to the mean for states that published data. *Source* of (ii): US Department of Commerce, 1987 Census of Manufacturing.

Public capital = estimated 1988 stock (in thousands of 1982 dollars) of state-owned and locally owned educational facilities, roads, sewerage, and utilities, computed and graciously supplied to the author by Douglas Holtz-Eakin.

Tax, earned income = combined effective state and federal (average) personal tax rate, expressed as a percentage of the personal income of the median state taxpayer in 1987.

Tax, unearned income = combined state and federal marginal tax rate on capital gains income in 1989.

Sources: National Association of State Development Agencies, *State Export Program Database (SEPD),* July 1988 (export promotion); US Department of Commerce, *Pollution Abatement Costs and Expenditures, 1988* (environmental cost); US Department of Commerce, 1987 Census of Manufacturing (environmental cost); Holtz-Eakin (1991) (public capital); Berliant and Strauss (1992) (tax, earned income); Bogart and Gentry (1992, table A-2) (tax, unearned income). See appendix C for details.

Environmental spending. States with high average pollution-abatement expenditures by firms were hypothesized to be those that cared more about the environment and that were willing to burden their exporters for a greater good. Yet such states seem to have greater exports of food and crops, chemicals, and electronics equipment relative to states with low pollution-abatement expenditure. While the states spending more on the environment also have relatively low exports of machinery and instruments, the negative coefficients in these sectors are smaller in absolute size than the anomalous positive coefficients.[45]

This is quite surprising if environmental spending really is an XD. Yet these results are also consistent with the nearly universal inability of statistical research to detect any significant negative effect of environmental regulation on international competitiveness,[46] including research that uses the same data on pollution abatement spending as the present study (US Congress, OTA 1992, 98). These results are also consistent with the opinion that environmental regulation creates significant opportunities as well as burdens; the opportunities are for internationally competitive exports of environmentally oriented goods, services, and technology (US Congress, OTA 1992, appendix D).

On the other hand, there are two possible reasons to reject these results as spurious, the first of which seems especially strong: These results are a consequence of the industry mix, in which states with heavy concentrations of exports in pollution-intensive industries seem to spend more on pollution abatement.[47] Second, the methodology is inappropriate because pollution abatement spending in 1989 was determined almost

45. A version of the regression in which average capital expenditures on pollution abatement was added to average operating expenditures generated quite similar results to those of table 5.4.

46. See Dean (1992), Pearce (1992), and US Congress, OTA (1992, appendix E) for surveys of the surprisingly inconclusive literature. Grossman and Krueger (1992), for example, find only quantitatively small tendencies for the United States to import more from Mexico in industries with higher US pollution abatement expenditure than other industries. By contrast, statistical research does detect significant tendencies for environmental regulation to reduce the level and growth rates of overall GDP. See Crandall (1992) for a survey.

47. Even though the ratio of pollution abatement spending to value added was a simple average across 19 2-digit SIC categories, and hence *not* subject to this bias directly, the underlying variation in 4-digit subcategories created the same bias *in*directly. Especially in food and kindred products, primary metals, and chemicals/pharmaceuticals, there is substantial variation in the pollution abatement ratios among 4-digit subsectors. If "dirty" subsectors bunch together in "lax" states, and "clean" subsectors in "fastidious" states, then 2-digit ratios of pollution abatement spending to value added would be high in the lax states and low in the fastidious states. This would completely invert the implicit hypothesis on which the regression experiment was based, that states with high average pollution abatement spending care more about the environment. I am indebted to Allen Lenz and Robert S. Dohner for documenting this point for me. A mystery remains, however. When industries for which variation across the 4-digit subcategories cause clear

entirely by federal, not state, mandate. Hence, cross-state differences in the average ratio of such spending to value added must be due to something other than state-to-state regulatory intensity.[48]

So can anything be said about the effects of environmental regulation on export competitiveness? A large literature cannot detect any effects, but most of this literature seems subject to measurement and methodological objections.

In an attempt to provide one more trial, the residual state exports that could not be explained by the natural endowments (residuals from the table C.1 regressions) were plotted against an independent ranking of states by the strength of their public environmental record.[49] The results are displayed in figures 5.1 and 5.2. Once again, there is no apparent suggestion that public environmental activism deters exports. If it did, the points should cluster around a line with a positive slope in figure 5.1, which relates unexplained manufactures exports to the state environmental ranking. But there is no evidence, either, that public environmental activism encourages high-technology exports. Figure 5.2 plots only the residuals from state high-tech exports against the state ranking. Once again, the points look more or less random. They do not cluster around any line with a negative slope, which is what the relationship would be if activism encouraged high-tech exports.

Public capital. Public infrastructure, by contrast, seems to relate to exports in a more-or-less straightforward way. States with larger public capital stocks have greater exports of manufactures, especially durables, and especially transportation equipment.[50]

Yet while a thousand dollars more public capital seems to generate $200 more state manufactures exports in table 5.4, a thousand dollars more private capital generates $500 more state manufactures exports in table C.1. Even a promising policy endowment for encouraging exports

---

problems are ignored, and a simple average is formed for the five 2-digit categories best represented in the data for all states, the qualitative results of Table 5.4 *still* hold. States with high environmental spending (in SIC 24, 30, 32, 34, and 37—lumber, rubber, stone, fabricated metal products, and transportation equipment) *still* tend to have higher exports in the categories suggested in Table 5.4.

48. This is a less persuasive explanation for the anomalous results of table 5.4 because, unlike the first explanation, it suggests only random, unsystematic variation across states in the environmental spending variable. Such a variable should have no explanatory power at all.

49. The ranking is due to Duerksen (1983). According to Meyer (1992, 10), who uses it, it is based on 23 environmental indicators, including the comprehensiveness of state environmental impact statements, the extent of state habitat and wildlife protection, state power plant regulations, and so on.

50. However, public capital stocks do not relate in the same way at all to state output (value added) of manufactures. It is not clear why public capital would influence exports but not output.

Figure 5.1 States' unexplained (residual) manufacturing exports against ranking of public environmental activism (1 = highest activism)

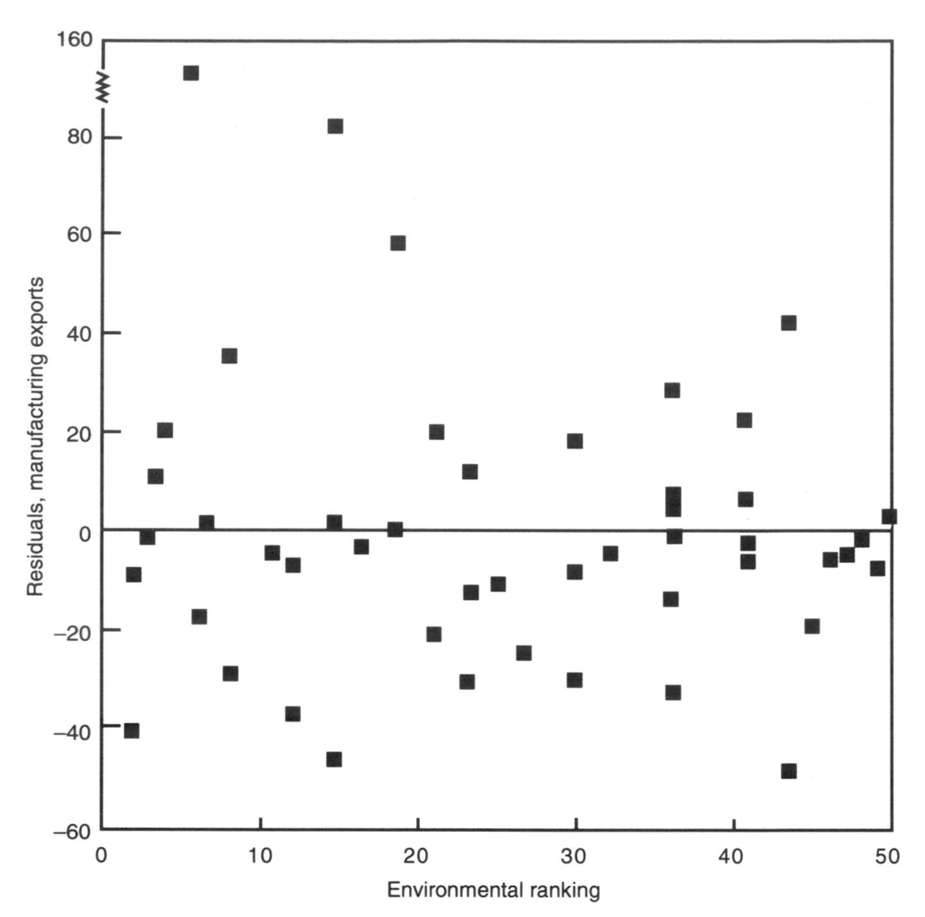

seems to be trumped by its private counterpart! In fact, an implicit conclusion from the two tables together is that policy support for generic, endowments-based sources of export competitiveness may be more potent and more promising than sectorally targeted policies (relief from taxes, regulation), vague policy promotion, or public infrastructure activism. The policy support that matters is that which encourages privately appropriable technology and private structural and human capital.

Box 5.2 highlights this perspective. The quantitatively important sources of large state exports of manufactures seem to be technology (reflected in patents), private structural capital, and a professional work force. Some of these coefficients are surprisingly large in absolute size. This is explained in part by how radically states differ among themselves in their category-by-category export performance. Coefficient size differs across sectors in sensible ways, however: patent coefficients are highest

Figure 5.2 States' unexplained (residual) high-technology exports against ranking of public environmental activism (1 = highest activism)

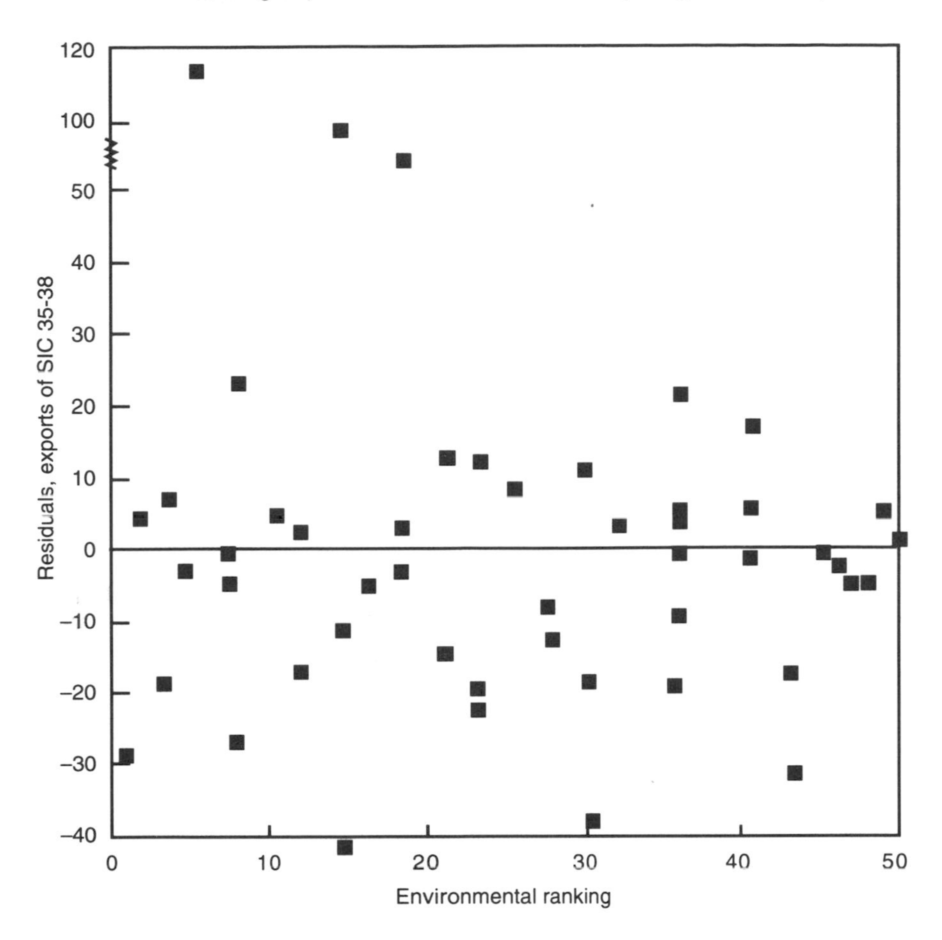

in the seemingly highest-tech sectors; the "export value" of a professional worker is also highest in such sectors; structural capital generates the most exports per dollar in transportation equipment.

The general implication is that the most effective approach is one that goes "back to basics." A government whose policies facilitate education, skill acquisition, capital formation, technological advance, and protection of intellectual property will find manufactures exports high, especially in the higher-technology categories. A government whose policies deter investment in skills, capital, and technology may find that it has saddled its manufacturers with insurmountable export disincentives, whatever more direct export promoting measures it adopts.

Taxes. Tax regulations are potentially both export-promoting and export-deterring, as we saw in chapter 3. Favorable treatment of foreign-source income promotes exports, and lack of border tax adjustment for

Box 5.2 How generic endowments contribute to sectoral export competitiveness

A US state, other things being equal, that has:

one more **patent** than other states will have an additional...

$46,000–$59,000[1] exports of rubber products (SIC 30)
$61,000–$79,000 exports of fabricated metal products (SIC 34)
$474,000–$491,000 exports of industrial machinery (SIC 35)
$1.25–$1.46 million exports of transportation equipment (SIC 37)
$160,000–$197,000[2] exports of instruments (SIC 38)
$1.61–$1.98 million exports of all manufactures

$1,000 more **private capital** than other states will have an additional...

$27–$30 exports of paper products (SIC 26)
$21–$58[2] exports of chemical products (SIC 28)
$88–$97 exports of industrial machinery (SIC 35)
$ 0–$94 exports of electrical equipment (SIC 36)
$80–$210[2] exports of transportation equipment (SIC 37)
$412–$556[2] exports of all manufactures

$1,000 more **public capital** than other states will have an additional...

$192–203[3] exports of transportation equipment (SIC 37)
$199–219[3] exports of all manufactures

one more **professional worker** than other states will have an additional...

$690–$1,606[2] exports of paper products (SIC 26)
$878–$1,313[2] exports of fabricated metal products (SIC 34)
$7,417–$8,415 exports of industrial machinery (SIC 35)
$7,809–13,673[2] exports of electrical equipment (SIC 36)
$20,571–$29,288[2] exports of all manufactures.

---

1. The first number in the range is taken from the regressions on 1989 data from tables 5.4 and C.1; the second is from regressions on 1987, 1988, and 1989 data that are "pooled"— i.e., forcing cross-state variation to be explained with the same intensity by the same determinants in each of the three years, but without including raw-material endowments (the three land variables, minerals, coal, oil, and gas) as explanatory variables.

2. The first number is from pooled regressions on 1987, 1988, and 1989 data; the second is from the regressions on 1989 data found in tables 5.4 and C.1.

3. The first number in the range is from regressions on 1989 data from tables 5.4 and C.1, 1988 public capital stock from Munnell (1990), courtesy of Douglas Holtz-Eakin; the second number is from regressions on 1989 data from tables 5.4 and C.1 and 1988 public capital stock from Holtz-Eakin (1989).

US direct taxes deters exports, at least according to some of the experts surveyed.[51] The two tax variables included in the cross-state regressions attempt to test the export-deterring claim about direct taxes. There is indeed some support for the claim, but it is on balance weak. States with high rates of income and capital-gains tax have lower exports of primary metal products, electrical equipment, electronics, and instruments. But the coefficients are relatively imprecise and do not sum into any significant effect on the manufacturing aggregates. That is, there is no evidence that high direct tax rates deter overall exports of manufactures, nor durables, nor nondurables.

Avoidability, Additionality, and the Econometric Approaches

Before summing up the results of our calculations below, it is worth repeating here the cautionary message from chapters 2 and 4. Many opportunities for offsetting exist whereby some exports may grow in response to XDs on others.

However, the message applies differently in light of the results from this chapter. The results confirm once more the importance of demand-constricting XDs relative to cost-inflicting XDs, especially in US high-technology sectors. Yet it is precisely in those sectors with flat or declining cost structures that one of the most important offsets does not work, as chapter 4 reminds us. In the case of flat cost structures, demand-constricting XDs do not lead to pressure to offset lost sales by more intense competition in unconstrained export markets. And in the case of declining costs, the possibility of perverse effects is strong—demand-constricting XDs toward some trading partners will make US exports less competitive toward all trading partners, by forcing US exporters up their cost curves. Such XDs are not only additive,[52] they multiply. Or, more accurately, they metastasize.

By contrast, there are many offset opportunities for avoiding cost-inflicting US XDs, and this chapter has found it difficult to detect any significant US export deterrence from such XDs. Of course, the second may be the result of the first. One should not expect forgone exports overall when opportunities for offsetting the burdens of XDs with export gains are large.

---

51. But see box 4.2 for reasons to doubt such experts.

52. The simple demand-constricting export embargoes described in chapter 4 are the cleanest example. Since there are zero offsets in this case, the aggregate effect of embargoing any given set of markets is the straightforward sum of exports across the embargoed markets.

Thus the results of this chapter are internally consistent and also consistent with previous chapters. The most severe US XDs seem to be those that foreclose markets for high-technology goods: export controls, sanctions, and to a lesser extent, inadequate export finance. The least severe in relative terms are those that impose extra costs on US exporters. But how do they all add up? In the next section, I try to answer that question.

Summing Up the Sizing-Up Calculations

It is now possible to look back on the results of this and previous chapters to ask the question with which we began. Just what are the most severe US export disincentives, what sectors do they affect, and how severe are they?

The most severe US XDs appear to be export controls on shipments to countries due to antiproliferation and Cold War considerations, often one and the same countries, and by US embargoes and sanctions aimed at enforcing foreign policy. Tables 5.1 and 5.2 suggest estimated ranges for forgone US exports of $1.7 billion to $19.9 billion for the first in 1989 and $2.4 billion to $3.1 billion for the second in 1989. The range from table 5.1 is wide because of both statistical variation and the nuances of disentangling unilateral from multilateral controls. The range from table 5.2 reflects statistical variation alone, although similar questions about unilateralism could be raised about these calculations.

These estimated shortfalls are concentrated in chemicals, machinery, equipment, instruments, and other high-tech sectors. Thus, one can feel fairly confident about disregarding offsets and adding them together, for the reasons given above. The same sectors, of course, are the chief beneficiaries of official support for US export finance. The numerical simulations of chapter 4 suggested US export shortfalls that ran from $0.5 billion to $3.1 billion for 1988–90 because of US support that fell short of equivalent support in major trading partners.

Cost-inflicting XDs such as US product-liability shortcomings were judged in box 2.1 and table 4.1 to have more modest, if any, deterrent effects on US exports. But because of their concentrated incidence on the same familiar sectors, they, too, might be assumed additive along the lines above, along with the small but high-profile exports deterred by US telecommunications deregulation in the 1980s and antidumping protection for flat-panel displays in 1992–93 (chapter 2 and box 3.1). The calculated ranges of export shortfalls on these products were (from earlier chapters), from zero to $2.4 billion from US product-liability shortcomings in the late 1980s, and from zero to $1.0[53] billion from miscellaneous high-profile deregulation and protection in the early 1980s and 1990s.

---

53. $1 billion seems a generous upper estimate, for reasons discussed earlier in the book.

Adding generic cost-inflicting XDs, such as the effects of heavy US workplace safety burdens and protection-induced steel price inflation, is more questionable because of additionality and avoidability considerations. But their estimated effects on US exports, discussed in box 3.1 and chapter 4, are quite modest in any case (and in the case of steel, probably zero): from zero to $2.5 billion in 1991 dollars from workplace safety burdens from zero to $0.7 billion (1986 maximum) from steel protection.

Little evidence could be mustered for significant effects of other alleged US XDs—environmental, antiboycott, and antibribery (Foreign Corrupt Practices Act) regulations; inadequate export promotion; taxation conventions; bans on exports of raw logs and Alaskan oil; and differences in standards and public infrastructure.

So at the end of the project, what is the answer to the key question? It seems very clear that the most severe US export disincentives are demand-constricting US export controls. It also seems clear that export losses from these XDs are concentrated on manufacturing sectors that are often described as "dynamic," or "leading," and that generate both technological impetus and high-paying jobs for skilled and professionally trained workers.

Export controls, of course, serve important national objectives that are hard to evaluate in such a way that export costs could be carefully compared to their benefits. But it seems timely to reopen a discussion of their costs and benefits. Exports in general, and those affected by US XDs in particular, are playing a growing role in US prosperity, as we have seen in chapter 1. And US export controls, whatever the merits of their objectives, are in danger of lapsing into mere symbolic display; rival exporters, not covered by multilateral controls or not enforcing them as strictly as we do, are increasingly undermining the ability of the United States to deny access to vital commodities and technologies. When the worthy objectives of US export controls are thereby unmet, the cost-benefit calculation becomes easy. The costs are forgone exports; the benefits are zero.

The project's estimated severity of US XDs is large, though necessarily imprecise. It is, after all, the first attempt to size them up. The final part of the answer is the range suggested by the additive XDs above: $4.6 billion to $29.5 billion, with a mid-point of $17.1 billion, of which two-thirds to three-quarters of the shortfall is in chemicals, machinery, and instruments.

This range was calculated with reference to a 1989 base. Between 1989 and 1991, however, US exports in these categories grew at an impressive 26 percent.[54] And we have seen in this chapter that estimated shortfalls

54. That is the growth in the SITC categories that include most high-technology goods in this chapter's regressions based on OECD data: SITC 7–78 + 87 + 88.

from US export controls are, if anything, larger in 1991 than in 1989, despite revolutionary reorientation in their purpose. A meaningful 1991 counterpart to the aggregate 1989 range might be the latter scaled up by 26 percent: $5.8 billion to $37.2 billion, with a mid-point of $21.5 billion.

And if the world economy were to return soon to a trajectory that would make 26 percent the relevant long-run biannual growth rate in US high-technology exports, then the relevant range for US exports lost to our own XDs *today*, in 1993, is $7.3 billion to $46.9 billion, with a midpoint of $27.1 billion.

Finally, these calculated ranges may still be underestimates for three reasons discussed above.[55] First and most important, exports of weapons and export controls on them have been excluded from consideration because of measurement inadequacies. Many similar concerns could be raised about them as about dual-use goods: arms exports usually come from the same familiar high-technology sectors, arms exports are sometimes undermined by foreign availability that is not covered by multilateral regimes, yet the objectives of controlling arms exports are laudable, and so on.

Second, no numerical effort was made to simulate the effects of scale, learning, and other dynamic economies that might cause declining (as opposed to flat) variable costs. For any US exports characterized by such dynamic economies, we have underestimated the perverse way that demand-constricting XDs multiply worldwide export losses by forcing firms to operate in uncompetitively high ranges on their cost curves.

Third, it has not been possible to calculate some of the indirect ways that US XDs affect US exports through operations of multinational affiliates. The direct effects of export diversion to affiliates are indeed sized up by the study. Two indirect effects are not sized up: even the affiliates' overseas sales may be held down by US XDs that apply extraterritorially, or by unilateral US pressures that force host countries to adopt parallel XDs, and the affiliates' capacity for generating complementary and follow-on US export business (a difficult thing to measure) may be blunted.[56]

Increasingly, American commentators reflect on the possibility that the best domestic stimulus program for the US economy is an export stimulus program. Often from that come concerns that the dollar is

---

55. Lack of consideration of export controls for short-supply reasons may be a fourth source of underestimation. But we have argued above that the goods covered by short-supply controls are almost never strategically vital and are almost always subject to strong offsets and/or avoidability.

56. See Bergsten and Graham (forthcoming) for evidence of and estimates for the complementarity of US exports and investment abroad. For investors forced abroad by US XDs, of course, it is not likely that indirectly induced complementary exports could ever replace directly deterred exports.

overvalued in real terms or that foreign trade barriers crimp our export opportunities. Maybe so: Cline (1989) finds that US exports fall $7.2 billion for every enduring 1 percent misalignment in the direction of a stronger dollar; Bergsten and Noland (1993) find that Japanese trade barriers cost US firms $9 billion to $18 billion of export business. But maybe these grievances about macroeconomics and foreign access are not the whole story.

This study suggests another conclusion: that we reconsider the ways that our own policies may be needlessly sacrificing our own exports. It estimates the potential for export gains of similar or greater magnitudes to those attainable from macroeconomic and market-opening activism. Without prejudging the important goals that US export-deterring policies seek to achieve, in the next chapter I suggest rationalization mechanisms and tests to ensure that national, political, and social security do not undermine US economic security.

6

Sizing Up the Export Disincentives Enterprise and the Policy Options

US market principles and economic performance once undergirded US global leadership. However, as the international competitiveness of important rivals has grown relative to the United States, the clash between its desire to leave markets free of unnecessary interference and its other important goals has been accentuated. Do US commitments to a democratic and peaceful world and the policies that enforce such commitments impose an undue economic burden on Americans? Do US controls and sanctions against "rogue" weapons producers, for example, cause a significant loss of export business in related dual-use goods? Or do US commitments to the environment and to safe products and workplaces cause significant losses of international competitiveness? Or do ideological US commitments to "free" markets cause its government sometimes to shun policies that could in fact enhance US competitiveness and thus benefit all Americans?

Americans are more concerned than they used to be about US international competitiveness. This is a good thing. But US policy concern often seems unduly reactive and focused on imports; it seems inadequately proactive and export-oriented. When exports are at issue, unfair foreign practices seem to dominate the typical US discussion, not our own policies that inhibit our own exports. These self-inflicted US export disincentives (XDs) have been the subject of this study, in which I argue that mitigating the burden XDs impose is crucial for market-centered economic prosperity.

This project is the first comprehensive attempt to catalog and to size up the costs of US policy commitments that deter its own exports. Many of these microeconomic XDs may be well worth the cost to exports because of the important goals they achieve, but it has always been hard to say so precisely or confidently or quantitatively. This study argues that exports and export sectors often have special economic value beyond what the market registers. Then forgone exports represent especially significant economic costs.

These are the sizing-up results: In general, XDs that foreclose markets or constrict demand, such as embargoes and export controls, appear to be quantitatively significant. But it is hard to detect significant export losses from tax systems or from many of the US regulatory policies with social, environmental, or other objectives. The next section of this chapter summarizes the detailed conclusions.

The subsequent section spells out the most important recommendations for US policy. They are, broadly, to mandate and report calculations of the export costs of relevant US policy objectives, to pursue these objectives with maximal market-minded multilateralism, and to support the fundamentals of export competitiveness proactively because of its importance for overall US prosperity.

The last section of the chapter sizes up the sizing-up project. The assessment is broadly encouraging. As a first attempt to establish comprehensive quantitative ranges for export shortfalls from a country's export-deterring policies, the XD project has links to the earliest quantitative evaluations of nontariff barriers to imports and to the common corporate exercise called benchmarking. The techniques employed are diverse and constitute a reasonable beginning for research aimed at documenting how integrated export and domestic markets affect national economic prosperity, especially in high-technology and other imperfectly competitive industries.

Ultimately, the sizing-up exercise contributes only the export cost component of a genuine benefit-cost evaluation of US export-deterring policies. Assessing the benefits of these policies and their other possible costs is a daunting project in its own right, requiring many subtle judgments, and is not attempted extensively here.

The Size and Range of US Export Disincentives

Aim and Methods

The aim of this project is to delimit quantitative ranges for the "cost" in forgone exports of US policies toward national security, foreign policy, taxation, and regulation, and of inadequate US policy support for exports. For purposes of the study, such policies are described as export disincentives (XDs); the often worthy objectives that they seek to achieve are not explicitly valued.

"Sizing up" is my characterization of the attempt to establish quantitative ranges for the effects of various US XDs on US exports—that is, order-of-magnitude estimates. I employ three broad techniques: surveys (of expert commentators, industry groups, other researchers); simulations (of basic XDs for hypothetical imperfectly competitive industries that serve as numerical benchmarks); and statistics (regressions across trading partners, and regressions across states). The three techniques generate very similar conclusions about the relative size of various XDs, but not about their absolute size.

But how much difference do US XDs make to overall export performance? Summing up the various sizing-up calculations requires an answer to the question of additionality and offsets: to what extent did XDs confronting only some product lines, firms, or industries, and those affecting only some sources or destinations, get offset by compensating exports of other products, firms, or industries from other sources or to other destinations? The study describes why industry cost and market structure negate the effect of certain important offsets for the XDs estimated to have the largest impact on leading US sectors.[1]

Conclusions

There are five important general conclusions from the sizing-up project:

- US government policies often get in the way of strong US export performance—sometimes by design, sometimes incidentally. In the mid 1990s I estimate that the United States forgoes as much as $40 billion of exports annually because of the policies covered here. The different estimates center on a range of $21 billion to $27 billion, of which I estimate that one-fifth to one-half is due to policies that the United States adopts multilaterally with important allies. Export controls for national security or antiproliferation purposes seem to be especially strong XDs, accounting for two-thirds to three-quarters of total exports forgone.[2]

---

1. There is even a possibility of "perverse offsets." In sectors with learning economies or other reasons for declining costs, US XDs that constrict sales to certain markets make US exports *globally* less competitive. Instead of offsets that make it inadvisable to add the effects of XDs together, there are "multiplier" effects that make $1 worth of direct XDs deter more than $1 worth of exports.

2. Export controls on pure weaponry, without commercial use, cause additional export shortfalls but are not covered in this study because of special problems of measurement and security.

- High-technology export sectors bear a disproportionate share of the resulting export shortfalls—sometimes by design, sometimes incidentally. Chemicals, machinery, equipment, and instruments account for two-thirds or more[3] of the shortfalls. These are also the sectors in which lost export sales are rarely recovered in offsetting product lines or to other customers.

- "Demand-constricting" XDs (such as sanctions) are more potent than "cost-inflicting" XDs (such as regulatory burdens). XDs that cut off demand (embargoes) are more potent than those that merely inhibit it (such as inadequate official support for export finance). XDs that inflict fixed costs on firms (such as legal/administrative support for export licensing departments) are more potent than those that inflict variable costs (such as product standards). It is hard to detect any significant export deterrence from US antiboycott, environmental, or other across-the-board regulatory burdens on US industry, or from inadequate export promotion, or from differences in direct taxes that are ineligible for border tax adjustments.

- Commentator perceptions of relative severity lined up well with subsequent rankings of the quantitative results. Export controls and sanctions topped almost everyone's list. Commentator perceptions of quantitative severity did not line up as well. Compared with subsequent quantitative experiments, commentators appeared to understate the severity of the most severe XDs, and overstated the severity of the least. The experiments indicate that controls and sanctions were even more significant XDs than the experts thought they were. They thought that taxes and regulatory burdens, though, were more significant XDs than any of our experiments suggest. The neglected implications of relatively flat or declining costs in imperfectly competitive, high-technology sectors is the most persuasive reason for the understatement; the neglected capacity for firms to remain competitive by passing on higher costs to workers, suppliers, and buyers is the most persuasive reason for the overstatement.

- The statistical results suggest the indirect export efficacy of familiar policies to boost capital, education and labor skills, and appropriable technology. Inadequacies in such policies can be considered important but indirect export disincentives.

There are also more specific quantitative conclusions. One way of summarizing them is to compare the results from simulations and statisti-

3. High-technology sectors accounted for two-thirds of the larger end of the range of estimated effect. At the smaller end, employing the most conservative assumptions about the way US XDs work, they accounted for virtually all the estimated effect.

cal analyses with those from the commentators that were surveyed. This produces three sets of results: surprisingly large numbers or ranges, unsurprising numbers/ranges, and surprisingly small numbers/ranges. After summarizing each, we propose a way of summing them up.

Surprisingly Large Estimates

Historic national-security export controls have imposed requirements for validated licenses on up to 50 percent of manufactured exports. Some of these controls were ostensibly multilateral and coordinated with COCOM partners. But some portion of these were almost certainly due to unilateral US pressure on its COCOM partners. This portion remains embedded in the figures that follow:

- The estimated US export shortfall in 1989 toward the former Soviet Union, China, and Eastern Europe from COCOM and other multilateral controls was $4.5 billion to $12.2 billion of chemicals, machinery, equipment, and instruments (SIC 28, 35–38) and $4.5 billion to $19.9 billion of total exports to the same countries. To the extent that multilateral controls reflected unilateral US pressure, a share of these figures should be added to the minimum unilateral estimates that follow.
- The estimated minimum US export shortfall in 1989 from unilateral controls toward the former Soviet Union, China, and Eastern Europe was $1.0 billion to $5.2 billion of chemicals, machinery, equipment, and instruments (SIC 28, 35–38) and $1.7 billion to $8.6 billion of total exports to the same countries. I estimate no export losses to COCOM allies (which are sometimes alleged to refuse to deal with US unilateralism and extraterritoriality).[4]
- The estimated US export shortfalls in 1991 from COCOM and unilateral controls toward these same countries were similar to or larger than the 1989 calculations, a surprising conclusion in light of COCOM liberalization during and before 1991.

Sizing up nascent and current export controls is almost impossible, and summarizing them is difficult. US controls have turned increasingly toward countering proliferation of weapons of mass destruction and the dual-use products that support such weaponry. Testimonial information and surveys of exporters suggest the potential for shortfalls of similar or only slightly smaller magnitude than before 1991 (30 to 40 percent of manufactured exports still require a validated license). The most important changes are that:

---

4. The important National Academy of Sciences study (1987a) found greater US export shortfalls to COCOM allies than to controlled countries. This study does not.

- there is now different trading-partner incidence, with the heaviest shortfalls occurring with trading partners suspected of pursuing or supporting proliferation[5];
- there is now a different industry incidence, with the heaviest export shortfalls on chemicals (chemical warfare bans), aerial guidance equipment, computation and communications hardware and software, and on any goods that might be used innocently to abet proliferators;
- there has been a shift in administrative cost from US agencies to US exporters through increased risk management costs (i.e., contingent costs against future liability for use of the export product) and increased compliance costs, for example, up to 1 percent higher variable cost of exports for a major high-tech firm to monitor export products, customers, and end uses for security/proliferation goals; or 0.11–0.66 percent higher cost of exports for the US chemical industry to comply with the January 1993 United Nations Chemical Weapons Convention.

Unsurprising Estimates

Foreign policy sanctions. The estimated US export shortfall in 1989 from foreign policy sanctions was $2.4 billion to $3.1 billion of all goods to Iran, Nicaragua, Syria, Libya, Cuba, North Korea, Myanmar, and Vietnam, which are the principal countries with commodity export sanctions. The estimated shortfall for Iran was large, $1.3 billion to $1.8 billion. Those for Myanmar and Vietnam were virtually imperceptible. The others were all in the neighborhood of $0.2 billion to $0.3 billion annually.

Low official export finance. The estimated US export shortfall in 1989 from low official support for export finance (relative to global norms) was $0.5 billion to $3.1 billion and was especially concentrated on exports subject to mixed-credit and tied-aid competition and on infrastructure-related equipment and services.

Sectoral regulatory burdens. Several sectoral regulatory burdens seemed potentially important with respect to the sector's own or related exports. In this regard, I discuss:

- the potential for small but high-profile effects of the mid-1980s US telecommunications regulation/deregulation and antitrust action. AT&T generated strong equipment exports; the regional Bell operating companies generated strong services exports and foreign direct investment.
- the basis for beliefs that product liability shortcomings caused from zero to $2.4 billion of export losses for chemicals and pharmaceuticals, machine tools, and aircraft.

---

5. Some of these are targets of historic national security controls as well.

- the extent to which import barriers (MBs) serve as XDs. I describe studies finding zero to $0.7 billion of export shortfalls from steel voluntary restraint agreements (VRAs) in the mid-1980s. I describe the brief, high-profile effects on laptop computer exports from temporary US antidumping duties on active-matrix liquid crystal displays.

Surprisingly Small Estimates

Across-the-board regulatory burdens, such as procedures mandated for all businesses by the Foreign Corrupt Practices Act, seemed generally unimportant. I found no quantitative evidence of significant export deterrence from:

- antiboycott regulation
- environmental control costs
- inadequate official export promotion programs
- taxes on earned incomes (direct taxes) and capital gains.

Taxes on corporate income from foreign sources also seemed unlikely to be an important US XD. The most thorough study, by Hufbauer and van Rooij (1992), finds offsetting influences of US treatment that is sometimes more favorable and sometimes less.

Workplace safety regulation, if a US XD at all, seems a modest one. The most thorough study, by Bayard and Rousslang (1980), estimates forgone exports of zero to $2.5 billion at most.

Increased public capital was found to have a positive impact on exports of transportation equipment and overall manufactures, so the case could be made that US infrastructural inadequacies were an XD. But $1 spent on private capital was found to have an even larger impact on US exports than $1 spent on public capital. In general, US exports were found to be significantly responsive to private endowments of patents and professional labor, suggesting indirect export expansion from policies to support these "basics" of US export competitiveness.

Adding Things Up: The Overall Effects

It is from these specific quantitative conclusions that I reach a general conclusion about the overall order of magnitude of US XDs. Others can, of course, use the specific conclusions and others to reach a different "bottom line."

I have taken seriously the consensus of the evidence in earlier chapters that demand-constricting XDs in typical imperfectly competitive sectors can be minimally offset by compensatory export competitiveness elsewhere, whereas such compensatory offsets are the rule for more traditionally competitive sectors producing standardized goods (e.g., logs).

That makes demand-constricting XDs in many high-technology, differentiated goods sectors additive. If I focus on demand-constricting XDs, with only a little attention to selected cost-inflicting XDs, then the overall accounting from this study is as follows:

- Export controls toward traditional national security targets cost the United States $1.7 billion to $19.9 billion in exports.
- Export controls toward targets of foreign policy sanctions cost $2.4 billion to $3.1 billion in exports.
- Inadequacies of official US support for export finance cost $0.5 to $3.1 billion in exports.
- Product liability shortcomings and high-profile deregulation and protection cost from zero to $3.4 billion in exports.

This amounts to a total export cost of $4.6 billion to $29.5 billion.

These calculations are based on and scaled to 1989 data. However, the calculations using 1991 data show no reason to diminish them; if anything, the estimated effects of US export controls were even larger in 1991, due in part to the rapid growth in typical US exports in the high-technology categories most affected by US export controls. If one took that growth—26 percent between 1989 and 1991[6]—and applied it to the total, the result would be a 1991 total (scaled up for 1989–91 growth) of $5.8 billion to $37.2 billion.

And if continued growth at that rate is likely once global recovery is under way, then we might think of scaling up again to come to a number suitable for the mid-1990s: so a mid-1990s total (scaled up twice for 1989–91 growth) would equal $7.3 billion to $46.9 billion.

Whatever one's doubts about scaling, all of the totals imply that the export costs of US XDs are sizable and suggest the merits of reconsidering how some of these policies may be needlessly undermining US exports and US prosperity.

Policy Implications

A concise summary of these results is that US export disincentives are indeed quantitatively significant but that some of the usual XD suspects have higher quantitative profiles than others. These high-profile XDs are the focus of the positive policy recommendations that follow. The section closes with remarks on low-profile XDs and the lack of strong support for policy remedies in their case.

---

6. US exports of machinery, equipment, and instruments (except road vehicles; SITC 7–78, 87, and 88) grew at this rate, according to OECD *Foreign Trade by Commodities*.

I suggest five areas of emphasis and reemphasis in policy principles below, then propose more detailed policy practices to implement them. Three of the principles concern export controls, one concerns export finance, and one concerns "export basics." I propose policy tactics and instruments when appropriate but believe that institutional experts in each area can extend, refine, and sharpen the instrumental recommendations more effectively than this study can. In most cases, the recommendations are aimed at reducing the economic cost of US XDs relative to some desired level of effectiveness in achieving the objectives the XDs were set up to meet. Assessing the net national benefits of XDs for these objectives is beyond the scope of this study.

Export Controls

Since US export controls seem still so strong, both quantitatively and relative to other alleged XDs, this project underscores two policy principles from a succession of National Academy of Sciences studies and workshops (1987a, 1991, 1992).

US export controls, whether designed to meet national security, antiproliferation, or foreign policy goals, should be implemented with:

- maximum multilateralism and
- increased sensitivity to economic security and to foreign availability, especially because export controls fall so heavily on leading sectors of the US economy.

In addition, I propose a third broad principle and some corresponding practices because antiproliferation concerns have themselves proliferated and because the demarcations between antiproliferation, national security, and foreign policy objectives have become increasingly blurred. US export controls should thus be accompanied by:

- auxiliary mechanisms to enhance the efficiency with which objectives are met—some corrective, some supportive.

A number of policy practices would help the United States adhere to these three principles. First and most obviously, I endorse the strong leadership that the United States has exercised in multilateral forums such as the Coordinating Committee on Multilateral Export Controls (COCOM), the Nuclear Suppliers Group, the Missile Technology Control Regime, and the Australia Group. But the United States must go even further, and must increase multilateral sensitivity to economic security. Liberalization of COCOM controls and their domestic US counterparts in 1990 only succeeded because the president stressed to his own government that this was a high priority. The same must happen again to alleviate negotiating inertia and US bureaucratic gridlock over export jurisdiction. President Clinton has an ideal opportunity to seize the initiative as the Export Administration Act (EAA) is thoroughly rewritten in 1993–94.

Second, the United States must be extremely cautious about taking unilateral initiatives in the name of symbolic leadership and in the hope that trading partners will follow suit. (Unilateral abstinence is in fact the safest posture!) The Enhanced Proliferation Control Initiative (EPCI) was launched in 1991 without enough of such caution, in part to show our trading partners that the United States was serious about depriving proliferators of easy access to weapons-building materials and technology. Almost two years later, neither the deterrence itself nor the multilateral support for the initiative are clearly detectable. Explicit trade in arms and dual-use subcomponents, and presumably in materials for weapons of mass destruction, continues to grow (*Economist*, 20 February 1993, 19–22; 20 June 1992) Membership in the multilateral antiproliferation control regimes has been expanding only slowly.

Third, the EAA should require timely annual reports on the quantitative effects of US export controls on US export competitiveness (Competitiveness Policy Council 1993a). This XD project provides some methods for doing so. Such reports should include sectoral and product detail and should also attempt to size up effects of export controls on US direct investment and corporate alliances abroad and on foreign direct investment and corporate alliances in the United States.

The fourth and fifth practical recommendations are complements. The fourth recommendation is that the United States should ease and broaden its foreign availability test for controls for national security, extending it to foreign policy sanctions and antiproliferation controls. The Export Administration Act currently permits US exporters to petition for disallowal of US national security controls when comparable goods or technology are available from uncontrolled suppliers (or presumably by diversion from uncontrolled buyers). But procedures are burdensome, and processing is slow and unpredictable (see chapter 2). When petitions are justified, no additional national security is attained by maintaining export controls. The economic costs are thus infinitely larger than the security benefits. Controls are then merely ineffectual symbols of US aims. Economic security is sacrificed; national security is not attained. Therefore, it makes sense to apply a more accessible availability test and, on the same grounds, to extend it to foreign policy sanctions or antiproliferation strictures.[7] The United States cannot afford economi-

---

7. Increasingly software, chemicals, missile parts, and other commercially available goods and technologies have dual uses in weapons. Such goods and technologies simply cannot be controlled, implying practically that availability tests might drastically shrink the length of control lists for antiproliferation.

cally costly symbolism, especially when the costs are borne by its most dynamic, technologically competitive sectors.[8]

Fifth, the EAA should enhance the effectiveness and predictability of those controls that remain, especially with regard to antiproliferation. The result sought, in conjunction with the fourth recommendation, would be the same or better level of benefits for controls but lower economic costs. This fifth recommendation has three facets:

- reassignment of at least some responsibility for monitoring end uses and end users of US exports to qualified US government agencies.[9] Under the EPCI guidelines, exporters themselves are responsible for virtually all monitoring and intelligence. Yet these are functions for which their own capabilities are limited and that divert resources from areas of corporate competitive strength.
- official support for technological and commercial innovations in intelligence capability, especially devices for monitoring at a distance.[10] Current technological inadequacies, coupled with the exporters' responsibilities for policing end uses and end users, lead all too often to an export constriction equivalent to an embargo. Firms consider certain products to be simply too risky to export to certain customers.
- increased efforts to make monitoring and intelligence functions multilateral efforts. Economic burdens on exporters for policing their own shipments could be reduced still further by intergovernmental cooperation. Currently, the International Atomic Energy Agency makes inspections under the Nuclear Non-Proliferation Treaty, and a UN agency will be charged with similar tasks under the 1993 UN Chemical Weapons Convention. Such cooperative inspection and verification should be extended to biological weapons and missile-building capability.

---

8. In practice, such broadening of the foreign availability test should also include "indexing"—a continuously updated list of the critical specifications of computers and other equipment subject to rapid technological change. The aim of such indexing would be to maintain a stable level of denial of the highest technology to targets of export controls while automatically easing controls on products with increasingly standard technology.

9. For example, the US Department of Justice, the US Customs Service, and the Central Intelligence Agency.

10. Examples might include satellite photography, encryption-defeating software, and monitoring mechanisms that cannot be separated from a product (such as a microprocessor) without destroying it.

Export Finance

Since officially supported export finance appears to have moderately strong effects on US exports in leading sectors, this project supports recommendations that:

- official US export finance programs be supplemented to make US capital goods and related services competitive in financial terms with overseas rivals, especially in projects and procurements where private financial markets are inadequate—for example, public infrastructure projects in developing and transition economies, often financed by mixed credits. Recent agreements on official finance should be respected and further strengthened.

Export Basics

Because this project finds indicators of indirect XDs that operate through inadequate public policy toward education, capital, and technology, it supports a "back-to-basics" recommendation that:

- growth-enhancing policies toward human, physical, and technological capital be endorsed not only in their own right, but also for their favorable US export spillovers.

The practical recommendations accompanying this principle are familiar and less intrinsically export-focused than those above. They include policies that increase the training of US professionals, especially scientists and engineers, or that increase net immigration of such workers. They include policy changes toward physical capital formation and technological impetus such as found in Competitiveness Policy Council (1993a): enhanced tax credits for research and development; accelerated depreciation schedules for productive investment; and a shift toward consumption taxes and improved governmental budget discipline to reduce the cost of capital. All of these increase US exports, especially of the high-technology goods and services that are already our leading sectors and that pay higher wages and enjoy more rapid technological progress than other sectors.

Finally, it is notable that this study is not mere mercantilist boosterism. It does not find strong support for any and every export-promoting policy. Official export-promotion programs, for example, seem to have very little quantitative impact on US exports, whatever their valuable contributions to export consciousness raising. More significant is the project's inability to find significant impacts from across-the-board tax and regulatory XDs.[11] Within the limits of the study, there is only very weak support for export-focused concern over policies that raise the variable costs of the nation's business as a whole. As leading business sectors, exporters may be able to bear the competitive variable costs of modest burdens better than other sectors do, without unduly sacrificing overseas sales.

There is somewhat more support, however, for concern over export licensing and other policies that raise fixed costs facing exporters. These seem to be larger XDs per dollar of extra costs than variable-cost XDs. They also concentrate exporting among larger and fewer firms, thereby undermining both competitive intensity and export consciousness. And they create political problems of equity for small exporters and compromised attitudes toward XDs for large incumbents.

Was the Enterprise Worthwhile?

Beyond its policy implications, in what senses has this project made a contribution? Three answers serve as the study's conclusion.

First, the project has contributed to the methodology of "measuring the hard-to-measure." It has illustrated the efficacy of several new techniques. More important, it has illustrated how an array of diverse techniques can sometimes reduce the imprecision attached to any one. Happily, the surveys, simulations, and statistical exercises instructed each other and ultimately supported each other. Though all the witnesses were imprecise, there were both enough of them and enough of a consensus among them that a verdict seemed possible. Imprecision still remains, of course. But it has been reduced enough perhaps to reassure the skeptic who claimed in one of the earliest study groups that the project reminded him of trying to record his daughter's temperature while standing across the room from her!

Second, the project has illustrated the value of quantitatively recognizing imperfections of real-world competition. Though employing extremely simple conceptions of fixed and variable costs and of the various market structures that govern small numbers of competitors, the study generates several sharp conclusions. The characterizations of imperfectly competitive markets ultimately explain why demand-constricting XDs were sharply more severe than cost-inflicting XDs. They also explain why XDs have especially sharp effects on high-technology compared with standard-technology industries. They explain why the

11. Sectorally burdensome XDs such as inadequacies in product liability law are seen to have significant sectoral effects, in that case on exports of chemicals, pharmaceuticals, aircraft, and machine tools. This is an especially serious policy concern to the extent that these are leading US export sectors.

conclusions of this study were occasionally at sharp variance with conclusions that rest on perfect competition.[12] They help explain how XDs affect not only the amount of competition, but its quality as well, measured by indexes of market power, the size and density of firms, and barriers to entry. Finally, they explain certain political economic features of XDs, such as ambivalence about XDs among incumbent firms that have learned to live with them and the lack of voice among would-be firms that are the unseen victims of "XD triage."

Finally, if the methods are at least somewhat reliable, and if the United States has indeed unduly sacrificed exports and related economic prosperity in the pursuit of other worthy goals, then perhaps the project can serve to guide the nation toward a more cost-effective pursuit of all that it values.

---

12. For example, XDs that embargo markets in a competitive model encourage exporters to recapture a large part of their losses in uncontrolled markets. The same embargo in imperfectly competitive models can raise exporter costs worldwide and cause losses in embargoed and uncontrolled markets alike.

Appendix A "Calibration Counterfactual": approaches to simulating export disincentives numerically

New data availability and the recent empirical resurgence in industrial organization (Bresnahan and Schmalensee 1987; Schmalensee 1988) have made simple numerical simulation possible for many industries. The easiest simulations "calibrate" an industry model to real data and to central estimates of important parameters, then alter the value of certain exogenous variables or parameters to calculate a "counterfactual" equilibrium. Such simulation models can cover multiple markets, quality differences, technological change, and a wide variety of imperfectly competitive industry structures, with flexibility to select alternative characteristics such as number of firms, freedom of entry or lack of it, type of competition (Cournot, Bertrand, etc.), static or dynamic settings, and so on. These models have been widely applied to quantify the effects of nontariff import barriers and liberalization experiments (Smith and Venables 1991) and of regulatory policies such as merger guidelines (e.g., Ordover and Willig 1986). They are generally thought to be instructive if not definitive. They have been recently surveyed by Helpman and Krugman (1989, chapter 8) and Richardson (1989, 1990, 1992).

An illustration of how the models are applied in chapter 4 follows.

Figure A.1 depicts a simple, highly stylized market suitable for illustrating how to simulate the effects of the most familiar types of XDs via calibration counterfactual approaches. The figure adopts the following extreme simplifications for graphical clarity. The algebraic industry model that is the counterpart to the figure can handle generalizations of most of these extreme simplifications quite easily.

- Countries 1 and 2 are two national suppliers of two differentiated, yet symmetric, goods, indexed 1 and 2.

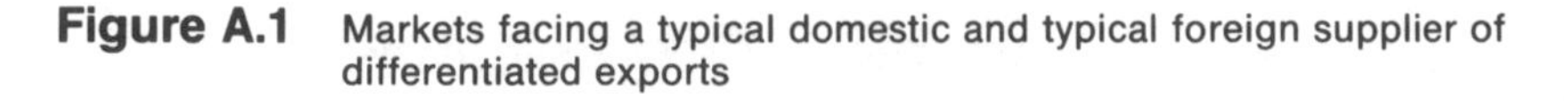

Figure A.1 Markets facing a typical domestic and typical foreign supplier of differentiated exports

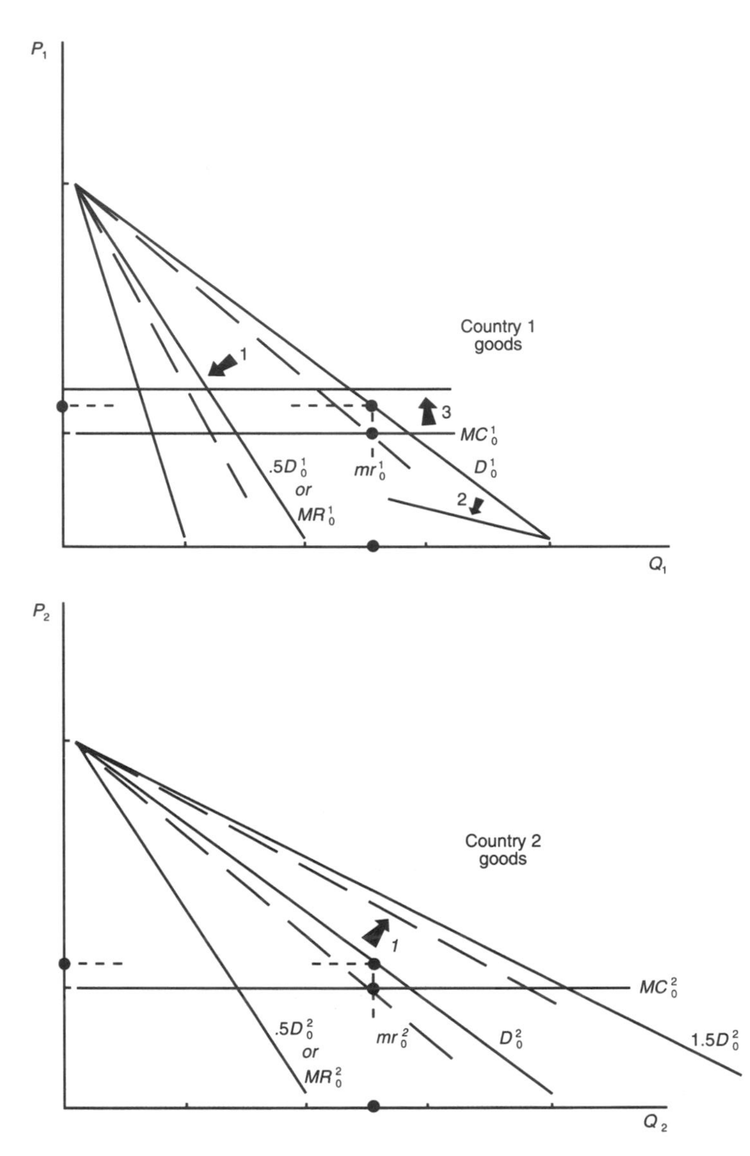

Country 1's goods and Country 2's goods are differentiated, though each of the export firms whose demand curve and marginal curves are shown produces the same homogeneous variety as its respective "kin," domestic or foreign. Changes in the price of 1's goods shifts all these curves in 2, and conversely. Dashed curves represent the marginal revenue a firm perceives given the exports of domestic rivals under Cournot competition and the price of the foreign substitute. Arrows 1, 2, and 3 illustrate, respectively, archetypical demand-constricting XDs, inadequate financial support for exports, and cost-inflicting XDs.

- Countries 3 and 4 are two symmetric national demanders of goods 1 and 2, each with initial demand curve $.5D_0$ per symmetric supplier firm. Since firms are assumed to be symmetric, each or any can be envisioned as a "representative firm" with the curves drawn, in the same fashion as the "representative household" that economists use frequently. The MR_0 curves are the initial marginal revenue curves to the initial total demand curves D_0 for each good per representative firm.
- mr_0 curves are initial "perceived" marginal revenue curves per firm (Helpman and Krugman 1989, 38–40) or Richardson (1989, 10–11), situated as drawn on the assumption of Cournot competition among a fixed number of symmetric firms. Each firm's perception is that its rivals' choices of sales volumes are given and unresponsive to the focus firm's own choice of sales volume. "Perceived" demand curves corresponding per firm are not drawn.
- MC_0 curves are initial marginal cost curves, assumed constant and common across firms. Initial equilibrium takes place at sales given by the intersection of mr_0 and MC_0 and at a price given by the height of D_0 above the intersection of mr_0 and MC_0.
- Average cost curves are not drawn but are the sum of marginal cost and a fixed cost f_0.

XDs of various sorts, say of country 1, can be analyzed graphically. Embargoes/controls can be taken to represent the closure of market 3 or 4 to suppliers from country 1 and the transferral of the corresponding demand to suppliers from country 2. The arrows labeled "1" illustrate. Demands "shift" in country 1 from D_0 to $.5D_0$, and in country 2 from D_0 to $1.5D_0$. Marginal revenue curves shift correspondingly, prices and sales adjust to new "quasi-equilibrium" levels (not shown), and demand curves may shift further as cross-price effects between countries 1 and 2 displace the quasi-equilibrium demand curves from $.5D_0$ and $1.5D_0$ (displacements that are not shown). The algebraic counterpart to these graphics is reasonably simple and can clearly decompose those shifts. One illustration is given below.

Export credit arrangements or ad valorem export subsidies in country 1 can be taken to represent a pivoting of the demand curve around its horizontal intercept. The arrow labeled "2" illustrates a reduction in export subsidies or credit support—that is, an XD. *MR* and *mr* curves, of course, shift, and ensuing price/sales adjustments through cross-price effects bring about subsequent further shifts in the curves that establish a new equilibrium.

Other subsidies, taxes, and various regulatory policies in country 1 can be taken to represent cost shocks. Arrow "3" illustrates a marginal cost shock that sets in motion price/sales adjustments through cross-price effects that bring about subsequent shifts in the demand curves that establish a new equilibrium. Fixed cost shocks are not illustrated, but many subsidy, tax, and regulatory policies can be analyzed as movements in f_0. These may affect entry and exit into the industries depicted, and hence the number of firms, which is in turn reflected in the location of the various demand and marginal revenue curves.

The model can be generalized fairly easily in the algebraic form that corresponds to figure A.1 (Helpman and Krugman 1989; Richardson 1989).

- There can be many suppliers of many differentiated goods, which need not be symmetric.
- There can be many demanders of each differentiated good, which need not be symmetric.
- Imperfect competition need not be modeled using Cournot assumptions, nor need it assume either a fixed number of firms or symmetry among them.
- Marginal costs may rise or fall with output, vary across firms, and move over time in response to "dynamic" scale economies such as learning by doing. Some simple "dynamic" versions of this model are almost as easy to manipulate as static versions.
- Alternative treatments of fixed costs allow the model to range from monopolistically competitive long-run equilibria to oligopolistic long-run equilibria, with supernormal profits that range correspondingly from zero on up.

Calibration of simpler or subtler versions of this model involve drawing parameter estimates (often of demand-curve and cost-curve slopes and shapes) from econometric industry research, and drawing data on costs, relative size, and number of firms from industry sources.

Counterfactual calculations then involve performing experiments, such as the XD experiments described above, on the calibrated counterpart of the algebraic model. The following sections illustrate.

The specific experiments carried out in chapter 4 are based on a calibration whose US industry is depicted in figure A.2. Two base-period equilibria are considered: one for a four-firm US industry, one for a ten-firm US industry. The rest-of-world industry could be depicted with five similar diagrams, illustrating another five national varieties of this good. These five are aggregated (since relative prices among the five are invariant to the XD experiments) into a single rest-of-world rival industry with five times the size of the US industry, five times the number of base-period firms, etc. Base-period demand curves facing the entire US and rest-of-world industries are linear and can be written:

$$nx = A - Bp + Cp^*;$$
$$n^*x^* = A^* - B^*p^* + C^*p;$$

Figure A.2 A typical firm and the US export industry under four- and ten-firm oligopoly

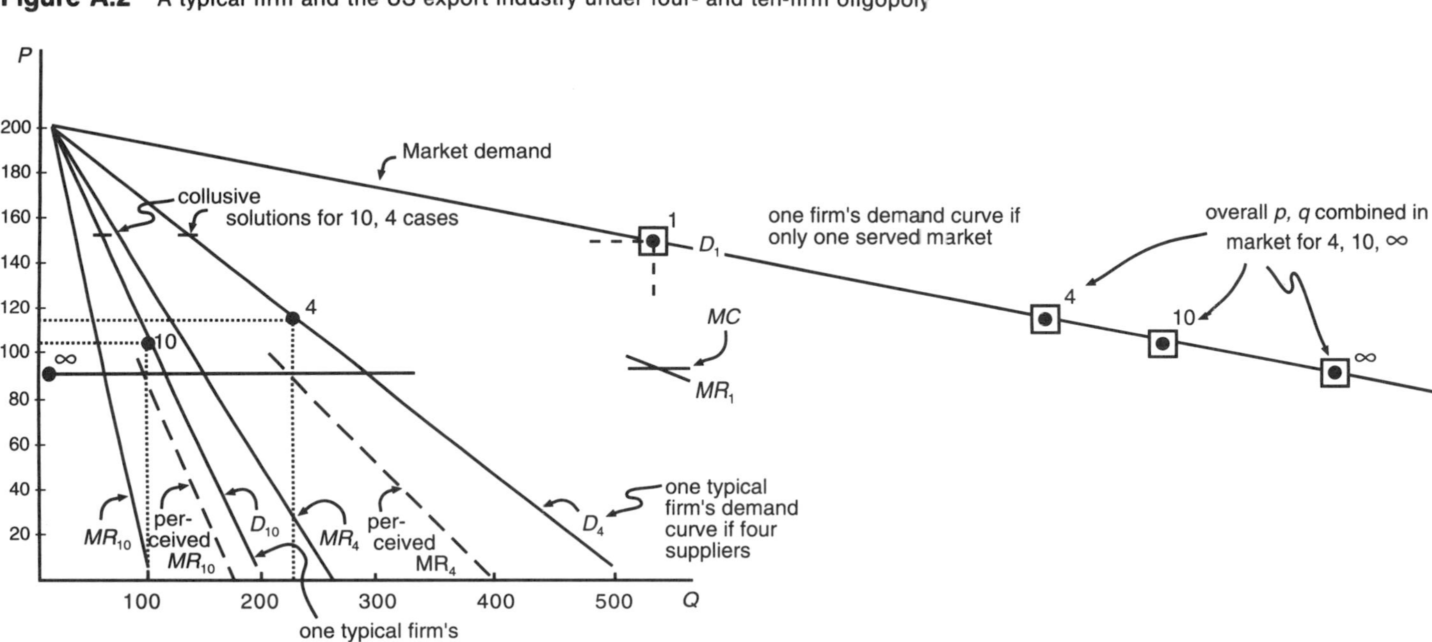

The outermost curve indicates industrywide demand for US exports. Inner curves represent the allocation of that demand to each of four competitors, or to each of ten. Under Cournot competition, the perceived marginal revenue curve, taking export sales of rivals as given, is the dashed line, lying three-quarters of the vertical distance between the demand curve and its conventional marginal curve, and nine-tenths of the counterpart distance, respectively, for the four- and ten-firm cases. Points 1 and ∞ denote monopolistic and perfectly competitive equilibria, respectively.

where

n, n^* = US and rest-of-world numbers of firms

x, x^* = US and rest-of-world export volume per firm

p = price of US variety

p^* = index of prices of five other varieties from rest-of-world suppliers

A, A^* = US and rest-of-world horizontal intercepts for industry demand curves;

Cp^* = sum of five $C_j p_j^*$ cross-price effects.

C^*p, Bp = response of rest-of-world and US demand to a change in US price alone;

B^*p^* = response of rest-of-world demand to simultaneous equal changes in the price of the five other varieties.[1]

Table A.1 gives base-period calibrated values for the relevant terms above, as well as values for base-period r, r^*, f, and f^*, where

r, r^* = (excess) profits per US and rest-of-world firm;

f, f^* = fixed costs per US and rest-of-world firm.

Marginal cost (c) was set equal to 90 in the base-period equilibrium.

The counterfactual XD experiments are conducted just as described in chapter 4:

For the 25 percent export embargo: A, B, A^*, and B^* are modified to rotate the US industry's demand curve around the vertical intercept one-fourth of the (radial) distance toward the vertical axis and to rotate the rest-of-world industry's demand curve out by the corresponding amount.

For export finance: B is increased 10 percent from its base value to rotate the US industry's demand curve around the horizontal intercept one-tenth of the (radial) distance toward the horizontal axis.

For regulatory burden, variable/marginal cost: c is increased 2 percent from its base value, shifting up the marginal cost curve.

For regulatory burden, fixed cost: f is increased 20 percent from its base value, shifting up the average cost curve.

Firms are assumed to optimize and reoptimize under Cournot assumptions only toward rivals producing their same variety; hence, they are assumed to take those rivals' sales volumes as given; by contrast, they are assumed to take the *prices* of the five alternative rest-of-world varieties as given. Under these assumptions, each firm works with a perceived demand curve whose elasticity is n or n^* times that of the relevant industry demand curve elasticity, and with the corresponding perceived marginal revenue curve. For algebraic details, see Richardson (1989, 7–50).

---

1. This term is a sum of variety-by-variety own-price terms, $B_j^* p_j^*$, and variety-by-variety cross-price terms, $C_j^* p_j^*$.

Table A.1 Base-period calibration for XD counterfactual experiments

Parameter	4 US firms; 20 RoW firms; no free entry/exit	4 US firms; 20 RoW firms; free entry/exit	10 US firms; 50 RoW firms; no free entry/exit	10 US firms; 50 RoW firms; free entry/exit
n	4	4	10	10
n^*	20	20	50	50
x	220.0	220.0	99.0	99.0
x^*	230.7	230.7	100.1	100.1
p	112	112	101	101
p^*	108	108	100	100
A	1,611.2	1,611.2	1,500	1,500
A^*	8,056.0	8,056.0	7,500	7,500
C	3.6	3.6	5	5
C^*	3.6	3.6	5	5
B	10	10	10	10
B^*	50	50	50	50
r	4,840[a]	484[b]	1,089[a]	49[b]
r^*	4,153[a]	415[b]	1,001[a]	41[b]
f	0[a]	4,356[b]	0[a]	1,040[b]
f^*	0[a]	3,738[b]	0[a]	960[b]
c,c^*	90	90	90	90

RoW = rest of world.

a. In no entry/exit regimes, fixed costs have no particular significance and were arbitrarily set to zero. The entirety of revenues above variable/marginal costs were arbitrarily assigned to profits.

b. In the free entry regimes, an attempt was made to control for the "integer problem" by setting base period (excess) profits at the average of zero and the level that would just prompt another entrant. The remainder of revenues above variable/marginal costs were correspondingly assumed to cover fixed costs.

Appendix B Gravity models of export variation across trading partners

J. DAVID RICHARDSON and PHILIP J. RUDER

Empirical cross-country gravity explanations of international trade patterns have a long history. Recent examples are Frankel (1992), Frankel and Wei (1992), Hamilton and Winters (1992), Wang and Winters (1991), and Brada and Mendez (1988). Chenery (1960), Linnemann (1966), and Leamer and Stern (1970) were among the first to formalize the model, specifying trade flows between nations as a function of origin and destination-country incomes, populations, and "resistance" factors between countries.

Though gravity models are only loosely based on any economic theory of trade, they have served as useful and accurate benchmarks for empirically predicting bilateral trade volumes. (Bilateral trade is often neglected by traditional theories of trade patterns that focus on some country's trade with the aggregated "rest of the world.") Gravity models do not violate trade theories, however, and are in fact consistent with them, as shown in a series of pioneering papers by Bergstrand (1985, 1989, 1990). Bergstrand's 1989 paper shows specifically how to estimate and interpret gravity models applied to bilateral trade flows for disaggregated industry groups. Our estimates are in Bergstrand's tradition, for both industry groups and aggregate trade.

The present study uses two specifications. The basic specification analyzes the exports of the United States to 130 countries in 1989. Aggregate exports and those in two-digit SIC categories are examined. An auxiliary specification analyzes exports of the United States, Britain, France, Germany, and Japan to 66 or 67 countries in 1989 and 1991. Aggregate exports and exports for a subaggregate of machinery, equipment, and instruments[1] are examined. The coefficients on the explanatory variables

1. The subaggregate is SITC 7–78 (road motor vehicles) + 87 + 88. Data are taken from various issues of the OECD's *Foreign Trade by Commodities*.

in the aggregate export equations are quite similar to those from other studies of aggregate trade flows. The results of the analysis establish the typical level of trade between the United States and its trading partners, given their size, prosperity, and location. Deviations from this level can be thought to reflect the presence of factors that increase or decrease the resistance to trade resulting from physical distance alone, such as, for example, XDs.

The version of the gravity model used here is:

$$\ln[X_{us,i}^{j}] = b_0^j + b_1^j[\ln(Y_i/N_i)] + b_2^j[\ln(N_i)] + b_3^j[\ln(D_i)] + u^j$$

The letters ln denote the natural logarithm of each variable. $X_{us,i}^{j}$ is US exports of commodity j to destination country i, Y_i is the real GDP) of country i, N_i is the population of country i, and D_i is the distance between Indianapolis, Indiana (the approximate economic center of the United States), and the capital of the destination country (a proxy for the economic center).

In this specification, b_1, b_2, and b_3 are all elasticities of US exports with regard to the respective explanatory variable. The intercept b_0 will be relatively large for industry groups in which the United States has global comparative advantage and small for groups in which it has global comparative disadvantage. US XDs that affect *all* trading partners equiproportionally will reduce b_0, but those that discriminate, such as export controls and embargoes, will reduce the estimated disturbance (u) for those trading partners that are targeted. Of course, that trading partner's own distinct comparative disadvantage or protection or politics or culture could also cause its purchases of US exports to be low. Chapter 5 describes forensic methods for disentangling the influence of US XDs from other "residual"determinants of US exports in the gravity-model approach.[2] The following describes the data employed.

---

2. The disturbance term u is assumed to be distributed normally for purposes of summarizing the estimated b coefficients and their standard errors in the text. The estimated shortfalls of tables 5.1 through 5.3 are the antilogs of each trading partner's residual. For goods with tight export controls, however, the assumption of a normal u gives too little weight to the strong likelihood of large negative residuals, and no weight at all to the chance that US exports would be zero, as they will for an embargo. For uncontrolled goods, the assumption of a normal u gives "too much weight" to positive residuals, in the sense that their antilogs are very large numbers. (In fact, the mean of the antilogs of the residuals is necessarily positive, not zero when u is distributed normally.) Since the industry groups on which we focus in chapter 5 are all mixes of controlled and uncontrolled goods, I cannot predict which of the two "mis-weighting" influences dominates *a priori*. But we can draw two other conclusions. First, standard hypothesis tests on coefficients will not be reliable. This explains the cautionary words in chapter 5 about trusting the precision of the range of estimated coefficients. Second, at higher levels of aggregation, the share of goods subject to export controls drops. For aggregates, therefore, the second mis-weighting influence dominates the first, and estimated shortfalls are in a sense "too small." This is why the estimated shortfalls from the regressions on the more aggregated OECD data in the auxiliary

Trade. Data for the basic specification are from the same source as is described in Appendix C. Data for the auxiliary specification are described above.

Income per person and population. Per capita GDP and population figures for countries in 1985 were obtained from Summers and Heston (1988). They provide internationally comparable estimates of GDP and population for 121 market economies and nine centrally planned economies, based on country data that conform to the System of National Accounts of the United Nations and on benchmark pricing studies of the United Nations International Comparison Project.[3] 1985 was the latest year for which internationally comparable data were available for so large a set of trading partners. If countries have largely maintained their positions relative to each other in terms of GDP and population between the years 1985 and 1989, the discrepancy between the years for which export and country data are available will not greatly affect the results of the study.

As an alternative to using the 1985 data, an attempt was made to bring 1980 Summers and Heston data up to 1988 by means of World Bank (*World Development Report,* 1990) data on average GNP growth rates between 1981 and 1988 and using 1988 population figures. The Summers and Heston 1980 GDP data were updated by multiplying the 1980 figures by one plus the appropriate annual growth rates to the eighth power. However, for many countries, including the Soviet Union and the East Bloc, the World Bank does not report growth rates, and an effort was made to fill the missing values from other data sources. For East Germany, Czechoslovakia, Poland, the USSR, Romania, and Bulgaria, per capita GDP figures were obtained from PlanEcon 1990 estimates reported in *The Economist* magazine (21 January 1991). For Iran and Afghanistan, the 1981–88 growth rates were approximated by taking the 1965–80 growth figures and adjusting them by the ratios of the 1981–88 growth rates to the 1965–80 rates for middle- and low-income countries, respectively. For Taiwan, the 1981–88 growth rate was taken from *The Economist* magazine (14 July 1990, 19).

In this alternative, population data for most countries were obtained from the World Bank (*World Development Report,* 1990). Information for several countries was omitted from the World Bank tables, however, and again, an effort was made to fill the missing values. For Afghanistan, population was assumed to be the 1980 Summers and Heston figure

---

specification are smaller than the summed estimated shortfalls from the regressions on two-digit SIC data in the basic specification.

3. To our knowledge, this is the first time the Summers-Heston data have been used in gravity approaches. It is generally acknowledged to be a much more accurate measure of comparative national real incomes than any alternative. But see Box 5.1 for a view to the contrary.

inflated by the average population growth of other low-income countries from 1980 to 1988. For Taiwan, 1988 population was taken from *The Economist* magazine (14 July 1990, 19).

Complete observations for 123 countries resulted from the effort to update the 1980 Summers and Heston data to 1988.

Resistance. Resistance was proxied by a measure of distance. Distances between the United States and the 130 destination countries were computed from the geographic coordinates of Indianapolis and the capital of each destination. Ideally, the coordinates used would be those of the economic centers of the countries—that is, an average of internal coordinates weighted by economic activity taking place at each location. These data are unavailable, however. Indianapolis was chosen as the approximate economic center of the United States, as it is north and east of the physical center, reflecting the concentration of population and economic activity in the northeast quadrant of the United States. Lacking much intuition about the distribution of population and industry for most other countries, the country capitals are used as proxies for the economic centers.

The source of the coordinates of Indianapolis and the 129 country capitals and the formula used to calculate great circle distances was Fitzpatrick and Modlin (1986).

Appendix C Generalized factor endowments models of export variation across trading regions

J. DAVID RICHARDSON and PAMELA J. SMITH

The Factor Endowments/Content Model

Empirical cross-country "factor content" explanations of international trade patterns based on national factor endowments have a long history. The most definitive recent examples are the monographs by Noland (1990, 1993) and Leamer and associates (Leamer 1984; Bowen, Leamer, and Sveikauskas 1987). They assess whether international trade in a commodity is essentially just embodied trade in countries' labor skills, capital endowments, land, and other resources. They find their hypothesis—that a commodity's trade varies linearly across countries with their factor endowments—moderately well-supported by the data, despite the seemingly stringent assumptions on which such a hypothesis rests. Maskus (1991) compares these endowments-based factor content approaches to other endowments-based approaches, such as attempts to relate a country's trade across industries to the industries' respective factor intensities. He finds the latter to perform equally well compared with the former for Germany, Japan, and the United States but to have inferior performance for the other 21 countries in his sample.

The regressions underlying chapter 5's discussion of tax and regulatory effects assess international trade of the US states in a manner similar to Leamer (1984) and Noland (1990), extending the analysis to "policy endowments" in the spirit but not the method of Noland (1993). Smith and Richardson (1990) contains a more detailed discussion.

Newly available trade data make this approach possible for the first time in studies of international trade determinants across states or regions (table C.1). The data are state-by-state international exports by

Table C.1 Effects of natural US state factor endowments on state exports, 1989 (export changes in thousands of dollars)

SIC Group		Patents	Capital	Labor1	Labor2	Labor3	Labor4	Labor5	Labor6
		(per patent)	(per millions of 1986 $)	(per worker)					
01	Crops				−12.749*			−5.944*	7.662*
20	Food					1.190*		−2.382*	6.308**
24	Lumber								
26	Paper	−168*	26.9*	1.606*		−0.654*		1.098*	
28	Chemicals		58.0*	−3.009*	−8.086**		5.733*		
30	Rubber	46*	6.3*		−0.432*			−0.224*	
33	Primary metal				−2.584*	−0.894*			−1.287*
34	Fabricated metal	61*		1.313*	−1.268*				−0.635*
35	Machinery	474*	88.3	7.417**		−1.411*			3.057*
36	Electronics			13.673*		−6.684*	17.739*		
37	Transport	1,245*	209.5*		−20.397*				
38	Instruments	197*		2.259**					
ND	Nondurables		157.8*		−10.244*		8.036*		5.949*
D	Durables	2,065*	398.5*	31.795	−27.669*		20.260*		
T	Total manufactures	1,609*	556.3*	29.288*	−37.894*		28.296*		

SIC Group		Land1	Land2	Land3	Minerals	Coal	Oil	Gas	R^2
		(per thousand acreas)			(per millions of dollars)	(per million short tons)	(per million barrels)	(per billion cubic feet)	
01	Crops	−14.40*			−1,016*				.146
20	Food	−6.83*		−6.14*	−396*				.403
24	Lumber								.260
26	Paper		1.72*						.463
28	Chemicals	−8.11*	−9.18**		−630**		768**	−29.0**	.495
30	Rubber				−38*				.451
33	Primary metal								.276
34	Fabricated metal							−4.6*	.338

35	Machinery					.461
36	Electronics					.267
37	Transport					.155
38	Instruments					.557
ND	Nondurables	−16.06*	−10.71*	−1,198**	969*	.384
D	Durables					.382
T	Total manufactures	−33.72*		−1,681*		.392

* = Estimate is one to two times standard error.
** = Estimate is more than two times standard error.
Nondurables = SIC 20-23, 26-31
Durables = SIC 24-25, 32-38
Total manufactures = nondurables + durables.

Column Headings:

Patents = total number of utility patents granted to state residents in 1989. *Source*: US Patent and Trademark Office, *Patenting Trends in the United States, State Country Report, 1963–1987*.

Capital = discounted sum of private, non-residential state construction in thousands of 1986 dollars from 1978 -1988; annual discount (depreciation) rate = 0.09. *Source*: Philip J. Ruder, *Construction Review, Survey of Current Business*. See Smith and Richardson (1990, appendix C).

Labor data = experienced civilian labor force. *Source*: US Bureau of Labor Statistics, *Geographic Profile of Employment and Unemployment*.
Labor1 = professional specialty, higher education required.
Labor2 = executive, administrative, managerial specialty, higher education advisable.
Labor3 = technicians, sales, and service occupations.
Labor4 = supervisors, construction workers, mechanics, repairers.
Labor5 = operators, fabricators, laborers.
Labor6 = farmers, forestry, fisheries workers.
Land data = thousands of acres. *Source: Statistical Abstract of the United States, 1989.*
Land1 = cropland.
Land2 = pastureland and rangeland.
Land3 = forestland.
Minerals = mining production in thousands of dollars. *Source: Survey of Current Business.*
Coal = demonstrative coal reserve base, million short tons. *Source*: US Department of Commerce, *Coal Production*.
Oil, Gas data from US Department of Commerce, *US Crude Oil, Natural Gas, and Natural Gas Liquids Reserves*, 12/1988.
Oil = million barrels of 42 US gallons, estimated reserves.
Gas = billion cubic feet at 14.73 psia and 60^0F, proved reserves.

two-digit Standard Industrial Classification (SIC) categories and are described at greater length below.[1]

There are some particular advantages to applying this factor content approach in a cross-regional context, especially for the United States. First, its validity rests on interregional factor-price equalization, on interregionally comparable technological opportunities and consumption patterns, and on reasonably similar, but not identical, relative factor endowments across regions.[2] We would maintain that each of these assumptions characterizes the 50 United States (plus the District of Columbia) more accurately than the 60 or so countries on which the usual studies are done.[3] Second, the endowments data for the US states are richer, and arguably of higher quality, than even the extensive national data compiled by Leamer and associates. As described below, we are able to disaggregate labor into six (and more) categories corresponding to types and levels of skill acquisition; to differentiate between regionally mobile and immobile capital;[4] to employ reserves data instead of production proxies for a number of natural-resource endowments; and to devise measures of technological capital that allow a flexible generalization of the assumption of identical technological opportunities.

On the other hand, there are some particular disadvantages in applying this factor content approach to the international trade of US states. First, the US Census Bureau does not collect import data that is comparable to their export data, which we employ. That makes it seem impossible to compute the *net* trade in each commodity that factor content studies purport to explain. We outline two methods for solving this problem, however, one of which we pursue in this research. Second, the cross-region factor content perspective hypothesizes a linear relation between a region's factor endowments and its net trade with *all* trading partners, not just a subset. There is no presumption that the same—or any—interpretation can be given to a linear relation between a region's factor endowments and its net trade with one, several, or even the majority of its trading partners. Our precise problem is that there is no available

1. The data are available for 1987 through 1992, and quarterly within those years, and also by country of destination, all cross-classified.

2. See Leamer (1984, 11–44). The last of these conditions ensures that state endowment vectors fall within the same "cone of diversification," as required by factor content theory.

3. The accuracy is not perfect, of course. Giese and Testa (1989) find, for example, that compared with other US regions, New England, the mid-Atlantic states, and the Pacific region employ production techniques that are more intensive in their use of high-tech labor in all industries. This makes suspect any assumptions of perfect comparability of technological opportunities and perfect factor price equalization.

4. As Leamer (1984) shows, only immobile endowments should be linear determinants of cross-regional trade. Each flow of a mobile factor in and out of a region should be treated as a form of trade itself and linearly related across states to their immobile endowments.

measure of a state's "exports" to other US states; if we had it, we should add it for each commodity group to our data on state exports to the "world." We retreat, as Leamer does at several junctures, to a rule of reason, or of judgmental inquisitiveness. We still find it a worthy question to ask how well factor content perspectives linearly "explain" cross-state variation in international exports alone.[5]

To solve the first problem of missing import data, we propose initially the following approach. Under the assumptions of the factor content approach, including comparable consumption patterns across regions, a region's net trade vector, $X - M$ (exports − imports), can be expressed as the following linear function of its endowment vector, V, and the world counterpart V_w:

$$X - M = A_0 + A_1(V - sV_w) + U, \qquad \text{(C.1)}$$

where A_1 = a matrix of (technological) coefficients, s = the region's share of world GNP (Leamer 1984, 9), and where U is a disturbance term representing measurement error in net trade and unmeasured determinants of net trade. M can be rewritten as

$$M = B(M_u/GNP_u)(GSP), \qquad \text{(C.2)}$$

where

$$B = (M/GSP)/(M_u/GNP_u), \qquad \text{(C.3)}$$

and where GSP = the region's gross state product, M_u = United States imports, and GNP_u = United States gross national product. Then the rewritten M can be added to both sides of equation C.1. We can see that a regression of *gross* exports on endowments plus (a constant-across-regions fraction of) regional gross product, entered as an additional regressor, is equivalent to equation C.1:

$$X = A_0 + A_1(V - sV_w) + B(M_u/GNP_u)(GSP) + U \qquad \text{(C.4)}$$

The fractional term involving US imports and GNP is, of course, measurable as well as constant across states. Then the hypothesis that the regression's estimated $B = 1$ can be tested in the normal way, providing a means of rejecting (or not) the fundamental maintained assumption of comparable consumption patterns across regions. (To be precise, M/GSP is comparable to M_u/GNP_u)

We have not attempted this approach but have implemented a closely related approach that leaves the assumption of comparable consumption

5. For example, if a state's (unobserved) export of some commodity to other states is also a linear function of its factor endowments and is the same linear function that generates its exports to the rest of the world, then our regressions will provide informative estimates of the signs and relative (but not absolute) sizes of the coefficients on each endowment in the true regression for total trade. While the "if" condition is admittedly hard to assess *a priori*, it is not fanciful on the face of it.

patterns as a maintained (that is, untested) hypothesis. This approach observes that if observations were to be scaled by GSP, as we do below to alleviate heteroskedasticity related to different state sizes,[6] then the right-hand term of equation C.4 would become a scalar that is constant across states. Hence, it would be incorporated into the estimated intercept of equation C.4. This is in fact the regression that we run in chapter 5.

Data

The trade data employed to implement the endowments model are described first, followed by the data on natural endowments and data on "policy endowments."

Trade. State export data are compiled by the Bureau of the Census from Shipper's Export Declarations. The state of export indicated on the Export Declarations is the state from which the merchandise begins its journey to the port of export. These data have been enhanced by the Massachusetts Institute for Social and Economic Research to reduce errors associated with the identification of the true originating state of export. The measure of state international exports is the total value of shipments based on free alongside ship (f.a.s.) value, which includes transaction price plus inland freight, insurance, and all other charges incurred getting goods to the point of export. The shipment value excludes overseas freight or any other charges beyond the port of export.

Export data procured from the Massachusetts State Data Center are in current dollars for 1987, 1988, and 1989. When data are pooled over all three years, US export price indexes provided by the Bureau of Labor Statistics, Division of International Prices, are used to transform the export data into constant 1986 dollar values.[7] Constant 1986 dollar export data are then pooled across 1987, 1988, and 1989, resulting in a sample of 153 observations (50 states plus the District of Columbia over three years) on gross exports.

Criticisms of these data, though widespread, seem overwrought, especially for manufacturing categories. The criticisms center on the fre-

6. See Leamer (1984, pp. 121–122, 162), who scales his observations by powers of GNP for the same reason.

7. The base year of 1986 was chosen in order to ensure comparability with the gross state product data which is used to scale exports to correct for heteroskedasticity. The price indexes used for the adjustments are two-digit SIC-based indexes when available, three-digit aggregate SIC-based indexes when the three-digit aggregate contributes substantially to the two-digit aggregate, and the index for manufactured goods otherwise. In using US-based price indexes to transform the state export data into real terms, it is assumed implicitly that price movements do not differ substantially across states.

quency with which the Shipper's Export Declarations are filled out by a consolidation rather than a producer, in a port or intermediary state, rather than in the state of final production or greatest value added. Coughlin and Mandelbaum (1991) is the most detailed critical treatment; see also Erickson and Hayward (1991, 372–74). Yet even they admit that the problems are less severe for manufactures than for agricultural and mined products (note 9, 68) and show that the data are highly correlated with more reliable Census Bureau data available from the *Annual Survey of Manufactures* with no destination detail and less frequency. They undermine their attempt to disparage this high correlation by incorrectly specifying, then rejecting, a constant arithmetic difference between the two data series as the *sine qua non* for using the suspect data series.[8] Furthermore Smith (1992a, 27) shows that the suspect export series is highly correlated across states for each industry group with output (value added by two-digit SIC).[9] Since measured output is not subject to consolidation problems, these high correlations cast doubt on quantitative severity of the admitted consolidation problems in measured exports.

The data underlying natural endowments are as follows:

Patents. Patents data are total numbers of utility patents granted to residents of US states in 1987, 1988, and 1989. Utility patents cover inventions of new and useful processes, machines, manufactures, and compositions of matter, and exclude patents for designs, botanical plants, and reissues. These data were provided by the US Patent and Trademark Office and are published by the Patent and Trademark Office in *Patenting Trends in the United States, State Country Report, 1963–1987*.

Several alternative patent "stock" variables were constructed, which in theory should have provided better measures of state endowments. Patents are a type of durable technological capital, similar to other capital, in that "units produced" in prior years still have current production values. In practice, discounted cumulations of patents over multiple-year intervals, our proxy for patent stocks, had the same or inferior explanatory power in our regressions.

Capital. Immovable capital stock data for the 50 states plus the District of Columbia are assembled by first recording the dollar value of the private nonresidential construction authorized annually in each state. These data are from various issues of *Construction Review*, published

8. Since states are very different from each other in size, one ought to have confidence in a suspect data series if it is a constant relative proportion (not an arithmetic difference) of a more reliable series. The suspect series passes this proper test with flying colors, as Coughlin and Mandelbaum admit (1991, note 3, 78), without apparently accepting that this undermines their criticism.

9. The lowest correlations are for SIC 20 (food and kindred products), 0.56; SIC 24 (lumber and wood products), 0.58; SIC 26 (paper and allied products), 0.47; and SIC 33 (primary metal products), 0.37. All other industry groups showed correlations greater than 0.70.

monthly by the US Department of Commerce. The data series collected covers the years 1978 through 1989.[10]

Next, the value of private nonresidential construction for each year and each state are converted from current dollars into both 1982 and 1986 constant dollars.[11] The adjusted constant dollar value of private nonresidential construction is then depreciated at an annual rate of 0.09. This depreciation rate was chosen on the assumption that buildings have a useful life of 50 years.[12]

A state's endowment stock of immovable capital, C, for the years 1987, 1988, and 1989 is then calculated as the sum of the depreciated value of authorized private nonresidential construction

$$C_{1987} = \Sigma_{i=1-8} \quad [c_{1978+i} (1 - 0.09)^{(8-i)}]$$
$$C_{1988} = \Sigma_{i=1-9} \quad [c_{1978+i} (1 - 0.09)^{(9-i)}]$$
$$C_{1989} = \Sigma_{i=1-10} \quad [c_{1978+i} (1 - 0.09)^{(10-i)}]$$

where C is the adjusted constant dollar value of private nonresidential construction and i denotes the year in which it is authorized.

Labor. Labor data are 1987, 1988, and 1989 annual averages of numbers, in thousands, in the experienced civilian labor force by occupation. Experienced is defined as persons with prior work experience. Data are from the *Geographic Profile of Employment and Unemployment*, published annually by the US Department of Labor, Bureau of Labor Statistics. These data are derived from the Current Population Survey (CPS) conducted by the Bureau of the Census.

In determining a meaningful aggregation scheme for the occupational categories, labor force data were supplemented with data on the significant sources of training for occupations. Data on training sources are from *Occupational Projection and Training Data, 1988* which is published by the US Department of Labor, Bureau of Labor Statistics. Information used to identify the significant sources of training for each occupation

---

10. Adjustments were made to improve comparability of the data across years that have varying numbers of permit-issuing places from which the data are collected. From 1978 through 1983, data on nonresidential construction were collected from 16,000 permit-issuing places. After 1984, the data were collected from 17,000 such places. Both the 17,000- and 16,000-place data are reported for 1984. To improve comparability, the pre-1984 number for each state was multiplied by the ratio of the 17,000- and 16,000-place 1984 numbers for that state.

11. These adjustments from current to constant dollar values are made using the Boeckh index for construction cost of commercial and factory buildings reported in the *Survey of Current Business* and published by the US Department of Commerce, Bureau of Economic Analysis.

12. The annual depreciation rate that reduces a building to 1 percent of its value after 50 years is 0.09. It is also assumed that construction authorized in one year is put into place in the following year—construction authorized this year adds to the capital stock next year.

was taken from responses to a supplemental questionnaire in the January 1983 CPS.

The labor endowments are defined as: Labor1, professional specialty; Labor2, executive, administrative, and managerial; Labor3, technical, sales, service, and administrative support; Labor4, precision production, craft, and repair; Labor5, operators, fabricators, and laborers; Labor6, farming, forestry, and fishing.

The occupation-training relationships that serve as the basis for these aggregates are as follows: Labor1 includes occupations generally requiring at minimum a four-year college degree or graduate/professional level training; Labor2 includes occupations generally requiring at most a four-year college degree; Labor3 includes occupations for which postsecondary school training but less than a bachelor's degree is sufficient, as well as occupations generally requiring high school vocational training, as the significant source of skills preparation; Labor4 includes occupations for which formal employer training is generally provided; Labor5 includes occupations generally requiring no formal training; and Labor6 includes farming, fishing, and forestry occupations for which there is no single principal source of formal training.

Land. Natural resource data are from a variety of sources. Data on land variables including cropland, pastureland and rangeland, and forestland are for 1982, measured in thousands of acres. These data were taken from the *Statistical Abstract of the United States, 1989,* which is published annually by the US Department of Commerce, Bureau of the Census.

Minerals. State mining production provides a proxy for state minerals endowments. The preferable measure of the mineral variable is state reserves of minerals. However, such data are not currently available at the state level. Mining data used in the current study are the sum of the current 1986 dollar value of production in the following two-digit SIC categories: metal mining and nonmetallic minerals except fuels. Mining production data were obtained from the US Department of Commerce, Bureau of Economic Analysis.

Coal. State data on coal endowments are measured as total recoverable coal reserves in million short tons. Recoverable reserves are the amount of coal that could be mined from the coal deposits at active producing mines as of the end of 1988. Data on recoverable reserves are from *Coal Production, 1988,* published by the US Department of Energy, Energy Information Administration. Data in this report were collected through a mandatory response survey of companies owning US mining operations that produced, processed, or prepared 10,000 or more short tons of coal in 1988.

Oil and gas. Data on state oil endowments are estimated crude oil proven reserves measured in million barrels of 42 US gallons as of 31

December 1988. Data on gas endowments are estimated total natural gas proven reserves, wet after lease separation, measured in billion cubic feet at 14.73 psia and 60 degrees Fahrenheit as of 31 December 1988. Proven reserves of both crude oil and natural gas are estimated quantities that have been demonstrated to be recoverable in future years from known reservoirs under existing economic and operating conditions. Data are from *US Crude Oil, Natural Gas, and Natural Gas Liquids Reserves, 1988,* which is published annually by the US Department of Energy, Energy Information Administration. Estimates of proved reserves are based on information provided by operators of oil and gas wells in the Annual Survey of Domestic Oil and Gas Reserves conducted by the Energy Information Administration.

"Policy endowments" were measured as follows:

Export promotion. Data on state "international budgets" appropriated for export and investment promotion, as recorded in National Association of State Development Agencies (1988), are erratic at best. Several states did not report such data at all, and others frequently excluded budget allocations for foreign offices. However, since almost all reported the number of staff devoted to such functions (a number treated as the variable X_1 below) and the number of foreign offices employed (X_2 below), the following method for cleaning and completing the data was adopted. For the 34 states with relatively complete data, an "auxiliary regression" was estimated across states to predict budget appropriations. The auxiliary regression used X_1 and X_2 as explanatory variables. The estimated regression, with $\hat{Y}$ standing for the estimated budget devoted to export and investment promotion, was

$$\hat{Y} = \underset{}{101.0} + \underset{(4.8)}{121.7\, X_1} - \underset{(-1.1)}{214.1\, X_2},$$

(t - values appear in the parentheses.) This equation was used, despite its peculiar negative coefficient on X_2, to predict the missing data or to replace the understated data for the 13 states not included in the regression. In replacing the understated data, we adopted the rule that the larger of either $\hat{Y}$ or the recorded figure would be treated as that state's export promotion.[13]

Environmental cost. The data on pollution abatement operating cost expenditure are estimates reported in *Pollution Abatement Costs and Expenditures, 1988,* published by the Current Industrial Reports Division of the Bureau of the Census of the US Department of Commerce. The estimates were formulated on the basis of a survey of a sample of about 20,000 manufacturing establishments with 20 employees or more selected as a subsample of the 1984 Annual Survey of Manufacturing (ASM),

13. Several $\hat{Y}$'s were, in fact, negative.

which itself was a sample of roughly 57,000 firms from the 1982 Census of Manufacturing.

Both capital and operating costs are reported for two-digit SIC manufacturing categories[14] (SIC 20 through 39, except 23) and for each state. Only limited data are reported for two-digit SIC categories of smaller states to avoid disclosing operations of individual companies. This affects small states much more than large ones, as such states are more likely to host only a few firms in many industries. The data were employed to obtain several measures of "environmental taxation"/environmental commitment across states:

- a simple average[15] for each state across its two-digit SIC industries of the industry's ratio of pollution abatement operating costs or operating plus capital costs to value added.
- a simple average, as previously, except that when a state provided no data on a two-digit category, the mean value of the two-digit industry's "environmental tax" across other states was substituted for the missing/secret observation.
- a simple average for each state across five two-digit SIC industries, as before, that were both well-represented in most states and that were not unduly subject to subindustry bias caused by excessive variation in "environmental taxes" across four-digit subcategories. The five industries were lumber and wood products (SIC 24); rubber and miscellaneous plastics products (SIC 30); stone, clay, and glass products (SIC 32); fabricated metal products (SIC 34); and transportation equipment (SIC 37).

Public Capital. Estimated public capital stocks by state from Holtz-Eakin (1989a,b; 1991), representing streets, highways, sewerage, utilities, and educational structures. Stocks were built up cumulating state-by-state investments over time net of discards and deflating properly. Deflation/discard techniques were based on Bureau of Economic Analysis, *Fixed Reproducible Tangible Wealth, 1929–1985*. See also Munnell (1990), especially Appendix A.[16]

---

14. Abatement expenditures for SIC 23, apparel and other textile products are not reported. Firms in these industries operate primarily out of rented quarters, and pollution abatement expenses are incurred by their landlord, not by the manufacturing plant.

15. A weighted average, with weights corresponding to industry value added was also tried, but was judged inferior. It is especially subject to direct industry-mix bias: states with large concentrations of dirty two-digit industries having high environmental spending will seem to spend and "care" more as a state than other states with smaller concentrations.

16. Munnell's data were used as well as Holtz-Eakin's with very little difference in the results of Table 5.4.

Tax, earned income. As described by Berliant and Strauss (1992, 15–19), net state personal income tax liabilities were simulated by the TAXSIM model of the National Bureau of Economic Research, using amplified versions of the 1985 and 1987 *Statistics of Income* of the US International Revenue Service. These were combined with reported federal taxes, both net of credits, and subdivided into more than 100 classes of effective tax rates and 25 intervals of economic income. The rate used for each state in our research was the median rate among the 100 or more rates in the combined state and federal table (Berliant and Strauss 1992, table 5.4, p. 24).

Tax, capital gains. As described by Bogart and Gentry (1992, 11–13, 22), calculated tax rates were "state-specific 'first-dollar' tax rates [on capital gains] for high-income individuals who itemize their deductions." Rates were calculated with due attention to states in which local taxes could be assessed as a proportion of state tax liabilities, states in which state taxes were assessed as a proportion of federal tax liabilities, and state differences in whether federal taxes were deductible.

References

Abraham, Filip, Inge Couwenberg, and Gerda Dewit. 1992. "Towards an EC Policy on Export Financing Subsidies: Lessons from the 1980s and Prospects for Future Reform." *The World Economy* 15: 389–405.

American Institute for Contemporary German Studies (AICGS). 1992. "German and American Export Controls." Paper no. 2 (September).

Anderson, James E. 1979. "A Theoretical Foundation for the Gravity Equation." *American Economic Review* 69, 1 (March): 106–16.

Anderson, Kym, and Richard Blackhurst, eds. 1992. *The Greening of World Trade Issues*. New York: Harvester Wheatsheaf.

Arce, Hugh M., and Charles W. Smithson. 1991. "An Empirical Analysis of Changing Liability Standards of New Product Introduction: The Effects of *Henningsen* and *Greenman* in the 1960s." Washington: US International Trade Commission, Research Division Working Paper 91-01-D (February).

Areeda, Phillip. 1993. "Antitrust Policies." In Martin Feldstein, ed., *American Economic Policy in the 1980s*. Chicago: University of Chicago Press.

Aschauer, David. 1989. "Is Public Expenditure Productive?" *Journal of Monetary Economics* 23 (March): 177–200.

Aschauer, David. 1990. "Why Is Infrastructure Important?" In Alicia Munnell, ed., *The Third Deficit: The Shortfall in Public Capital Investment*. Boston: Federal Reserve Bank of Boston.

Balassa, Bela. 1986. "Japanese Trade Policies Towards Developing Countries." *Journal of International Economic Integration* 1 (Spring): 1–19.

Balassa, Bela, and Marcus Noland. 1988. *Japan in the World Economy*. Washington: Institute for International Economics.

Baldwin, Robert E. 1970. *Nontariff Distortions of International Trade*. Washington: The Brookings Institution.

Baldwin, Robert E. 1989. "Measuring Nontariff Trade Policies." National Bureau of Economic Research Working Paper No. 2978 (May). Cambridge, MA: NBER.

Barnett, William, Bernard Cornet, Claude d'Asprenont, Jean Gabszewiez, and Andrew Mas-Collell, eds. 1991. *Equilibrium Theory and Applications*. Cambridge: Cambridge University Press.

Bayard, Thomas O., and Rousslang, Donald J. 1980. "The Effects of Environmental Protection and Occupational Safety and Health Regulations on U.S. Trade." Unpublished paper.

Beeson, Patricia E., and Steven Husted. 1989. "Patterns and Determinants of Productive Efficiency in State Manufacturing." *Journal of Regional Science* 29, 1: 15–28.

Bergsten, C. Fred. 1974. *Completing the GATT: Toward New International Rules to Govern Export Controls*. British-North American Committee, National Planning Association (USA), C. D. Howe Research Institute (Canada).

Bergsten, C. Fred. 1988. *America in the World Economy: A Strategy for the 1990s*. Washington: Institute for International Economics.

Bergsten, C. Fred, Thomas Horst, and Theodore H. Moran. 1978. *American Multinationals and American Interests*. Washington: The Brookings Institution.

Bergsten, C. Fred, and William R. Cline. 1987. *The United States–Japan Economic Problem*. POLICY ANALYSES IN INTERNATIONAL ECONOMICS 13. Washington: Institute for International Economics.

Bergsten, C. Fred, and Edward M. Graham. N.d. *The Globalization of Industry and National Governments*. Washington: Institute for International Economics. Forthcoming.

Bergstrand, Jeffrey H. 1985. "The Gravity Equation in International Trade: Some Microeconomic Foundations and Empirical Evidence." *The Review of Economics and Statistics* 67 (August): 474–81.

Bergstrand, Jeffrey H. 1989. "The Generalized Gravity Equation, Monopolistic Competition, and the Factor-Proportions Theory in International Trade." *The Review of Economics and Statistics* 71 (February): 143–53.

Bergstrand, Jeffrey H. 1990. "The Heckscher-Ohlin-Samuelson Model, the Linder Hypothesis and the Determinants of Bilateral Intra-Industry Trade." *The Economic Journal* 100 (December): 1216–29.

Berliant, Marcus C., and Robert P. Strauss. 1992. "State and Federal Tax Equity: Estimates Before and After the Tax Reform Act of 1986." Presented at a National Bureau of Economic Research Conference on State and Local Taxes after TRA 86 (1 June 1991). Manuscript.

Berry, Steven, Vittorio Grilli, and Florencio López-de-Silanes. 1992. "The Automobile Industry and the Mexico-U.S. Free Trade Agreement." National Bureau of Economic Research Working Paper No. 4152 (August). Cambridge, MA: NBER.

Bertsch, Gary K., and Steven Elliott-Gower, eds. 1992. *Export Controls in Transition: Perspectives, Problems, and Prospects*. Durham, North Carolina: Duke University Press.

Besharov, Douglas J. 1987. "Liability for Foreign Torts: Whose Law Should Apply?" Prepared for a Roundtable Conference on "The Impact of US Product Liability Laws on US Export Trade and International Competitiveness." The Fletcher School of Law and Diplomacy, 4–6 October. Copyrighted manuscript.

Bogart, William T., and William M. Gentry. 1992. "Capital Gains Taxes and Realizations: Evidence from Interstate Comparisons." Manuscript (March).

Bowen, Harry P., Edward E. Leamer, and Leo Sveikauskas. 1987. "Multicountry, Multifactor Tests of the Factor Abundance Theory." *American Economic Review* 77 (December): 791–809.

Brada, Josef C., and José A. Méndez. 1988. "Exchange Rate Risk, Exchange Rate Regime and the Volume of International Trade." *Kyklos* 41, 2: 263–80.

Brainard, S. Lael. 1993. "A Simple Theory of Multinational Corporations and Trade with a Trade-Off Between Proximity and Concentration." National Bureau of Economic Research, Inc., Working Paper No. 4269 (February). Cambridge, MA: NBER.

Bregman, Arie, Melvyn Fuss, and Haim Regev. 1991. "High Tech and Productivity, Evidence from Israeli Industrial Firms." *European Economic Review* 35: 1199–1221.

Bresnahan, Timothy F., and Peter C. Reiss. 1991. "Entry and Competition in Concentrated Markets." *Journal of Political Economy* 99 (October): 977–1009.

Bresnahan, Timothy F., and Richard Schmalensee. 1987. "The Empirical Renaissance in Industrial Economics: An Overview." *The Journal of Industrial Economics* 35 (June): 371–77.

Bryen, Steven, and Michael Ledeen. 1991. "Breaching Export Controls." *The American Enterprise* 2, no. 4 (July/August): 64–72.

Caves, Richard E., and David R. Barton. 1990. *Efficiency in U.S. Manufacturing Industries*. Cambridge, MA: MIT Press.

Cavusgil, S. Tamer, and Michael R. Czinkota, eds. 1990. *International Perspectives on Trade Promotion and Assistance*. New York: Quorum.

Chenery, Hollis. 1960. "Patterns of Industrial Growth." *American Economic Review* 50 (September): 624–54.

Christman, Keith A. 1992. "The Effect of the Tort Liability System On U.S. International Competitiveness." Chemical Manufacturers Association manuscript (February).

Clements, Kenneth W., and Larry A. Sjaastad. 1984. *How Protection Taxes Exporters*. Thames Essay No. 39. London: Trade Policy Research Centre.

Committee for Economic Development. 1989. *Who Should Be Liable? A Guide to Policy for Dealing with Risk*. New York: CED Research and Policy Committee.

Competitiveness Policy Council. 1992. *Building a Competitive America*. First Annual Report to the President & Congress of the United States. Washington: CPC (March 1).

Competitiveness Policy Council. 1993a. *A Competitiveness Strategy for America*. Second Report to the President of the United States. Washington: CPC (March).

Competitiveness Policy Council. 1993b. "Reports of the Subcouncils." Washington: CPC (March).

Cooney, Stephen. 1991. *Can the U.S. Export Drive Continue?* National Association of Manufacturers Report. Washington: National Association of Manufacturers, International Economic Affairs Department (December).

Coughlin, Cletis C., and Oliver Fabel. 1988. "State Factor Endowments and Exports: An Alternative to Cross-Country Studies." *The Review of Economics and Statistics* 70 (November): 696–701.

Coughlin, Cletis C., and Thomas B. Mandelbaum. 1991. "Measuring State Exports: Is There a Better Way?" *Federal Reserve Bank of Review* 73: 65–79.

Crandall, Robert. 1992. "Why Is the Cost of Environmental Regulation So High?" Policy Study No. 110. St. Louis: Washington University Center for the Study of American Business (February).

Dean, Judith M. 1992. "Trade and the Environment; A Survey of the Literature." In Patrick Low, ed., 1992. *International Trade and the Environment*. World Bank Discussion Papers No. 159.

DeHamel, Beth, James R. Ferry, William W. Hogan, and Joseph S. Nye, Jr. 1983. *The Export of Alaskan Crude Oil: An Analysis of the Economic and National Security Benefits*. Cambridge, MA: Putnam, Hayes, and Bartlett, Inc.

Dempster, Arthur P. 1988. "Employment Discrimination and Statistical Science." *Statistical Science* 3, with commentary by Franklin M. Fisher, Harry V. Roberts, Stephen E. Fienberg, and Dempster Rejoinder: 149–95.

Denzau, Arthur T. 1987. *How Import Restraints Reduce Employment*. Formal Publication No. 80. St. Louis: Washington University, Center for the Study of American Business (June).

Destler, I. M., and John S. Odell, assisted by Kimberly Ann Elliott. 1987. *Anti-Protection: Changing Forces in United States Trade Politics*. POLICY ANALYSES IN INTERNATIONAL ECONOMICS 21. Washington: Institute for International Economics (September).

Dick, Andrew R. 1991. "Are Export Cartels Efficiency-Enhancing or Monopoly-Promoting?" Manuscript (August).

Duerksen, Christopher J. 1983. *Environmental Regulation of Industrial Plant Siting: How to Make It Work Better*. Washington: The Conservation Foundation.

Emerson, Michael, Michel Aujean, and Michel Catinat. 1988. "The Economics of 1992. An Assessment of the Potential Economc Effects of Completing the Internal Market of the European Community." *European Economy* 35 (March). Luxembourg: Commission of the European Communities.

England-Joseph, Judy A. 1990. "Alaskan Crude Oil Exports." US General Accounting Office testimony, GAO/T-RCED-90-59 (April).

Erickson, Rodney A. 1989. "Export Performance and State Industrial Growth." *Economic Geography* 65, 4 (October): 280–92.

Erickson, Rodney A., and David J. Hayward. 1991. "The International Flows of Industrial Exports from U.S. Regions." *Annals of the Association of American Geographers* 81, 3: 371–90.

Feldstein, Martin, and Paul Krugman. 1990. "International Trade Effects of Value-Added Taxation." In Assaf Razin and Joel Slemrod, eds., *Taxation in the Global Economy*. Chicago: University of Chicago Press.

Finan, William F. 1986. "Estimate of Direct Economic Costs Associated with US National Security Controls." Manuscript. Revision appearing as Appendix D of National Academy of Sciences (1987a).

Finan, William F., and Karen M. Sandberg. 1986. "Analysis of the Effects of US National Security Controls on US-Headquartered Industrial Firms." Manuscript. Background paper for National Academy of Sciences (1987a).

Fitzpatrick, Gary L., and Marilyn J. Modlin. 1986. *Direct-Line Distances: International Edition*. Metuchen, NJ, and London: The Scarecrow Press.

Frank, Isaiah. 1990. *Breaking New Ground in US Trade Policy*. Washington: Committee for Economic Development Research and Policy Committee.

Frankel, J. 1992. "Is Japan Creating a Yen Bloc in East Asia and the Pacific?" In J. Frankel and M. Kahler, eds., *Regionalism and Rivalry: Japan and the US in Pacific Asia*. Presented at a National Bureau of Economic Research Conference, 3–5 April, Del Mar, CA.

Frankel, J., and S. Wei. 1992. "Yen Bloc and Dollar Bloc: Exchange Rate Policies of the East Asian Economies." Third Annual East Asian Seminar on Economics, organized by Takatoshi Ito and Anne Krueger, held in Sapporo, Japan, 17–19 June.

Giese, Alenka S., and William A. Testa. 1989. "Regional Specialization and Technology in Manufacturing." Federal Reserve Bank of Chicago Working Paper WP-1989-6 (July).

Goldstein, Donald. N.d. "Japan's Strategic Trade Controls: A New Era." Manuscript. Background paper for National Academy of Sciences (1991).

Graham, Edward M., and Michael E. Ebert. 1991. "Foreign Direct Investment and National Security: Fixing the Exon-Florio Process." Manuscript.

Graham, Edward M., and Paul R. Krugman. 1991. *Foreign Direct Investment in the United States*. Washington: Institute for International Economics.

Gravelle, Jane G. 1987. "International Competitiveness and the Tax Reform Act of 1986." Congressional Research Service Paper 87-428 E. Washington: CRS.

Greenaway, David, and Chris R. Milner. 1987. " 'True Protection' Concepts and Their Role in Evaluating Trade Policies in LDCs." *Journal of Development Studies* 23 (January): 200–19.

Grossman, Gene M., and Elhanan Helpman. 1991. *Innovation and Growth in the Global Economy*. Cambridge, MA: The MIT Press.

Grossman, Gene M., and Alan B. Krueger. 1992. "Environmental Impacts of a North American Free Trade Agreement." National Bureau of Economic Research Working Paper No. 3914 (November). Cambridge, MA: NBER.

Gruber, Jonathan. 1992. "The Efficiency of a Group-Specific Mandated Benefit: Evidence from Health Insurance Benefits for Maternity." National Bureau of Economic Research Working Paper No. 4157 (September). Cambridge, MA: NBER.

Hamilton, C., and A. Winters. 1992. "Opening Up International Trade in Eastern Europe," *Economic Policy* 14 (April): 77–116 .

Hattis-Rolef, Susan, ed. 1985. *Freedom of Trade and The Arab Boycott*. Jerusalem: Anti-Defamation League of B'nai Brith in cooperation with the Israel Institute of Co-existence.

Hazilla, Michael, and Raymond J. Kopp. 1990. "Social Cost of Environmental Quality Regulations: A General Equilibrium Analysis." *Journal of Political Economy* 98 (August): 853–73.

Heinz, John. 1991. *U.S. Strategic Trade: An Export Control System for the 1990s*. Boulder, CO: Westview Press.

Helpman, Elhanan, and Paul R. Krugman. 1990. *Trade Policy and Market Structure*. Cambridge, MA: The MIT Press.

Hickok, Susan, and Juann Hung. 1992. "Explaining the Persistence of the U.S. Trade Deficit in the Late 1980s." Federal Reserve Bank of New York *Quarterly Review* (Winter 1991–92): 29–41.

Holtz-Eakin, Douglas. 1989a. "The Spillover Effects of State-Local Capital." Columbia University Department of Economics Discussion Paper Series No. 435 (July).

Holtz-Eakin, Douglas. 1989b. "Private Output, Government Capital, and the Infrastructure 'Crisis.' " Manuscript (January).

Holtz-Eakin, Douglas. 1991. "Public-Sector Capital and the Productivity Puzzle." Manuscript (July).

Hooper, Peter, and J. David Richardson. 1991. *International Economic Transactions: Issues in Measurement and Empirical Research*. Conference on Research in Income and Wealth Series No. 53. Chicago: University of Chicago Press.

Horiba, Yutaka. 1979. "Testing the Demand Side of Comparative Advantage Models." *American Economic Review* 69 (September): 650–61.

Horiba, Yutaka, and Rickey C. Kirkpatrick. 1981. "Factor Endowments, Factor Proportions, and the Allocative Efficiency of US Interregional Trade." *The Review of Economics and Statistics* 63 (February): 178–87.

Hufbauer, Gary Clyde, and A. Hammond Tooke. 1988. *US Export Competitiveness and Source-of-Income Rules*. Washington: US Export Source Coalition.

Hufbauer, Gary Clyde. 1990. "The Impact of U.S. Economic Sanctions and Controls on U.S. Firms." A Report to the National Foreign Trade Council (April).

Hufbauer, Gary Clyde, Diane T. Berliner, and Kimberly Ann Elliott. 1986. *Trade Protection in the United States: 31 Case Studies*. Washington: Institute for International Economics.

Hufbauer, Gary Clyde, Kimberly Elliott, and Eduardo Maldonado. 1988. *Tax Treaties and American Interests*. A Report to the National Foreign Trade Council (August).

Hufbauer, Gary Clyde, Jeffrey J. Schott, and Kimberly Ann Elliott. 1990. *Economic Sanctions Reconsidered: History and Current Policy*, 2nd edition. Washington: Institute for International Economics.

Hufbauer, Gary Clyde, and Joanna M. van Rooij. 1992. *US Taxation of International Income: Blueprint for Reform*. Washington: Institute for International Economics.

Hufbauer, Gary Clyde, Kimberly Ann Elliott, Yoko Sazanami, Shujiro Urata, and Hiroki Kawai. N.d. *Measuring the Costs of Protection in the United States and Japan*. Washington: Institute for International Economics. Forthcoming.

Hulten, Charles R. 1991. "Getting on the Right Road." *The American Enterprise* 2 (May/June): 39–43.

Hulten, Charles R., and Robert M. Schwab. 1991. "Is There Too Little Public Capital? Infrastructure and Economic Growth." Presented at an American Enterprise Institute Conference on Infrastructure Needs and Policy Options for the 1990s, Washington, 4 February 1991.

Industry Commission, Government of Australia. 1991. *Review of Overseas Export Enhancement Measures*. *Report* 1. *Country Studies* 2. Canberra.

International Business-Government Councillors, Inc. 1986. "A Study of Foreign Country Export Control Systems." Manuscript. Background paper for National Academy of Sciences (1987b).

International Business-Government Councillors, Inc. 1990. "National Security and Foreign Policy Export Controls." Manuscript. Background paper for National Academy of Sciences (1991).

International Monetary Fund, The World Bank, Organization for Economic Cooperation and Development, and European Bank for Reconstruction and Development. 1990. *The Economy of the USSR: Summary and Recommendations*. Washington: The World Bank.

Jepma, Catrinus J. 1990. *The Tying of Aid*. Paris: Organization for Economic Cooperation and Development, Development Centre Studies.

Jorgenson, Dale W., and Peter J. Wilcoxen. 1989. "Environmental Regulation and U.S. Economic Growth." Harvard Institute of Economic Growth, Discussion Paper No. 11458 (October).

Keesing, Donald B., and Andrew Singer. 1992. "Why Official Export Promotion Fails: A Survey of Experience and Interviews with Experts." *Finance and Development* 29, 1 (March): 52–53.

Kotabe, Masaaki, and Michael R. Czinkota. 1991. "State Government Promotion of Manufacturing Exports: A Gap Analysis." *Journal of International Business Studies* 23 (Fourth Quarter): 637–58.

Kravis, Irving B., and Robert E. Lipsey. 1992. "Sources of Competitiveness of the United States and of Its Multilateral Firms." *The Review of Economics and Statistics* 74 (May): 193–201.

Kravis, Irving B., and Robert E. Lipsey. 1989. "Technological Characteristics of Industries and the Competitiveness of the US and its Multinational Firms." National Bureau of Economic Research Working Paper No. 2933. Cambridge, MA: NBER.

Krueger, Anne O. 1990. "The Political Economy of American Protection in Theory and in Practice." National Bureau of Economic Research Working Paper No. 3544 (December). Cambridge, MA: NBER.

Krugman, Paul. 1984. "Import Protection as Export Promotion." In H. Kierzkowski, ed., *Monopolistic Competition in International Trade*. Oxford: Oxford University Press.

Krugman, Paul. 1992. "Does the New Trade Theory Require a New Trade Policy?" *The World Economy* 15 (July): 423–41.

Kuttner, Robert. 1990. *Export Controls: Industrial Policy in Reverse*. Washington: Economic Policy Institute.

Kuttner, Robert. 1991. *The End of Laissez-Faire: National Purpose and the Global Economy After the Cold War*. New York: Alfred A. Knopf.

Lawrence, Robert Z. 1987. "Imports in Japan: Closed Markets or Minds?" *Brookings Papers on Economic Activity* 2: 517–54.

Leamer, Edward E. 1974. "The Commodity Composition of International Trade in Manufactures: An Empirical Analysis." *Oxford Economic Papers* 26, 350–74.

Leamer, Edward. 1984. *Sources of International Comparative Advantage: Theory and Evidence*. Cambridge, MA: The MIT Press.

Leamer, Edward. 1990. "The Structure and Effects of Tariff and Nontariff Barriers in 1983." In Ronald W. Jones and Anne O. Krueger, eds., *The Political Economy of International Trade*. Cambridge, MA: Basil Blackwell.

Leamer, Edward E., and Robert M. Stern. 1970. *Quantitative International Economics*. Chicago: Aldine Publishing Company.

Lenz, Allen J., assisted by Hunter K. Monroe and Bruce Parsell. 1992. *Narrowing the U.S. Current Account Deficit: A Sectoral Assessment*. Washington: Institute for International Economics (June).

Linnemann, Hans. 1966. *An Econometric Study of International Trade Flows*. Amsterdam: North-Holland Publishing Company.

Lipsey, Robert E. 1989. "The Internationalization of Production." National Bureau of Economic Research Working Paper No. 2923. Cambridge, MA: NBER.

Lipsey, Robert E. 1991a. "Foreign Direct Investment in the US and US Trade." Annals of the American Academy of Political and Social Sciences. No. 516 (July): 76–90.

Lipsey, Robert E. 1991b. "The Competitiveness of the U.S. and of U.S. Firms." Prepared for the 11th Ministry of Finance-National Bureau of Economic Research Joint Conference on "The Competitiveness of US Industries and its Implications on US-Japan Relationships in the Future," Tokyo, Japan (10–11 September).

Lipsey, Robert E., and Irving B. Kravis. 1985. "The Competitive Position of U.S. Manufacturing Firms." *Banca Nazionale del Lavaro Quarterly Review* 153: 127–54.

Lipsey, Robert E., and Irving B. Kravis. 1986. "The Competitiveness and Comparative Advantage of US Multinationals, 1957-1983." National Bureau of Economic Research Working Paper No. 2051 (October). Cambridge, MA: NBER.

Lipsey, Robert E., and Irving B. Kravis. 1987. "The Competitiveness and Comparative Advantage of U.S. Multinationals 1957–1984." *Banca Nazionale del Lavaro Quarterly Review* 161: 147–65.

Lipsey, Robert E., and Irving B. Kravis. 1991. "Production and Exports by Overseas Operations of U.S. Firms in High-Technology Industries." Prepared for Conference on Deindustrialization, Columbia University, 15 and 16 November.

Litan, Robert E. 1991. "The Liability Explosion and American Trade Performance Myths and Realities." *Tort Law and the Public Interest: Competition, Innovation, and Consumer Welfare*. New York: W.W. Norton & Company.

Long, William J. 1989. *U.S. Export Control Policy*. New York: Columbia University Press.

Low, Patrick, ed. 1992. *International Trade and the Environment*. World Bank Discussion Papers No. 159.

MacDonald, Stuart. 1990. *Technology and the Tyranny of Export Controls: Whisper Who Dares*. New York: St. Martin's Press.

Marin, Dalia. 1992. "Is the Export-Led Growth Hypothesis Valid for Industrial Countries?" *Review of Economics and Statistics* 74, 4: 678–88.

Markusen, James R., and Lars E. O. Svensson. 1990. "Factor Endowments and Trade with Increasing Returns: Generalizations and Extensions." *International Economic Journal* 4 (Autumn): 1–20.

Maskus, Keith E. 1991. "Comparing International Trade Data and Product and National Characteristics Data for the Analysis of Trade Models." In Hooper and Richardson, eds., *International Economic Transactions: Issues in Measurement and Empirical Research*. Chicago: The University of Chicago Press.

Maskus, Keith E., and Denise Eby Konan. 1991. "Trade-Related Intellectual Property Rights: Issues and Exploratory Results." Presented at Conference on Analytical and Negotiating Issues in the Global Trading System, Institute of Public Policy Studies and Department of Economics, the University of Michigan, 31 October–1 November.

McCulloch, Rachel, and J. David Richardson. 1986. "US Trade and the Dollar: Evaluating Current Policy Options." In Robert E. Baldwin and J. David Richardson, eds., *Current US Trade Policy: Analysis, Agenda, and Administration*. Cambridge, MA: National Bureau of Economic Research.

McGuire, E. Patrick. 1988. *The Impact of Product Liability*. New York: The Conference Board, Research Report No. 908.

Meyer, Stephen M. 1992. "Environmentalism and Economic Prosperity: Testing the Environmental Impact Hypothesis." Massachusetts Institute of Technology Project on Environmental Politics and Policy. Manuscript (5 October).

Morici, Peter, and Laura J. Megna. 1980. *US Economic Policies Affecting Industrial Trade*. Washington: National Planning Association.

Morrison, Wayne M. 1993. "The Economics of Export Promotion." *CRS Report for Congress*. Washington: Congressional Research Service (9 March).

Munnell, Alicia. 1990a. "How Does Public Infrastructure Affect Regional Economic Performance?" In Alicia Munnell, ed., *Is There a Shortfall in Public Capital Investment*? Boston: Federal Reserve Bank of Boston.

Munnell, Alicia, ed. 1990b. *Is There a Shortfall in Public Capital Investment*? Boston: Federal Reserve Bank of Boston.

Munnell, Alicia. 1990c. "Why Has Productivity Declined? Productivity and Public Investment." *New England Economic Review* (January/February): 3–22.

Munnell, Alicia H., with the assistance of Leah M. Cook. 1990. "How Does Public Infrastructure Affect Regional Economic Performance?" *New England Economic Review* (September-October): 11–32.

Murrell, Peter. 1990. *The Nature of Socialist Economies: Lessons from East European Foreign Trade*. Princeton, NJ: Princeton University Press.

Mutti, John H. 1978. "The Presence of Americans Abroad and US Exports." US Department of the Treasury, OTA Paper 33 (October).

Mutti, John H., and Richardson, J. David. 1977. "International Competitive Displacement from Environmental Control: The Quantitative Gains from Methodological Refinement." *Journal of Environmental Economics and Management* 4: 135–52.

National Academy of Sciences. 1987a. *Balancing the National Interest*. Washington: National Academy Press.

National Academy of Sciences. 1987b. *Balancing the National Interest Working Papers*. Washington: National Academy Press.

National Academy of Sciences. 1991. *Finding Common Ground: US Export Controls in a Changed Global Environment*. Washington: National Academy Press.

National Academy of Sciences. 1992. *The New Era in U.S. Export Controls: Report of a Workshop*. Washington: National Academy Press.

National Association of Manufacturers. 1990. *US Manufacturers in World Export Markets*. Washington: International Economic Affairs Department.

National Association of Manufacturers. 1993. *Export Financing: A Key to US Export Success*. Washington: NAM (March).

National Foreign Trade Council. 1988. *Creating the Capacity to Finance U.S. Exports*. Washington: NFTC (December).

Nelson, Richard R. 1993. "Retrospective." In Richard R. Nelson, ed., *National Innovation Systems: A Comparative Analysis*. New York: Oxford University Press.

Nicholson, Walter. 1989. *Microeconomic Theory: Basic Principles and Extensions*. Chicago: The Dryden Press.

Nishimizu, Mieko, and John Page. 1991. "Trade Policy, Market Orientation, and Productivity Change in Industry." In Jaime de Melo and André Sapir, eds., *Trade Theory and Economic Reform: North, South, and East—Essays in honor of Bela Balassa*. Cambridge, MA: Basil Blackwell.

Noland, Marcus. 1987. "A Cross-Country Model of International Trade Protection." Manuscript.

Noland, Marcus. 1990. *Pacific Basin Developing Countries: Prospects for the Future*. Washington: Institute for International Economics.

Noland, Marcus. 1993. "The Impact of Industrial Policy on Japan's Trade Specialization." *Review of Economics and Statistics*. Forthcoming.

Nollen, Stanley D. 1987. "Business Costs and Business Policy for Export Controls." *Journal of International Business Studies* 18, 1 (Spring): 1–18.

Oliveira-Martins, Joaquim, Jean-Marc Burniaux, and John P. Martin. 1992. "Trade and the Effectiveness of Unilateral CO_2-Abatement Policies: Evidence From Green." *OECD Economic Studies* 19 (Winter): 123–40.

Ordover, Janusz A., and Robert D. Willig. 1986. "Perspectives on Mergers and World Competition." In Ronald E. Grieson, ed., *Antitrust and Regulation*. Lexington: DC Heath.

Organization for Economic Cooperation and Development. 1985. *Environment and Economics: Results of the International Conference on Environment and Economics, 18–21 June 1984*. Paris: OECD.

Organization for Economic Cooperation and Development. 1990. *The Export Credit Financing Systems in OECD Member Countries*. Paris: OECD.

Pearce, D. 1992. "Should the GATT Be Reformed for Environmental Reasons?" CSERGE Working Paper GEC 92-06, University College London and University of East Anglia.
Preeg, Ernest H. 1989a. "Trade, Aid, and Capital Projects." *The Washington Quarterly* (Winter): 173-185.
Preeg, Ernest H. 1989a. *The Tied Aid Credit Issue: U.S. Export Competitiveness in Developing Countries*. Washington: Center for Strategic and International Studies.
Quigley, Kevin F.F., and William J. Long. 1989. "Export Controls: Moving Beyond Economic Containment." *World Policy Journal* 6, 1 (Winter): 165–188.
Radspieler, Anthony, and Georg Mehl. 1991. "The Myth of State Trade Balances." Manuscript (25 June).
Ray, John E. 1986. "The OECD 'Consensus' on Export Credits." *The World Economy* 9 (September): 295–309.
Razin, Assaf, and Joel Slemrod, eds. 1990. *Taxation in the Global Economy*. Chicago: University of Chicago Press.
Reich, Robert B. 1990. "Who is US?" *Harvard Business Review* (January/February): 53–64.
Reinicke, Wolfgang H. 1990. "Political and Economic Changes in the Eastern Bloc and their Implications for COCOM: West German and European Community Perspectives." Copyrighted manuscript. Background paper for National Academy of Sciences (1991).
Reinicke, Wolfgang H. 1992. "Arms Sales Abroad: European Community Export Controls Beyond 1992." *The Brookings Review* (Summer): 22–25.
Richardson, J. David. 1989. "Empirical Research on Trade Liberalization with Imperfect Competition: A Survey." *OECD Economic Studies* 12 (Spring): 7–50.
Richardson, J. David. 1990. "International Trade, National Welfare, and the Workability of Competition: A Survey of Empirical Estimates." In Colin Carter, Alex McCalla, and Jerry A. Sharples, eds., *New Developments in Trade Theory: Implications For Agricultural Trade Research*. Boulder, CO: Westview.
Richardson, J. David. 1993. "The Case for Trade: A Modern Reconsideration." Washington: Institute for International Economics. Forthcoming.
Robison, H. David. 1988. "Industrial Pollution Abatement: the Impact on Balance of Trade." *Canadian Journal of Economics* 21 (February): 187–99.
Ruder, Philip J. 1990. "State Environmental Policy and State Exports: A Factor Content Approach." Manuscript (December).
Ruder, Philip J. 1991. "The Effects of Political Ties on the Resistance to Trade." Manuscript (June).
Sarna, Aaron J. 1986. *Boycott and Blacklist: A History of Arab Economic Warfare Against Israel*. Totowa, NJ: Rowman & Littlefield.
Saxonhouse, Gary R. 1983. "The Micro- and Macroeconomics of Foreign Sales to Japan." In William R. Cline, ed., *Trade Policy for the 1980s*. Washington and Cambridge, MA: Institute for International Economics and the MIT Press.
Saxonhouse, Gary R. 1986. "What's Wrong with Japanese Trade Structure?" *Pacific Economic Papers* 137 (July): 1–45.
Saxonhouse, Gary R., and Robert M. Stern. 1988. "An Analytical Survey of Formal and Informal Barriers to International Trade and Investment in the United States, Canada, and Japan." *Seminar Discussion Paper 215*. Ann Arbor: Seminar in International Economics, University of Michigan.
Schmalensee, Richard. 1988. "Empirical Studies of Rivalrous Behavior." Associazione Borsisti Luciano Jona Working Paper No. 18 (May). In Giacomo Bonanno and Dario Brandolini, eds., *Industrial Structure in the New Industrial Economics*. Oxford: Oxford University Press (1990).
Schmalensee, Richard, and Robert Willig. 1989. *Handbook of Industrial Organization*, 2 vols. Amsterdam, North-Holland.
Schuck, Peter H., ed. 1991. *Tort Law and the Public Interest: Competition, Innovation, and Consumer Welfare*. New York: W.W. Norton & Company.

Schultz, Siegfried, Joachim Volz, and Christian Weise. 1991. "Die Aubenwirtschaftsförderung der wichtigsten Konkurrenzlander Deutschlands—Frankreich, Grobbritannien, Japan und USA im Vergleich." Deutsches Institut for Wirtschaftsforschung Beiträge Zur Strukturforschung, Heft 124.
Selden, Thomas M., and Daqing Song. 1992. "Environmental Quality and Development: Is There a Kuznets Curve for Air Pollution?" Manuscript (January).
Smith, Alasdair, and Anthony J. Venables. 1991. "Trade Policy Modeling with Imperfectly Competitive Market Structures." Manuscript.
Smith, Pamela J., and J. David Richardson. 1990. "Factor-Content Determinants of US State Exports: An Empirical Exploration." Manuscript (November).
Smith, Pamela J. 1991. "Explaining U.S. State Trade Performance in Manufactured Goods: An Empirical Study." Manuscript (November).
Smith, Pamela J. 1992a. "Knowledge Capital, Geographic Scale Economies and U.S. State Comparative Advantage: An Econometric Study." Unpublished Ph.D. dissertation. University of Wisconsin-Madison (10 August).
Smith, Pamela J. 1992b. "Geographic Scale Economies in an Endowments-Based Trade Model: An Empirical Analysis of the U.S. States." Manuscript (16 October).
Smith, Pamela J. 1993. "Estimation of Inter-Industry and Inter-Regional Knowledge Spillovers Using Patents Data." Manuscript.
Srinivasan, T.N., and Koichi Hamada. 1990. "The US-Japan Trade Problem." Presented to the Japan Economic Seminar of the East Asian Institute of Columbia University, New York, 21 April.
Stern Group, The. 1989. *Rebuilding American Manufacturing in the 1990s: The Case Against Steel VRAs*. Washington: The Stern Group (February).
Sturgis, Robert W. 1989. *Tort Cost Trends: An International Perspective*. Washington: Tillinghast, a Towers Perrin company.
Summers, Lawrence H. 1989. "Some Simple Economics of Mandated Benefits." *American Economic Review* 79 (May): 177–83.
Summers, Robert, and Alan Heston. 1988. "A New Set of International Comparisons of Real Product and Price Levels Estimates for 130 Countries, 1950-1985." *The Review of Income and Wealth* 34, 1: 1–25.
Tait, Alan A., ed. 1991. *Value-Added Tax: Administrative and Policy Issues*. International Monetary Fund Occasional Paper 88. Washington: IMF (October).
Tatom, John A. 1991a. "Should Government Spending on Capital Goods Be Raised." *Federal Reserve Bank of St. Louis Review* 73 (March/April): 3–15.
Tatom, John A. 1991b. "Public Capital and Private Sector Performance." *Federal Reserve Bank of St. Louis Review* 73 (May/June): 3–15.
Tobey, James A. 1990. "The Effects of Domestic Environmental Policies on Patterns of World Trade: An Empirical Test." *Kyklos* 43, 2: 191–209.
Tybout, James R. 1991. "Linking Trade and Productivity: New Research Directions." *The World Bank Economic Review* 6, 2 (May 1992): 189–211.
Tyson, Laura D'Andrea. 1991. "They Are Not US: Why American Ownership Still Matters." *The American Prospect* 4 (Winter): 37–48.
Tyson, Laura D'Andrea. 1992. *Who's Bashing Whom? Trade Conflict in High-Technology Industries*. Washington: Institute for International Economics.
US Congress, Office of Technology Assessment. 1992. *Trade and Environment: Conflicts and Opportunities*. Washington: OTA (May).
US Department of Commerce. 1980. *Report of the President on Export Promotion Functions and Potential Export Disincentives*. Washington: Department of Commerce (September).
US Department of Labor Office of Foreign Economic Research. 1980. *Report of the President on U.S. Competitiveness*. Washington: Department of Labor (September).
US Export Disincentives Task Force. 1980. "Report of Working Party V to the Chairman of the Interagency Export Disincentives Task Force." Unpublished task force report (February).

US Export-Import Bank. 1989. *Report to the U.S. Congress on Tied Aid Credit Practices* (April).
US General Accounting Office. 1989a. *Export Controls: Assessment of Commerce Department Foreign Policy Reports to Congress*. NSIAD-89-44 (September). Washington: GAO.
US General Accounting Office. 1989b. *Export Controls: Extent of DoD Influence on Licensing Decisions*. NSIAD-89-190 (December). Washington: GAO.
US General Accounting Office. 1992a. *Export Controls: Multilateral Efforts to Improve Enforcement*. NSIAD-92-167 (May). Washington: GAO.
US General Accounting Office. 1992b. *Export Promotion: Federal Programs Lack Organizational and Funding Cohesiveness*. NSIAD-92-49 (January). Washington: GAO.
US General Accounting Office. 1992c. *Export Promotion: A Comparison of Programs in Five Industrialized Nations*. GGD-92-97 (June). Washington: GAO.
US International Trade Commission. 1985. *The Effects of Restraining U.S. Steel Imports on the Exports of Selected Steel Consuming Industries*. USITC Publication 1788 (December). Washington: USITC.
US International Trade Commission. 1986. *Effects of Proposed Tax Reforms on the International Competitiveness of US Industries*. USITC Publication 1832 (April). Washington: USITC.
US International Trade Commission. 1989. *The Effects of the Steel Voluntary Restraint Agreements on U.S. Steel-Consuming Industries*. Report to the Subcommittee on Trade of the House Committee on Ways and Means on Investigation No. 332-270 Under Section 332 of the Tariff Act of 1930. USITC Publication 2182 (May). Washington: USITC.
US President's Export Council. 1980. *The Export Imperative* 1 and 2. Washington: USPEC (December).
US President's Export Council. 1984. *Coping With The Dynamics of World Trade in the 1980s* 1 and 2. Washington: USPEC (December).
US President's Export Council. 1988. *US Trade in Transition: Maintaining the Gains* 1 and 2. Washington: USPEC (November).
US Trade Representative. 1992. "US Exports Create High-Wage Employment." Washington: USTR (June).
Viscusi, W. Kip, and Michael J. Moore. 1991. "Rationalizing the Relationship between Product Liability and Innovation." In Schuck, ed., *Tort Law and the Public Interest: Competition, Innovation, and Consumer Welfare*. New York: W.W. Norton & Company.
Wang, Z.K., and A. Winters. 1991. "The Trading Potential of Eastern Europe." Centre for Economic Policy Research Discussion Paper No. 610, London (November).
Weidenbaum, Murray L. 1990. *Business, Government, and the Public*. Englewood Cliffs, NJ: Prentice Hall.

Index

Other Publications from the

Institute for International Economics

POLICY ANALYSES IN INTERNATIONAL ECONOMICS Series

1 **The Lending Policies of the International Monetary Fund**
John Williamson/*August 1982*
ISBN paper 0-88132-000-5 72 pp.

2 **"Reciprocity": A New Approach to World Trade Policy?**
William R. Cline/*September 1982*
ISBN paper 0-88132-001-3 41 pp.

3 **Trade Policy in the 1980s**
C. Fred Bergsten and William R. Cline/*November 1982*
(out of print) ISBN paper 0-88132-002-1 84 pp.
Partially reproduced in the book *Trade Policy in the 1980s.*

4 **International Debt and the Stability of the World Economy**
William R. Cline/*September 1983*
ISBN paper 0-88132-010-2 134 pp.

5 **The Exchange Rate System, Second Edition**
John Williamson/*September 1983, rev. June 1985*
(out of print) ISBN paper 0-88132-034-X 61 pp.

6 **Economic Sanctions in Support of Foreign Policy Goals**
Gary Clyde Hufbauer and Jeffrey J. Schott/*October 1983*
ISBN paper 0-88132-014-5 109 pp.

7 **A New SDR Allocation?**
John Williamson/*March 1984*
ISBN paper 0-88132-028-5 61 pp.

8 **An International Standard for Monetary Stabilization**
Ronald I. McKinnon/*March 1984*
ISBN paper 0-88132-018-8 108 pp.

9 **The Yen/Dollar Agreement: Liberalizing Japanese Capital Markets**
Jeffrey A. Frankel/*December 1984*
ISBN paper 0-88132-035-8 86 pp.

10 **Bank Lending to Developing Countries: The Policy Alternatives**
C. Fred Bergsten, William R. Cline, and John Williamson/*April 1985*
ISBN paper 0-88132-032-3 221 pp.

11 **Trading for Growth: The Next Round of Trade Negotiations**
Gary Clyde Hufbauer and Jeffrey J. Schott/*September 1985*
ISBN paper 0-88132-033-1 109 pp.

12 **Financial Intermediation Beyond the Debt Crisis**
Donald R. Lessard and John Williamson/*September 1985*
ISBN paper 0-88132-021-8 130 pp.

13 **The United States-Japan Economic Problem**
C. Fred Bergsten and William R. Cline/*October 1985, 2d ed. January 1987*
ISBN paper 0-88132-060-9 180 pp.

14 **Deficits and the Dollar: The World Economy at Risk**
Stephen Marris/*December 1985, 2d ed. November 1987*
ISBN paper 0-88132-067-6 415 pp.

15 **Trade Policy for Troubled Industries**
Gary Clyde Hufbauer and Howard F. Rosen/*March 1986*
ISBN paper 0-88132-020-X 111 pp.

16 **The United States and Canada: The Quest for Free Trade**
Paul Wonnacott, with an Appendix by John Williamson/*March 1987*
ISBN paper 0-88132-056-0 188 pp.

17 **Adjusting to Success: Balance of Payments Policy in the East Asian NICs**
Bela Balassa and John Williamson/*June 1987, rev. April 1990*
ISBN paper 0-88132-101-X 160 pp.

18 **Mobilizing Bank Lending to Debtor Countries**
William R. Cline/*June 1987*
ISBN paper 0-88132-062-5 100 pp.

19 **Auction Quotas and United States Trade Policy**
C. Fred Bergsten, Kimberly Ann Elliott, Jeffrey J. Schott, and Wendy E. Takacs/*September 1987*
ISBN paper 0-88132-050-1 254 pp.

20 **Agriculture and the GATT: Rewriting the Rules**
Dale E. Hathaway/*September 1987*
ISBN paper 0-88132-052-8 169 pp.

21 **Anti-Protection: Changing Forces in United States Trade Politics**
I. M. Destler and John S. Odell/*September 1987*
ISBN paper 0-88132-043-9 220 pp.

22 **Targets and Indicators: A Blueprint for the International Coordination of Economic Policy**
John Williamson and Marcus H. Miller/*September 1987*
ISBN paper 0-88132-051-X 118 pp.

23 **Capital Flight: The Problem and Policy Responses**
Donald R. Lessard and John Williamson/*December 1987*
ISBN paper 0-88132-059-5 80 pp.

24 **United States-Canada Free Trade: An Evaluation of the Agreement**
Jeffrey J. Schott/*April 1988*
ISBN paper 0-88132-072-2 48 pp.

25 **Voluntary Approaches to Debt Relief**
John Williamson/*September 1988, rev. May 1989*
ISBN paper 0-88132-098-6 80 pp.

26 **American Trade Adjustment: The Global Impact**
William R. Cline/*March 1989*
ISBN paper 0-88132-095-1 98 pp.

27 **More Free Trade Areas?**
Jeffrey J. Schott/*May 1989*
ISBN paper 0-88132-085-4 88 pp.

28 **The Progress of Policy Reform in Latin America**
John Williamson/*January 1990*
ISBN paper 0-88132-100-1 106 pp.

29 **The Global Trade Negotiations: What Can Be Achieved?**
Jeffrey J. Schott/*September 1990*
ISBN paper 0-88132-137-0 72 pp.

30 **Economic Policy Coordination: Requiem or Prologue?**
Wendy Dobson/*April 1991*
ISBN paper 0-88132-102-8 162 pp.

31 **The Economic Opening of Eastern Europe**
John Williamson/*May 1991*
ISBN paper 0-88132-186-9 92 pp.

32 **Eastern Europe and the Soviet Union in the World Economy**
Susan M. Collins and Dani Rodrik/*May 1991*
ISBN paper 0-88132-157-5 152 pp.

33 **African Economic Reform: The External Dimension**
Carol Lancaster/*June 1991*
ISBN paper 0-88132-096-X 82 pp.

34 **Has the Adjustment Process Worked?**
Paul R. Krugman/*October 1991*
ISBN paper 0-88132-116-8 80 pp.

35 **From Soviet disUnion to Eastern Economic Community?**
Oleh Havrylyshyn and John Williamson/*October 1991*
ISBN paper 0-88132-192-3 84 pp.

36 **Global Warming: The Economic Stakes**
William R. Cline/*May 1992*
ISBN paper 0-88132-172-9 128 pp.

37 **Trade and Payments After Soviet Disintegration**
John Williamson/*June 1992*
ISBN paper 0-88132-173-7 96 pp.

BOOKS

IMF Conditionality
John Williamson, editor/*1983*
ISBN cloth 0-88132-006-4 695 pp.

Trade Policy in the 1980s
William R. Cline, editor/*1983*
ISBN cloth 0-88132-008-1 810 pp.
ISBN paper 0-88132-031-5 810 pp.

Subsidies in International Trade
Gary Clyde Hufbauer and Joanna Shelton Erb/*1984*
ISBN cloth 0-88132-004-8 299 pp.

International Debt: Systemic Risk and Policy Response
William R. Cline/*1984*
ISBN cloth 0-88132-015-3 336 pp.

Trade Protection in the United States: 31 Case Studies
Gary Clyde Hufbauer, Diane E. Berliner, and Kimberly Ann Elliott/*1986*
ISBN paper 0-88132-040-4 371 pp.

Toward Renewed Economic Growth in Latin America
Bela Balassa, Gerardo M. Bueno, Pedro-Pablo Kuczynski, and Mario Henrique Simonsen/*1986*
(out of stock) ISBN paper 0-88132-045-5 205 pp.

Capital Flight and Third World Debt
Donald R. Lessard and John Williamson, editors/*1987*
(out of print) ISBN paper 0-88132-053-6 270 pp.

The Canada-United States Free Trade Agreement: The Global Impact
Jeffrey J. Schott and Murray G. Smith, editors/*1988*
ISBN paper 0-88132-073-0 211 pp.

World Agricultural Trade: Building a Consensus
William M. Miner and Dale E. Hathaway, editors/*1988*
ISBN paper 0-88132-071-3 226 pp.

Japan in the World Economy
Bela Balassa and Marcus Noland/*1988*
ISBN paper 0-88132-041-2 306 pp.

America in the World Economy: A Strategy for the 1990s
C. Fred Bergsten/*1988*
ISBN cloth 0-88132-089-7 235 pp.
ISBN paper 0-88132-082-X 235 pp.

Managing the Dollar: From the Plaza to the Louvre
Yoichi Funabashi/*1988, 2d ed. 1989*
ISBN paper 0-88132-097-8 307 pp.

United States External Adjustment and the World Economy
William R. Cline/*May 1989*
ISBN paper 0-88132-048-X 392 pp.

Free Trade Areas and U.S. Trade Policy
Jeffrey J. Schott, editor/*May 1989*
ISBN paper 0-88132-094-3 400 pp.

Dollar Politics: Exchange Rate Policymaking in the United States
I. M. Destler and C. Randall Henning/*September 1989*
ISBN paper 0-88132-079-X 192 pp.

Latin American Adjustment: How Much Has Happened?
John Williamson, editor/*April 1990*
ISBN paper 0-88132-125-7 480 pp.

The Future of World Trade in Textiles and Apparel
William R. Cline/*1987, 2d ed. June 1990*
ISBN paper 0-88132-110-9 344 pp.

Completing the Uruguay Round: A Results-Oriented Approach to the GATT Trade Negotiations
Jeffrey J. Schott, editor/*September 1990*
ISBN paper 0-88132-130-3 256 pp.

Economic Sanctions Reconsidered (in two volumes)
Economic Sanctions Reconsidered: History and Current Policy
(also sold separately, see below)
Economic Sanctions Reconsidered: Supplemental Case Histories
Gary Clyde Hufbauer, Jeffrey J. Schott, and Kimberly Ann Elliott/*1985, 2d ed. December 1990*
ISBN cloth 0-88132-115-X 928 pp.
ISBN paper 0-88132-105-2 928 pp.

Economic Sanctions Reconsidered: History and Current Policy
Gary Clyde Hufbauer, Jeffrey J. Schott, and Kimberly Ann Elliott/*December 1990*
ISBN cloth 0-88132-136-2 288 pp.
ISBN paper 0-88132-140-0 288 pp.

Pacific Basin Developing Countries: Prospects for the Future
Marcus Noland/*January 1991*
ISBN cloth 0-88132-141-9 250 pp.
ISBN paper 0-88132-081-1 250 pp.

Currency Convertibility in Eastern Europe
John Williamson, editor/*October 1991*
ISBN cloth 0-88132-144-3 396 pp.
ISBN paper 0-88132-128-1 396 pp.

Foreign Direct Investment in the United States
Edward M. Graham and Paul R. Krugman/*1989, 2d ed. October 1991*
ISBN paper 0-88132-139-7 200 pp.

International Adjustment and Financing: The Lessons of 1985-1991
C. Fred Bergsten, editor/*January 1992*
ISBN paper 0-88132-112-5 336 pp.

North American Free Trade: Issues and Recommendations
Gary Clyde Hufbauer and Jeffrey J. Schott/*April 1992*
ISBN cloth 0-88132-145-1 392 pp.
ISBN paper 0-88132-120-6 392 pp.

American Trade Politics
I. M. Destler/*1986, rev. June 1992*
ISBN cloth 0-88132-164-8 400 pp.
ISBN paper 0-88132-188-5 400 pp.

Narrowing the U.S. Current Account Deficit
Allen J. Lenz/*June 1992*
ISBN cloth 0-88132-148-6 640 pp.
ISBN paper 0-88132-103-6 640 pp.

The Economics of Global Warming
William R. Cline/*June 1992*
ISBN cloth 0-88132-150-8 416 pp.
ISBN paper 0-88132-132-X 416 pp.

U.S. Taxation of International Income: Blueprint for Reform
Gary Clyde Hufbauer, assisted by Joanna M. van Rooij/*October 1992*
ISBN cloth 0-88132-178-8 304 pp.
ISBN paper 0-88132-134-6 304 pp.

Who's Bashing Whom? Trade Conflict in High-Technology Industries
Laura D'Andrea Tyson/*November 1992*
ISBN cloth 0-88132-151-6 352 pp.
ISBN paper 0-88132-106-0 352 pp.

Korea in the World Economy
Il Sakong/*January 1993*
ISBN cloth 0-88132-184-2 328 pp.
ISBN paper 0-88132-106-0 328 pp.

NAFTA: An Assessment
Gary Clyde Hufbauer and Jeffrey J. Schott/*February 1993*
ISBN paper 0-88132-198-2 92 pp.

Pacific Dynamism and the International Economic System
C. Fred Bergsten and Marcus Noland, editors/*May 1993*
ISBN paper 0-88132-196-6 424 pp.

Economic Consequences of Soviet Disintegration
John Williamson, editor/*May 1993*
ISBN paper 0-88132-190-7 664 pp.

Reconcilable Differences? United States–Japan Economic Conflict
C. Fred Bergsten and Marcus Noland/*June 1993*
ISBN paper 0-88132-129-X 296 pp.

Does Foreign Exchange Intervention Work?
Kathryn M. Dominguez and Jeffrey A. Frankel/*September 1993*
ISBN 0-88132-104-4 192 pp.

Sizing Up U.S. Export Disincentives
J. David Richardson/*September 1993*
ISBN 0-88132-107-9 192 pp.

SPECIAL REPORTS

1 **Promoting World Recovery: A Statement on Global Economic Strategy by Twenty-six Economists from Fourteen Countries/**
December 1982
(out of print) ISBN paper 0-88132-013-7 45 pp.

2 **Prospects for Adjustment in Argentina, Brazil, and Mexico: Responding to the Debt Crisis**
John Williamson, editor/*June 1983*
(out of print) ISBN paper 0-88132-016-1 71 pp.

3 **Inflation and Indexation: Argentina, Brazil, and Israel**
John Williamson, editor/*March 1985*
ISBN paper 0-88132-037-4 191 pp.

4 **Global Economic Imbalances**
C. Fred Bergsten, editor/*March 1986*
ISBN cloth 0-88132-038-2 126 pp.
ISBN paper 0-88132-042-0 126 pp.

5 **African Debt and Financing**
Carol Lancaster and John Williamson, editors/*May 1986*
(out of print) ISBN paper 0-88132-044-7 229 pp.

6 **Resolving the Global Economic Crisis: After Wall Street**
Thirty-three Economists from Thirteen Countries/*December 1987*
ISBN paper 0-88132-070-6 30 pp.

7 **World Economic Problems**
Kimberly Ann Elliott and John Williamson, editors/*April 1988*
ISBN paper 0-88132-055-2 298 pp.

Reforming World Agricultural Trade
Twenty-nine Professionals from Seventeen Countries/*1988*
ISBN paper 0-88132-088-9 42 pp.

8 **Economic Relations Between the United States and Korea: Conflict or Cooperation?**
Thomas O. Bayard and Soo-Gil Young, editors/*January 1989*
ISBN paper 0-88132-068-4 192 pp.

FORTHCOMING

Reciprocity and Retaliation: An Evaluation of Tough Trade Policies
Thomas O. Bayard and Kimberly Ann Elliott

The Globalization of Industry and National Economic Policies
C. Fred Bergsten and Edward M. Graham

The New Tripolar World Economy: Toward Collective Leadership
C. Fred Bergsten and C. Randall Henning

The United States as a Debtor Country
C. Fred Bergsten and Shafiqul Islam

The Dynamics of Korean Economic Development
Soon Cho

Third World Debt: A Reappraisal
William R. Cline

Equilibrium Exchange Rates for Global Economic Growth
Rudiger Dornbusch

Global Competition Policy
Edward M. Graham and J. David Richardson

International Monetary Policymaking in the United States, Germany, and Japan
C. Randall Henning

The New Europe in the World Economy
Gary Clyde Hufbauer

The Costs of U.S. Trade Barriers
Gary Clyde Hufbauer and Kimberly Ann Elliott

Measuring the Costs of Protection in the United States and Japan
Gary Clyde Hufbauer, Kimberly Ann Elliott, Yoko Sazanami, Shujiro Urata, and Hiroki Kawai

Toward Freer Trade in the Western Hemishpere
Gary Clyde Hufbauer and Jeffrey J. Schott

A World Savings Shortage?
Paul R. Krugman

Trade and Migration: NAFTA and Agriculture
Philip L. Martin

Adjusting to Volatile Energy Prices
Philip K. Verleger, Jr.

The Future of the World Trading System
John Whalley

Trading and the Environment: Setting the Rules
John Whalley and Peter Uimonen

Equilibrium Exchange Rates: An Update
John Williamson

The Politics of Economic Reform
John Williamson

For orders outside the US and Canada please contact:

Longman Group UK Ltd.
PO Box 88
Harlow, Essex CM 19 5SR
UK

Telephone Orders: 0279 623925
Fax: 0279 453450
Telex: 817484